Cambridge Studies in French

SARTRE:
LITERATURE AND THEORY

Cambridge Studies in French

General editor: MALCOLM BOWIE

Also in the series

J. M. COCKING
Proust. Collected Essays on the Writer and his Art

LEO BERSANI
The Death of Stéphane Mallarmé

MARIAN HOBSON
The Object of Art.
The Theory of Illusion in Eighteenth-Century France

LEO SPITZER
Essays on Seventeenth-Century French
Literature, translated and
edited by David Bellos

NORMAN BRYSON
Tradition and Desire. From David to Delacroix

A. MOSS
Poetry and Fable. Studies in Mythological
Narrative in Sixteenth-Century France

SARTRE:
LITERATURE AND THEORY

RHIANNON GOLDTHORPE

Fellow of St Anne's College, Oxford

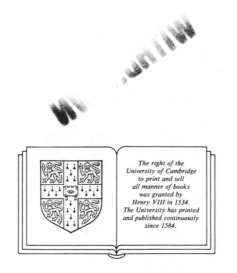

The right of the
University of Cambridge
to print and sell
all manner of books
was granted by
Henry VIII in 1534.
The University has printed
and published continuously
since 1584.

CAMBRIDGE UNIVERSITY PRESS

CAMBRIDGE

LONDON   NEW YORK   NEW ROCHELLE

MELBOURNE   SYDNEY

Published by the Press Syndicate of the University of Cambridge
The Pitt Building, Trumpington Street, Cambridge CB2 1RP
32 East 57th Street, New York, NY 10022, USA
296 Beaconsfield Parade, Middle Park, Melbourne 3206, Australia

First published 1984

Printed in Great Britain at The Pitman Press, Bath

Library of Congress catalogue card number: 83–24055

British Library Cataloguing in Publication Data
Goldthorpe, Rhiannon
Sartre. – (Cambridge Studies in French)
1. Sartre, Jean-Paul – Criticism and interpretation
I. Title
848′.91209   PQ2637.A82Z
ISBN 0 521 23791 2

PP

For Siân and David

CONTENTS

GENERAL EDITOR'S PREFACE

This series aims at providing a new forum for the discussion of major critical or scholarly topics within the field of French studies. It differs from most similar-seeming ventures in the degree of freedom which contributing authors are allowed and in the range of subjects covered. For the series is not concerned to promote any single area of academic specialisation or any single theoretical approach. Authors are invited to address themselves to *problems*, and to argue their solutions in whatever terms seem best able to produce an incisive and cogent account of the matter in hand. The search for such terms will sometimes involve the crossing of boundaries between familiar academic disciplines, or the calling of those boundaries into dispute. Most of the studies will be written especially for the series, although from time to time it will also provide new editions of outstanding works which were previously out of print, or originally published in languages other than English or French.

ACKNOWLEDGEMENTS

The first two parts of Chapter 1 and the whole of Chapter 3 first appeared in *French Studies* (vols XXII (1968), XXV (1971) and XXXIV (1980) respectively). An earlier version of Chapter 5 was published in the *Journal of the British Society for Phenomenology* (vol. IV (1973)). I am indebted to the editors of these journals (Professor Malcolm Bowie and Dr Wolfe Mays) for permission to use this material. A version of the third part of Chapter 1 was read to a colloquium on 'La Fiction de Sartre' at the University of Warwick in January 1981; Chapter 2 and the first part of Chapter 6 grew out of papers read to the Society of French Studies in March 1968 and March 1981. I am grateful to the organisers of those meetings for giving me the opportunity to present and discuss my views. The second section of Chapter 6 first appeared in *Baudelaire, Mallarmé, Valéry. New Essays in Honour of Lloyd Austin*, ed. Malcolm Bowie, Alison Fairlie and Alison Finch (Cambridge University Press, 1982). My thanks go to Professor Austin, and to the editors and publishers, for permission to reprint. I am also grateful to the Principal and Fellows of St Anne's College, Oxford, for a period of sabbatical leave which gave me time to write and rewrite.

It gives me particular pleasure to thank the following: Malcolm Bowie, for the generous encouragement and help which made this book possible, and John Goldthorpe, for his unfailing sense of proportion. Finally, I owe a long-standing debt of gratitude to Professor Ian Alexander, who first helped me to read Sartre, and whose teaching I recall with deep appreciation.

ABBREVIATIONS

References to Sartre's works are given in the text, with the
following abbreviated titles:

CRD	*Critique de la raison dialectique*
EM	*L'Engagement de Mallarmé*
EN	*L'Etre et le Néant*
ETE	*Esquisse d'une théorie des émotions*
GM	*La Grande Morale*
IF	*L'Idiot de la famille*
Im.	*L'Imaginaire*
O.r.	*Œuvres romanesques*
S i–x	*Situations*, vols i to x
SG	*Saint Genet, comédien et martyr*
TE	*La Transcendance de l'Ego*
TS	*Un Théâtre de situations*

When a sequence of references is given to the same text, the abbreviated title appears with the first reference only.

INTRODUCTION

It may verge upon paradox to suggest that a writer as voluminous as Sartre is a master of ellipsis. But his explicit recognition of the power of ellipsis in expression and his own recourse, whether conscious or unconscious, to the unsaid or to the unwritten mean that the task of the reader is often one of unfolding the highly implicit. The essays which follow, although written over a number of years, share a common preoccupation. They aim primarily to explore the not always overt relationships between Sartre's theoretical and literary writing. The first term is taken broadly. It refers mainly to his philosophical and psychological works, but also includes aspects of his dramatic theory and his theory of commitment. Although the opening section of each essay tends to be expository, my discussion of theoretical issues does not claim to be systematic or exhaustive, and it later becomes more allusively interwoven with an analysis of a specific literary work, whether fictional, dramatic or critical. The literary texts themselves are not primarily discussed as illustrations or examples of a philosophical position. They may be seen to anticipate, confirm or question the authority of theoretical discourse. Each mode implicates the other. Indeed, there are times when the form of the literary writing itself crystallises theoretical issues which are thematically dispersed throughout Sartre's works and which are not of necessity those which may at first sight appear to be dominant in a given literary text. Thus, *La Nausée*, which powerfully dramatises the relationships between consciousness and the world explicitly analysed later in *L'Etre et le Néant*, also dramatises the philosophical problems involved in thinking and writing about such relationships – problems which are the subject of theoretical discussion (or sometimes, more accurately, of allusion) in a wide range of earlier, contemporary and later works.

But although, in Sartre, theoretical and literary writing may implicate each other, they do not necessarily validate each other.

1

There are frequent episodes of tension, questioning and subversion between the two. A flaw in traditional dramatic effect may highlight problems or inconsistencies within aspects of Sartre's theory of emotion and reflection (*Les Mouches*). The rhetoric of a theory of dramatic style may run counter to a more strictly philosophical theory of language and action, and both theories may be called into question by the play which most overtly enacts them (*Les Mains sales*). Another play, exemplifying a theory of theatrical distance and a parodic relationship to a literary tradition, may be seen to subvert not so much Sartre's philosophy itself, as a formulaic version of that philosophy (*Huis clos*). The confrontation of an evolving theory of commitment, superficially assertive but potentially self-questioning, with a recently discovered critical essay on Mallarmé, reveals a reorientation in Sartre's thinking which disturbs existing views of his intellectual development.

Despite these indications of disruption and discontinuity, the essays will also explore continuities in Sartre's thought and writing. Certain themes recur with variations. I shall discuss his theory of reflection, which is central to his early work, with different emphases in different contexts. His theory of imagination, which links the theme of transcendence and the practice of writing in *La Nausée*, is also seen to be fundamental to the problems of historical responsibility represented in *Les Séquestrés d'Altona*, and to its dramatic effects. My discussion of emotion in *Les Mouches* complements that of a more generalised affectivity in *La Nausée*. Sartre's notion of the magical is recurrently relevant, as is his closely related and even more dominant theory of poetry. The latter is implicated in the language attributed to Roquentin in *La Nausée*, in the over-categorical definitions of *Qu'est-ce que la littérature?*, to which I shall allude in different essays, and in Sartre's reflections on subversive and critical poetry in 'Orphée noir' and *L'Engagement de Mallarmé*. More generally, three of the longer essays trace a progression. *La Nausée*, as I have indicated, enacts the relationship not only between consciousness and world but between writer and writing; *Les Mains sales* dramatises the relationship between agent and act and between speaker and speech, while Sartre's essays on commitment explore the relationship between writing and action.

This last preoccupation suggests that style is functional in the work of Sartre. The metaphors and metamorphoses of *La Nausée*, the more ritualised rhetoric of *Les Mouches* and the distancing stylisation of *Huis clos* are all integral to their investigation of

2

philosophical problems. But at the same time, the literary quality of their language is underlined by its insistent and wide-ranging allusions to other literary texts and styles. *Les Mains sales* is no exception, although, perhaps more than any other work of Sartre's, it is a play written in and about 'ordinary language'. For this reason, the essay in which it is discussed refers briefly to theories other than those of Sartre. An excursion into speech-act theory may be justified by those aspects of Sartre's philosophy which are concerned with language as a mode of action, and by J. L. Austin's description of his own analyses as a form of 'linguistic phenomenology'.[1]

Otherwise, I shall consider the interplay of theory and literature purely in terms of Sartre's own work. But, as I have said, this should not be taken to imply a closed circuit of mutual confirmation. Sartre's philosophy rejects stability and closure. His literary writing prises apart forms that on the surface may seem traditional. The interaction of literature and theory generates new questions which are themselves open-ended.

1

LA NAUSÉE

La Nausée may be read at two levels. First, it can be taken to be an expression 'sous une forme littéraire des vérités et des sentiments métaphysiques'.[1] In such a reading, the novel would be construed as a fictional transposition, exploration or anticipation of the theories which were being elaborated by Sartre during its period of composition and which were to find their fullest conceptual exposition in *L'Etre et le Néant* in 1943.[2] A second level of reading would concentrate upon the problems of writing explored in Roquentin's diary, upon the extent to which they promote or frustrate the production of meaning and the possibility of paraphrase, and upon the question of whether they thereby confirm, correct or subvert the novel's ostensible arguments and concerns. The two levels might therefore be complementary, but their complementarity might generate tensions and ambiguities not only within each level, but between them.

The essay which follows attempts a reading at both levels. Since Sartre's thinking at either level operates through intricate textual and intertextual relationships,[3] I have chosen to look at its arguments and at its strategies in the three passages of the novel which seem to dramatise most acutely the problems of enacting, in writing, a theory of consciousness and of existence.

Reflection and facticity

The complex structure of *La Nausée* is paradoxically designed to demonstrate the inadequacy of the structures which men seek to impose upon the external world. Roquentin discovers, as he contemplates a tram-seat, that words no longer seem to confer identity upon the object designated; the fragile control of language over the world of things is undermined. He also realises that the existence of particular objects can no longer be explained in terms of the functions which we expect them to perform. He sees, as he walks

4

one Sunday in Bouville, that social conventions are arbitrary and absurd impositions upon the world of human reality. Finally, Roquentin discovers that there is indeed no inherent structure or necessity in the external world itself. From this point of view, the revelation of contingency which assails Roquentin as he sits in the public park can be taken – and usually is taken – to be the climax of the novel. It is certainly vital, in that it presents exhaustively, but allusively and organically, an intuition of the nature of non-conscious being – the *en-soi* – and of its contingency, which obviously completes and clarifies Roquentin's earlier experiences in the episodes of the pebble, the beer-glass and the tram-seat. It also dislocates still further the linguistic, functional, even perceptual patterns which consciousness seeks to impose upon the world of the *en-soi* in order to create a human world within it. Its status as a climax is reinforced by the fact that it is relatively accessible; the revelation which it conveys is structured through recollection, and the implications of the revelation seem to be followed through in a highly ordered and detailed sequence.

Yet this passage by no means summarises the import of *La Nausée*. In the novel, as in his theoretical work, Sartre is as preoccupied with the nature and activity of the *pour-soi* – human consciousness – as with the world of the *en-soi*.[4] The revelation of the nature of consciousness is experienced acutely at two particular points. The first follows the visit to the picture gallery and Roquentin's discovery that he can no longer write his biography of the marquis de Rollebon (pp. 113–22); the second, briefer, but if anything more complete, follows the parting with Anny and the disgrace of the Autodidacte (pp. 199–202). The former episode follows the annihilation of a project, the latter the breakdown of human relationships. It is significant, too, that these passages flank the *Jardin public* episode, which is so often regarded as being, dramatically, the climax of the work, and, philosophically, the crucial passage in the elucidation of the nature of existence. For the point would seem to be that the preceding and succeeding passages complete the experience and the analysis by presenting the nature of human consciousness – of the *pour-soi* – in a purer form as an essential complement to the discussion of the *en-soi*. The three passages are, therefore, inseparable, and convey three essential aspects of Sartre's thought. The sequence could be summarised thus: the first passage is concerned chiefly with the presentation of human consciousness devoid of a project, and gradually overwhelmed by the contingency and facticity which are sustained within it by its own bodily, material, 'factual' situation.[5] Secondly, in the public-park episode, the absolute and universal contingency of the external world is revealed to consciousness. Then finally, in the third passage, Sartre tries to show how the absolute freedom of consciousness is related to its extreme, pure, depersonalised transparency as 'intentionality', devoid of identity but nevertheless aware of itself through the constant secondary awareness of the 'pre-reflective cogito' – 'conscience, hélas! de la conscience' (*O.r.*, p. 202). Or, even more briefly, the first passage emphasises the contingency of the *pour-soi*, revealed through its awareness of its physical existence, the second presents the impact of the contingency of external objects upon the consciousness, and the third underlines man's inability to escape the self-perpetuating 'freedom' of consciousness and its constant ambiguity.

The presentation of such a range of human consciousness must obviously involve considerable technical difficulty, particularly in the first and third passages, in which consciousness appears to be disintegrating, reduced to a formless flicker, to a stream of undifferentiated, involuntary responses. Sartre takes up the challenge of expressing what must remain on the very limits of the possibility of expression, of giving form in order to create an impression of formlessness. He must in addition convey a sense of immediacy, of present-ness, unmediated by the retrospective journal form in which much of the novel is cast – the form responsible for the sense of structure apparent in the *Jardin public* episode, but impossible to sustain in a 'stream of consciousness' context. He must therefore lead us to accept what is in effect an arbitrary suspension of the journal form, sacrificed in the interests of apparently immediate transcription. The impression of a lowered, unstructured consciousness must furthermore be conveyed to the reader with a sense of urgency, as an organic experience, yet it must at the same time allow for the possibility of evaluation on the part of the reader. The range of Sartre's techniques in formulating and dramatising such intractable material commands first a fascinated response, followed by a curious interest in the actual techniques employed, and, perhaps, by a suspicion that, in the first passage at least, Sartre has over-compensated for the otherwise possibly colourless and abstract nature of his material in the apparently gratuitous obscenity of Roquentin's responses to the account of the child's death. However, further investigation suggests that the modulations of Sartre's presentation of consciousness in these passages are not only functional in the sense that they vary and heighten otherwise refractory material;

they, and indeed the images in which they are conveyed, are functional also in that they illustrate allusively, but with considerable range and rigour, the analyses of the nature of consciousness set out in Sartre's theoretical work. They have, in the first place, to be seen against the background of Sartre's more general pronouncements. These for the present purpose must be taken as axiomatic: the 'intentional' nature of consciousness (i.e. the fact that it is directed towards an object or referent), its freedom, the definition of consciousness as a 'lack', the fact that consciousness, being conscious of 'what it is not', is radically separated from the material world, and yet, being incarnate, participates in the material world through the body. These ideas are present by implication in all three passages, but analysis will show that the correspondences between the literary expression and the detailed philosophical theory are far more elaborate than one might at first suppose.

The passage which immediately follows the abandonment of the Rollebon project (*O.r.*, pp. 113–22) embraces several levels of consciousness. There is, first, the experience of existence through direct awareness of the body, followed by an attempt to end the reflection which is implied by that awareness: 'si seulement je pouvais m'arrêter de penser' (p. 118). Then, an effort to return to a deliberately heightened purely physical awareness is represented by the self-inflicted wound. Finally, the attempt at distraction through buying the newspaper is frustrated as Roquentin reads of the rape and murder of a little girl; he is again invaded by a sense of physical existence as his consciousness subsides into an increasingly hysterical whirl of desire, shame, fear, disgust, pain, fear, fainting. The sequence is presented in the novel in terms of an intense individual experience; each modulation in fact illustrates a fundamental and universal tension between consciousness and its facticity (the contingent situation over which the individual has no control, which limits the freedom of consciousness; the 'given' basis beyond which consciousness must choose to project itself). The sequence moves from the abandoned project to 'coenaesthetic' awareness of the body; thence to the relationship between reflection, affectivity and the body; finally, it has as its climax an intuition of the self as pure flesh, involving a growing 'objectifying' of consciousness in a parody of being-for-others. The modulations will often be conveyed in imagery, befitting the intuitive nature of the experience, but we shall see that, viewed in a theoretical perspective, the imagery often lends itself to a quite literal interpretation.

The revelation of facticity through awareness of the body is, in *La Nausée* as in Sartre's theoretical work, closely related to the breakdown of a project. We normally transcend our situation by projecting ourselves beyond the 'given' contingency of our material situation towards our possibilities; we freely commit ourselves to a certain course of action in order to realise our possibilities, but we are free to continue or to suspend such a project. Normally, in our everyday acts, we are not explicitly aware that our freedom of choice and responsibility are involved, for we do not even posit our possibilities and the acts which are intended to fulfil them as specific spheres for evaluation and decision. 'Je puis aussi me trouver engagé dans des actes qui me révèlent mes possibilités dans l'instant même où ils les réalisent' (*EN*, p. 73). 'Nous saisissons nos possibles comme tels dans et par la réalisation active de ces possibles' (p. 73). Consciousness engaged in action in this way is essentially non-reflective consciousness, and it implies a particular relationship both with the world and with the body. In his theoretical work, Sartre elaborates these relationships with reference to the act of writing – an illustration which reinforces a comparison of these arguments with the breakdown of Roquentin's project as the biographer of Rollebon. In the action of writing, the world presents itself as a series of objects organised as instruments within the sphere of my project: 'Dans le cadre même de l'acte, un complexe indicatif d'ustensiles se révèle et s'organise (plume- encre- papier- lignes- marge etc.) [. . .] Ainsi, dans la quasi-généralité des actes quotidiens, je suis engagé, j'ai parié et je découvre mes possibles en les réalisant et dans l'acte même de les réaliser comme des exigences, des urgences, des ustensilités' (p. 74).

Elsewhere, Sartre also analyses the place of the body among these 'rapports complexes d'ustensilité', again with reference to the act of writing, and again with relevance to this passage of *La Nausée*. For the body is evidently closely involved in the world of tools, of instruments, of things requiring to be acted upon ('exigences passives'). The body is firstly a *condition* of consciousness and of its powers of transcendence and project. But it is not *known* as such in action, nor is it known as an instrument in the series 'paper, pen, hand', in writing. Our relationship to the body *pour-moi* is existential, not cognitive; our consciousness (of) the body is pre-reflective:[6]

Je ne suis pas, par rapport à ma main, dans la même attitude utilisante que par rapport au porte-plume; je *suis* ma main. [. . .] En ce sens elle est à la fois le terme inconnaissable et inutilisable qu'indique l'instrument dernier de la série 'livre à écrire – caractères à tracer sur le papier – porte-plume', et, à la fois, l'orientation de la série tout entière [. . .]. Mais je ne puis la saisir – en tant qu'elle agit du moins – que comme le perpétuel renvoi évanescent de toute la série. (p. 387)

This is one of the characteristics of the body *pour-moi*, the body as I live it. Normally, 'la conscience (du) corps est latérale et rétrospective; le corps est le *négligé*, le *"passé sous silence"* ' (p. 395). But the body has another characteristic: 'Ou bien il est le centre de référence indiqué à vide par les objets-ustensiles du monde, ou bien il est *la contingence que le pour-soi existe*' (p. 405). This contingency is also 'passed over' in our day-to-day activities: 'Cette contingence, nous ne pouvons jamais la saisir comme telle, en tant que notre corps est *pour nous*' (p. 393).

But there is another dimension of the body – that of the body *pour-autrui* – in which the contingency of the body, and hence the facticity of the self, is fully revealed, bringing about a dreaded 'objectifying' of consciousness in which the *pour-soi* and its freedom are petrified and engulfed by the *en-soi*, as we become objects for the consciousness of others. Moreover, between the contingency 'passed over' in our experience of the body *pour-nous* and the fully revealed contingent facticity of our *être-pour-autrui*, there are several intermediary stages, exemplified allusively, but with surprising rigour, in Roquentin's experience.

For Roquentin, Rollebon, the subject of his biography, had existed as a 'structure d'exigence' of the world, constituting, for the realisation of the task, a whole 'complexe indicatif d'ustensiles'. Roquentin defines this past situation in what might be a paraphrase of the extracts of *L'Etre et le Néant* already quoted: 'chacun de mes mouvements avait son sens au-dehors, là, juste en face de moi, en lui; je ne voyais plus ma main qui traçait les lettres sur le papier, ni même la phrase que j'avais écrite – mais, derrière, au-delà du papier, je voyais le marquis, qui avait réclamé ce geste' (*O.r.*, p. 117). But the calling into question and the rejection of the Rollebon project now sets in motion a sequence of experiences explicable, even predictable, in terms of Sartre's analyses in *L'Etre et le Néant*. There, Sartre defines such a situation in terms of the experience of freedom as anguish. The *mise en question* of a project is seen to leave us face to face with our liberty to continue or end the project, the liberty, in fact, to destroy the self which had previously existed as 'voulant écrire ce livre'. 'L'angoisse [. . .] se constitue lorsque la conscience se voit coupée de son essence par le néant ou séparée du futur par sa liberté même' (*EN*, p. 73). This is illustrated by Roquentin's distress when he experiences an

9

inexplicable and apparently involuntary discontinuity of the self. He remembers with foreboding his change of heart in Mercier's office in Hanoi, his curiously passive decision not to go to Bengal; his successive projects have the consistency of dreams, compared with the weight of pure existence which threatens to follow their break-down. This sense of discontinuity and the experience of liberty have another corollary: 'la liberté qui se manifeste par l'angoisse se caractérise par une obligation perpétuellement renouvelée de re-faire le *Moi* qui désigne l'être libre' (p. 72). For Sartre, the freedom of the *pour-soi* involves the total responsibility of the *pour-soi* in recreating and sustaining its own possibilities. Hence the vocabulary of guilt, self-disgust and dehumanisation, suggesting an anguished need for moral self-justification and self-recreation, with which Roquentin registers the breakdown of his project and its effects. At this point, it should be noted, Roquentin does not postulate his freedom openly and consciously; this stage will be reached only later in the evolution of his self-awareness, following the break with Anny, in the passage which, as already suggested, seems to constitute the third climax of the novel. At this earlier point the intuition of liberty and disengagement is implied quite obliquely, and is transferred, thus emphasising Roquentin's passivity, to existence itself. The sense of existence is given a positive, animistic consistency and autonomy: 'La Chose, qui attendait, s'est alertée, elle a fondu sur moi, elle se coule en moi, j'en suis plein. – Ce n'est rien: la Chose, c'est moi. L'existence, libérée, dégagée, reflue sur moi' (*O.r.*, p. 117). At the same time, in the imagery of fullness and nothingness – 'j'en suis plein. – Ce n'est rien, [. . .] c'est moi' – Roquentin illustrates the oscillation between the *en-soi* density of existence, which consciousness recognises as its own facticity, and the 'nihilating' effect of consciousness seeking to tear itself away from this facticity. Theoretically, Sartre expresses this oscillation thus: 'Cette néantisation de l'En-soi par le Pour-soi et le ressaisissement du Pour-soi par l'En-soi qui alimente cette néantisation même' (*EN*, p. 399).[7]

The oblique awareness of freedom is accompanied by a change in Roquentin's awareness of the body, a transition from awareness of the body as 'le centre de référence indiqué à vide par les objets-ustensiles du monde' (p. 405) to awareness of the body as '*la contingence que le pour-soi existe*' (p. 405). This contingency, moreover, is no longer 'surpassed'[8] ('dépassé') as it is in action. The oblique, non-reflective consciousness of the body *pour-moi* gives way to awareness of the body as an independent *en-soi*. Roquentin's movements, no longer purposive, become involuntary: 'Ce mouvement d'épaules, je n'ai pas pu le retenir' (*O.r.*, p. 117). His consciousness focuses upon his body's torpid warmth, viscous secretions and dead weight. His hand, no longer 'passée sous silence' (*EN*, p. 395) in the act of writing, becomes an object apparently beyond his control, no longer limited, even in form, by its function: 'Je vois ma main, qui s'épanouit sur la table' (*O.r.*, p. 117); it becomes a grotesque, dehumanised object, a dead crab. At the same time, the contingency of the body, hitherto 'dépassée', is openly revealed: 'où que je la mette [his hand], elle continuera d'exister et je continuerai de sentir qu'elle existe; je ne peux pas la supprimer, ni supprimer le reste de mon corps' (p. 118).

Another aspect of Roquentin's experience of his body as an inert demonstration of facticity is clarified if we refer to Sartre's analyses of 'coenaesthesia' – the general sense of existence arising from the sum of our bodily impressions – and of affectivity. Sartre takes the view that our consciousness of the body is inseparable from our affectivity: 'La conscience du corps se confond avec l'affectivité originelle' (*EN*, p. 395). But a distinction must be made between different levels of affectivity. For Sartre, as we have seen, the body and its facticity can be transcended by becoming involved in our projects as a 'centre instrumental des complexes ustensiles' (p. 390). Similarly, our affectivity can take the form of a project, as an 'affectivité constituée':

Je puis découvrir en moi une affectivité intentionnelle dirigée vers ma douleur pour la 'souffrir', pour l'accepter avec résignation ou pour la rejeter, pour la valoriser (comme injuste, comme méritée, comme purifiante, comme humiliante, etc.) pour la fuir. Ici, c'est l'intention même qui est affection, elle est acte pur et déjà projet, pure conscience *de* quelque chose. Ce ne saurait être elle qui peut être considérée comme conscience (du) corps. (p. 395)

Yet just as the body 'passé sous silence' in a project refers us back to the body as contingent facticity, so does our 'affectivité constituée' refer us back to a basic affectivity as *its* contingent facticity.

Il existe des qualités affectives pures qui sont dépassées et transcendées par des projets affectifs. [. . .] Ce peut être la douleur pure, mais ce peut être aussi l'humeur, [. . .] l'agréable pur, le désagréable pur; d'une façon générale, c'est tout ce que l'on nomme le *cœnesthésique*. Ce 'cœnesthésique' paraît rarement sans être dépassé vers le monde par un projet transcendant du Pour-soi. (p. 396)

But in the passage under discussion, as we have seen, Roquentin's project has collapsed, leaving him with an awareness of his body as pure contingency, and, moreover, as a pure 'affectivité cœnesthésique', of which his tiny involuntary movements, his warmth, his sickly sweet saliva, are precisely the symptoms. In *L'Etre et le Néant* Sartre chooses the example of physical pain to illustrate his analysis of affectivity at different levels of awareness, but he concludes his account with a paragraph particularly relevant to the passage of *La Nausée* which concerns us here, and with a reference to the novel itself. He claims that there is one fundamental 'pure affectivity', in the absence of any specific pain, pleasure or unpleasantness, which reveals our pure facticity to us.

L'affectivité cœnesthésique est alors pure saisie non-positionnelle d'une contingence sans couleur, pure appréhension de soi comme existence de fait. Cette saisie perpétuelle par mon pour-soi d'un goût *fade* et sans distance qui m'accompagne jusque dans mes efforts pour m'en délivrer et qui est *mon* goût, c'est ce que nous avons décrit ailleurs sous le nom de *Nausée*. Une nausée discrète et insurmontable révèle perpétuellement mon corps à ma conscience: il peut arriver que nous recherchions l'agréable ou la douleur physique pour nous en délivrer, mais dès que la douleur ou l'agréable sont existés par la conscience, ils manifestent à leur tour sa facticité et sa contingence et c'est sur fond de nausée qu'ils se dévoilent. (p. 404)

The attempt to deliver oneself, through the specific experience of physical pain, from the basic, colourless contingency of Nausea (here the sickly *fadeur* of Roquentin's own taste of himself) is precisely illustrated by Roquentin's self-inflicted wound when he drives his pen-knife into his hand; this action suggests too the desire, impossible of fulfilment, to be the responsible foundation of one's own facticity. But Roquentin's momentary illusion of meaningful pattern following the wound ('quatre lignes sur une feuille blanche, une tache de sang, c'est ça qui fait un beau souvenir' (*O.r.*, p. 119)) soon fades, absorbed into a sense of colourless contingency: 'il ne reste qu'une petite sensation pareille aux autres, peut-être encore plus fade' (p. 119).

A further relationship between affectivity and consciousness in *L'Etre et le Néant* has its significant counterpart in *La Nausée*; it is centred upon Sartre's concepts of the 'objet psychique' and the 'corps psychique'. In this connection, some reference must be made to the distinctions which Sartre establishes between different levels of consciousness and reflection.[9] There is first, accompanying our consciousness of the world, 'la conscience préréflexive', or 'conscience non-thétique (de) soi', or 'présence à soi' (*EN*, pp. 116–21 passim); the last of these terms suggests that even within this pre-reflective consciousness there is a duality separated by a 'néant', a lack of self-coincidence and identity. This duality is characterised by Sartre as the interplay of a 'reflet' and a 'reflétant' in which, however, consciousness does not posit itself as an object of reflection. This form of consciousness is not positional in any sense, but it accompanies other forms of positional consciousness. Sartre conveys this pre-reflective consciousness through the typographical device 'conscience (de) quelque chose' (we have already seen it as non-positional consciousness (of) the body in action), as opposed to the positional 'conscience *de* quelque chose'.

The second level of reflection is 'la réflexion pure' (pp. 201–5 passim). It is a form of consciousness in which the *pour-soi* reflects upon itself in an attempt to grasp itself, to realise a form of identity. The *pour-soi* attempts to achieve the status of a totality while remaining a *pour-soi*. But this identity and this totality remain forever out of reach, for in reflecting upon itself (as the 'réflexif' and the 'réfléchi'), the *pour-soi* can only perpetuate and intensify the gap which separates the two terms of its duality. Also, although this form of reflection is positional (p. 202), the 'réfléchi' which is posited by the 'réflexif' is only a quasi-object, for it is never posited as external and transcendent; it remains intra-subjective. This attempt to reflect upon consciousness in its activity remains, for Sartre, beyond the sphere of description and definition; 'la réflexion pure' can only be attained through a form of catharsis (pp. 201 and 206).

This second level of reflection is not as relevant to the present discussion as the third level postulated by Sartre, that of 'la réflexion impure' or 'la réflexion complice' (pp. 207–8 passim). In Sartre's theoretical arguments, this is a concept essential to his distinction between the *pour-soi* and the ego, and is closely related to the facticity of the *pour-soi*. Whereas reflection is 'pure présence du pour-soi réflexif au pour-soi réfléchi', in impure reflection, the 'pour-soi réfléchi' is posited as an object: the 'pour-soi réflexif' aims to 'saisir le réfléchi comme en-soi'; an *en-soi* which is 'susceptible d'être déterminé, qualifié' (p. 207). Thus the *pour-soi*, instead of trying to grasp itself in its constant movement towards its own possibilities, posits the reflected consciousness as an *en-soi*, a transcendent object, thereby intensifying still further the distance between the 'réflexif' and the 'réfléchi'. For Sartre, this process constitutes an example of *mauvaise foi*; reflective consciousness 'objectifies' reflected consciousness in order to make an affirmation of identity: 'affirmer de cet en-soi que "je *le* suis"' (p. 208). Reflective consciousness organises reflected consciousness as a series of definable qualities, states or acts – what Sartre calls 'des faits psychiques'. These constitute the Ego, or the Psyche, or 'le Moi', and can be regarded as an object of knowledge in a way in which the *pour-soi* – constantly torn from itself in its project towards its possibilities, constantly undermined by its freedom, haunted by the 'néant' at its core – can never be.[10] The Ego thus constituted by the 'réflexion impure' seems partly a welcome refuge from the anguished freedom and responsibility of the *pour-soi*, partly a reprehensible act of 'complicity' with the *en-soi* in a denial of that freedom. The Ego also possesses a particular temporal dimension and an inner consistency and cohesion denied to the *pour-soi*; moreover, in impure reflection, the Self is at an intermediary stage between the *pour-soi* and the *pour-autrui* (p. 218). In our *être-pour-autrui* we are reduced almost irremediably to the status of an object by the consciousness of another. But 'la réflexion complice' does not only attempt to reduce the *pour-soi* to a number of 'faits psychiques' which constitute the Ego; there is also a particular relationship between 'la réflexion complice', affectivity and the body, which concerns us more immediately here (pp. 395–404 passim).

We saw previously that our affectivity can take either the form of an 'affectivité constituée' – an affective project directed towards the world to apprehend it as pleasant, intolerable, etc. – or the form of a more basic 'coenaesthesia', for which Sartre takes pain or nausea as his examples. These forms of coenaesthesia can themselves be experienced in different ways. In *L'Etre et le Néant*, these are discussed with reference to the experience of pain, but they are equally relevant to Roquentin's experience of nausea. First, pain is experienced not as an object of reflection, but simply as the basis from which consciousness tears itself away (in what Sartre calls an 'arrachement de soi') 'vers une conscience ultérieure qui serait vide de toute douleur' (p. 399). This attitude could be said to correspond to the level of 'la conscience préréflexive' or 'irréfléchie'. It is to this non-reflective surpassing of nausea that Roquentin unsuccessfully aspires: a surpassing in which the contingent facticity of nausea, or pain, is nihilated within the consciousness as *pour-soi*. But it is possible also to apprehend pain (or nausea) at a reflective level; the character of the affective state then changes. It seems to acquire an independent status and its own time-scale; it comes, goes, returns, and it has its own spontaneous animism as the 'illness' into which momentary pains are absorbed (p. 401). The relevance of this analysis to the imagery of nausea which runs throughout the novel is immediately apparent; the sick, insipid taste is sometimes nihilated, sometimes posited as an object for reflection; in the latter case it becomes an entity in itself, apparently with its own volition and consistency – an entity in regard to which the individual seems to remain passive. It becomes an 'objet psychique' for 'la réflexion complice'. (It would seem then to follow from this that the animistic imagery of nausea attributed to Roquentin is not simply individual and idiosyncratic, designed for literary effect, but is regarded by Sartre as a fundamental and universal structure of consciousness reflecting upon an 'objet psychique'.) However, the 'objet psychique' does not share all the characteristics of a pure object of consciousness; it is 'transcendant mais *sans distance*' (p. 402).[11] It is in fact a *quasi*-object. 'Il est hors de ma conscience, comme totalité synthétique et déjà tout près d'être ailleurs, mais d'un autre côté il est en elle, il pénètre en elle, par toutes ses dentelures, par toutes ses notes qui *sont ma conscience*' (p. 402). (Hence the oscillation of Roquentin's imagery between the transcendent and the immanent; nausea has its independent existence, and yet *is* himself.)[12] Moreover, this 'objet psychique' of pain or nausea is the object of a certain form of 'réflexion complice' which is in itself affective rather than cognitive: 'la réflexion qui cherche à saisir la conscience douloureuse n'est pas encore cognitive. [. . .] Elle saisit bien le mal comme un objet, mais comme un objet affectif. On se dirige d'abord sur sa douleur pour la haïr, pour l'endurer avec patience, [. . .] pour la valoriser de quelque façon' (p. 403).

Affectivity, then, can be 'dépassée' by non-reflective consciousness, or posited as an 'objet psychique'. But there is a further stage in Sartre's argument in which affectivity is seen to be related to what he calls the 'corps psychique'. This has two particular characteristics; it is experienced as passive, and it is closely related to the *en-soi*. We saw that affectivity as an 'objet psychique' is experienced as both independent of me and yet as part of me; it is the link of the 'objet psychique' with the body which leads me to experience the 'objet psychique' as 'mine'. Sartre again uses the experience of illness as an example.

Il [le mal] est *mien* en ce sens que je lui donne sa matière. Je le saisis comme soutenu et nourri par un certain milieu passif, dont la passivité est l'exacte projection dans l'en-soi de la facticité contingente des douleurs et qui est *ma* passivité. [. . .] C'est mon corps sur un nouveau plan d'existence, c'est-à-dire comme pur corrélatif noématique d'une conscience réflexive. Nous l'appellerons *corps psychique*.   (p. 402–3)[13]

The passivity of the body bears a curious relationship to the quasi-independence of the affective state, in that the strength of the latter increases in direct relation to the passivity of the former. This definition of the 'corps psychique' as a 'milieu passif' finds convincing expression in Roquentin's experience, particularly in his passive helplessness vis-à-vis his looming sense of existence. Sartre, however, fails to rationalise this relationship between the passivity of the body and affective states in his theoretical analysis in *L'Etre et le Néant*. 'Il [i.e. the 'milieu passif' of the body] est *la passivité que ronge le mal* et qui lui donne magiquement de nouvelles forces, comme la terre à Antée' (p. 403). The curious synthesis of quasi-spontaneity and passivity in the affective states of the Ego is perhaps more clearly expressed in *La Transcendance de L'Ego*, although the relationship of affective states to the body is not elaborated there:

la conscience projette sa propre spontanéité dans l'objet Ego pour lui conférer le pouvoir créateur qui lui est absolument nécessaire. Seulement cette spontanéité, *représentée et hypostasiée* dans un objet, devient une spontanéité bâtarde et dégradée, qui conserve magiquement sa puissance créatrice tout en devenant passive. [. . .] En vertu de cette passivité l'Ego est susceptible d'être *affecté*. Rien ne peut agir sur la conscience, parce qu'elle est cause de soi. Mais, au contraire, l'Ego qui produit subit le choc en retour de ce qu'il produit. Il est 'compromis' par ce qu'il produit. Il y a ici inversion de rapport: l'action ou l'état se retourne sur l'Ego pour le qualifier. Ceci nous ramène encore à la relation de participation. Tout nouvel état produit par l'Ego teinte et nuance l'Ego dans le moment où l'Ego le produit. L'Ego est en quelque sorte envoûté par cette action, il en participe.   (*TE*, pp. 63–5)

We shall meet again Sartre's recourse to anthropological notions of the magical and of 'participation' in order to explain irrational forces within the psyche and within specific modes of expression and of creativity.[14] In the meantime, his analysis of the Ego as a 'synthèse irrationnelle d'activité et de passivité' (p. 65) will help to account for the passive fascination and helpless disgust with which Roquentin contemplates the apparently spontaneous evolution of his affective state. It will also suggest that such a response is not, for Sartre, purely idiosyncratic.

We saw earlier that pain or nausea, as quasi-objects, are in fact objects of affective rather than cognitive awareness. Similarly, the 'corps psychique' as the passive milieu of an affective state is 'suffered', rather than known. Knowledge would be possible only if we could adopt the point of view of the other in a purely external relationship. This affective awareness of the 'corps psychique' has an important corollary, as it reinforces the threat of the *en-soi* and of facticity:

Tout de même que le corps originel était existé par chaque conscience comme sa contingence propre, le corps psychique est *souffert* comme la contingence de la haine ou de l'amour, des actes et des qualités, mais cette contingence a un caractère neuf: en tant qu'existée par la conscience, elle était le ressaisissement de la conscience par l'en-soi; en tant que soufferte, *dans* le mal ou la haine ou l'entreprise, par la réflexion elle est *projetée dans* l'en-soi. (*EN*, p. 403)

The sense of the qualification 'complice' now becomes clearer; in this form of reflection and affective awareness, in this passive 'suffering' of my 'corps psychique' I 'objectify' myself and my physical contingency more and more, eclipsing the free spontaneity of my consciousness; I enter into a reprehensible pact with the *en-soi*. Only the gaze of the other can transform me totally into an object, but I move dangerously near this nadir in the 'réflexion complice' which reveals my facticity to me.

We see, then, that the relationship between different levels of reflection, different levels of affectivity and different levels of awareness of the body is complex and highly systematised. The distinction between 'la conscience préréflexive' and 'la réflexion complice' is echoed in the distinction between affectivity 'dépassée' in an affective project, and affectivity as an 'objet psychique' (or between coenaesthesia 'dépassée' and coenaesthesia as an 'objet psychique'). This distinction in turn is paralleled by that between the body 'passé sous silence' and the body as 'corps psychique'. Furthermore the second term in each distinction is seen as intermediary between the subjectivity of the *pour-soi* and the objectivity of the *être-pour-autrui*.

In what way, then, do these highly systematised theoretical structures find an organic expression in Sartre's presentation of Roquentin? I have already shown how the end of Roquentin's project, in which the facticity of the body is surpassed by its existence as a 'centre de référence indiqué à vide par les objets-ustensiles du monde' (p. 405), reveals the contingency of the body in a fundamental coenaesthesia experienced as nausea. The oblique experience of freedom and anguish also released by the end of the project is eclipsed by a sickening awareness of the body itself; as this awareness is prolonged in reflection, consciousness seems to be sucked down into the *en-soi*. Consciousness in reflection, far from being a means whereby Roquentin can project himself beyond his contingency, becomes the means of accentuating that contingency: 'si seulement je pouvais m'arrêter de penser, ça irait déjà mieux' (*O.r.*, p. 118). Reflection itself becomes contaminated by an overwhelming sense of facticity, inseparable even from coenaesthetic taste: 'Les pensées, c'est ce qu'il y a de plus fade. Plus fade encore que de la chair. Ça s'étire à n'en plus finir et ça laisse un drôle de goût' (p. 118). Reflection's powers of *dépassement* are now engulfed, to the extent that it fails to fulfil even its own projected thought-sequences; it disintegrates into disconnected fragments: 'Et puis il y a les mots, au-dedans des pensées, les mots inachevés, les ébauches de phrase qui reviennent tout le temps: "Il faut que je fini. . . J'ex. . . Mort. . . M. de Roll est mort. . . Je ne suis pas. . . J'ex. . ."' (p. 118). Moreover, this reflection is affective rather than cognitive; it posits its own facticity, and existence itself, as 'affective objects', thus reinforcing their apparently independent power: 'En ce moment même – c'est affreux – si j'existe, *c'est parce que* j'ai horreur d'exister [. . .]: la haine, le dégoût d'exister, ce sont autant de manières de *me faire* exister, de m'enfoncer dans l'existence' (p. 119). This recalls Sartre's analysis of the way in which affective reflection, 'suffering' the *corps psychique* as the contingent facticity of affective states, thereby *projects* one's contingency into the *en-soi*: 'en tant que soufferte, *dans* le mal ou la haine ou l'entreprise, par la réflexion elle [contingency] est *projetée dans* l'en-soi' (*EN*, p. 403). This projection explains, as we saw, Sartre's use of the expression 'la réflexion complice', and Roquentin's use of the term as he considers his own powers of reflection: 'C'est pis que le reste parce que je me sens responsable et complice' (*O.r.*, p. 118). 'Responsable', because human consciousness should sustain the tension, the power of nihilation which constitutes its freedom to realise itself in its chosen projects; 'complice' because the relaxation of that tension suggests a morally reprehensible complicity with one's own facticity. This complicity is mingled with a sense of self-disgust and of helplessness as Roquentin realises that reflection alone is sufficient to sustain the grip of facticity. It is mingled too with a hopeless aspiration for the *néant* of pure consciousness which would nihilate this facticity and project him again beyond it: 'C'est moi, *c'est moi* qui me tire du néant auquel j'aspire' (p. 119). Reflection, too, is accompanied by a curious passivity, by a transference of spontaneity to the 'pensées' which are themselves objects of a fascinated affective reflection: 'si je cède, elles vont venir là devant, entre mes yeux – et je cède toujours, la pensée grossit, grossit et la voilà, l'immense, qui me remplit tout entier et renouvelle mon existence' (p. 119). This recalls with precision Sartre's analysis of the *objet psychique* – pain in illness, or nausea – or, as here, reflection itself in its relation to the *corps psychique* as a *milieu passif*. The *objet psychique* is experienced both as an 'individualité transcendante', as thought is by Roquentin, and as an integral part of the self: 'transcendante mais sans distance' (*EN*, p. 402). 'Ma pensée c'est *moi*' (*O.r.*, p. 119). This simultaneous experience of the *objet psychique* as both spontaneity and passivity is closely related to the projection of consciousness into the *en-soi* which we have already noted: 'en même temps qu'il est objet passif, le mal, en tant qu'il est vu à travers une spontanéité absolue qui est la conscience, est projection dans l'En-soi de cette spontanéité' (*EN*, p. 401). In this way the *objet psychique* is endowed with a certain animism: 'il se donne comme un être vivant qui a sa forme, sa durée propre, ses habitudes' (p. 401). The animistic imagery with which Roquentin posits his own thought as an object of affective reflection is not, therefore, purely a literary device or an element of characterisation; it constitutes, or gives rise to, an essential element of Sartre's thought, which he regards as being of universal validity. The relation of apparently transcendent thought to the *milieu passif* of the body gives a further literal significance to the imagery in which Roquentin's consciousness is rendered insipid and glutinous by his facticity: 'Les pensées, c'est ce qu'il y a de plus fade. Plus fade encore que de la chair. Ça s'étire à n'en plus finir et ça laisse un drôle de goût' (*O.r.*, p. 118).

This last sentence also suggests that the quality of time now experienced by Roquentin is no longer the time of the *pour-soi*, which nihilates its past in order to project itself towards the future. It now appears as a glutinous stagnation, dominated by the past – an experience of time which Sartre rationalises thus:

du fait que le psychique est en-soi, son présent ne saurait être fuite ni son avenir possibilité pure. Il y a, dans ces formes d'écoulement, une priorité essentielle du Passé, qui est ce que le Pour-soi *était* et qui suppose déjà la transformation du Pour-soi en En-soi. Le réflexif projette un psychique pourvu des trois dimensions temporelles, mais il constitue ces trois dimensions uniquement avec ce que le réfléchi *était*. Le Futur *est* déjà: [. . .] il perd donc son caractère de *possibilité-que-j'ai-à-être*. [. . .] Le Présent, pareillement, est saisi dans sa qualité réelle d'*être-là*. Seulement, cet être-là est constitué en ayant-été-là. (*EN*, p. 212)

Hence the imagery of undifferentiated, stagnant duration; 'ça s'étire à n'en plus finir', 'Oh, le long serpentin, ce sentiment d'exister', 'On n'en finira donc jamais?' and the sense of being overwhelmed by an attack from behind (a frequent image in *L'Etre et le Néant* as well as in *La Nausée*), which suggests not only helpless passivity, but the pre-eminence of the past: 'Les pensées naissent par-derrière moi, comme un vertige, je les sens naître derrière ma tête' (*O.r.*, p. 119).

Roquentin's attempt to distract himself by going out and buying a newspaper fails to draw him out of his sense of growing facticity. Overwhelming physical sensations, on the other hand, accentuate it; the smell of newsprint and the feel of paper reinforce his intuition of pure existence, and as he reads the *fait divers* of Lucienne's death, his consciousness reaches its nadir in images of sadism and desire. From the theoretical point of view, this is a logical progression for Sartre: the 'empâtement de la conscience', the pull of the *en-soi*, is most complete in the form of being-for-others exemplified in sexual desire. But for Roquentin, desire is not stimulated by the physical presence of another; how is this apparently gratuitous modulation explained? In *L'Etre et le Néant*, Sartre investigates the transitions that predispose consciousness for the invasion of desire; these transitions follow closely those of Roquentin's experience. For instance, the revelation of the flesh culminating in desire is closely related to the breakdown of a project and the disintegration of the 'instrumentality' of the world. Both these elements are exemplified in Roquentin's experience. If the body ceases to be 'passé sous silence' in action and is revealed as flesh, consciousness will become more aware of the matter and contact of objects (and, by extension, of other people), than of their form or instrumentality (*EN*, p. 461). A further shift in the relationship of consciousness and world will confirm this incarnation – a process reinforced in desire: 's'il [le corps] est vécu comme chair, c'est comme renvois à ma chair que je saisis les objets du monde. Cela signifie que je me fais passif par rapport à eux, et que c'est du point de vue de cette passivité, dans et par elle qu'ils se révèlent à moi' (p. 461). Desire, indeed, reveals an uneasy relationship between spontaneous, responsible choice and passivity – a relationship which leaves ample opportunity for a sense of guilt and disgust. Consciousness, in fact, *chooses* to remain passive, and *chooses* facticity: 'Le Pour-soi [. . .] se détermine [. . .] à se faire empâter par sa facticité' (p. 461). Through desire, then, consciousness is doubly threatened by the *en-soi*: 'Le désir n'est pas seulement empâtement d'une conscience par sa facticité, il est corrélativement l'engluement d'un corps par le monde' (p. 461). This sense of materiality and passive *engluement* assails Roquentin in a crescendo of hysterical disgust, ranging from the feel of his shirt, the smell of printers' ink, the overpowering sense of material presence eclipsing spontaneity ('les maisons se referment sur moi', 'le long du long mur j'existe' (*O.r.*, p. 120)) – to his own uncontrolled reflexes of desire.

Despite the apparent helplessness of Roquentin, for Sartre the ideas of 'complicity' and of responsibility are again related to the experience of desire – a relationship expressed in Roquentin's self-disgust:

le désir me *compromet*; je suis complice de mon désir. Ou plutôt le désir est tout entier chute dans la complicité avec le corps. [. . .] Dans le désir sexuel la conscience est comme empâtée, il semble qu'on se laisse envahir par la facticité, qu'on cesse de la fuir et qu'on glisse vers un consentement *passif* au désir. À d'autres moments, il semble que la facticité envahisse la conscience dans sa fuite même et la rende opaque à elle-même.

(*EN*, p. 457)

In such a situation the body is experienced as pure flesh: 'je me fais chair *en présence d'autrui pour m'approprier la chair d'autrui*' (p. 458).

The 'empâtement' of Roquentin's consciousness is nevertheless not sufficiently complete for the possibility of flight to be totally eliminated.[15] However, Roquentin's flight from desire departs to some extent from the theoretical analysis of *L'Etre et le Néant*. There Sartre makes a distinction between desire and other forms of consciousness: 'La facticité de la conscience douloureuse, par exemple, est facticité découverte dans une fuite perpétuelle' (p. 455); 'dans le désir la conscience choisit d'exister sa facticité sur un autre plan. Elle ne la fuit plus, elle tente de se subordonner à sa propre contingence, en tant qu'elle saisit un autre corps – c'est-à-dire une autre contingence – comme désirable' (p. 457). The fact that the object of Roquentin's desire exists only in imagination may account for this divergence. But, phantasy though it may be, other images – those particularly of dizziness and fainting – seem to confirm, at least at first, the view that Roquentin's consciousness is threatened by complete submergence in the facticity of desire. For Sartre claims that in desire the *pour-soi* passively 'existing' the body experiences it as vertigo; this theory finds its immediate correspondence in Roquentin's experience: 'il subit le vertige de son propre corps ou, si l'on préfère, ce vertige est précisément sa manière d'exister son corps. La conscience non thétique [. . .] *veut être* corps et n'être que corps' (p. 458), 'la chair qui tourne tourne tourne l'eau douce et sucrée de ma chair le sang de ma main j'ai mal doux à ma chair meurtrie qui tourne marche' (*O.r.*, p. 121). Again, for Sartre, the image of fainting ('Antoine Roquentin n'est pas mort, m'évanouir' (p. 122)) can signify the 'dernier degré de consentement au corps' and thus 'le dernier degré du désir' (*EN*, p. 458).

However, Roquentin's experiences of flight and fainting remain ambiguous. For the transitions from fear to flight to the threat of fainting seem to refer to Sartre's theory of emotional behaviour in general even more clearly than to his specific analysis of desire. For Roquentin, the almost irresistible fascination of facticity is counter-balanced by a fear that consciousness will be irremediably engulfed – and this fear, paradoxically, culminates in a desire to annihilate consciousness in another manner. Sartre analyses the relationship between fear, flight and fainting in his *Esquisse d'une théorie des émotions*. Fear is 'une conscience qui vise à nier, à travers une conduite magique, un objet du monde extérieur' (*ETE*, p. 44). Flight is 'une conduite magique qui consiste à nier l'objet dangereux avec tout notre corps' (p. 44). But escape is impossible for Roquentin because his fear is precisely fear of his own consciousness and of facticity exemplified not only in the world but within himself. Flight alone is not enough. But in fear 'une conscience [. . .] ira jusqu'à s'anéantir, pour anéantir l'objet avec elle' (p. 44). So fainting, for Sartre (and here for Roquentin), is a conscious but non-reflective 'conduite *d'évasion*': 'faute de pouvoir éviter le danger par les voies normales et les enchaînements déterministes, je l'ai nié. J'ai voulu l'anéantir. [. . .] Je peux le supprimer comme objet de conscience mais je ne le puis qu'en supprimant la conscience elle-même' (p. 43–4). It is this that Roquentin aspires, and fails, to do.

In this passage, then, Roquentin fails to sustain that 'pure' reflection, that 'refus d'être en-soi' (*EN*, p. 204), which reveals to us our freedom and our possibilities – '[qui] découvre les possibles *en tant que possibles*, allégés par la liberté du pour-soi' (p. 204). Instead, facticity, exemplified here by an overwhelming sense of physical existence, and induced by 'impure' reflection, has engulfed his freedom and obscured his possibilities. The *pour-soi* has become 'hypostatised' into the *en-soi* of facticity. Yet the process is not complete: Roquentin's consciousness remains capable of sensing and expressing, if not of fully and explicitly evaluating, the moral reprehensibility of his experience. However, the reader's response remains ambiguous. Is Roquentin's passivity in fact inherent in the nature of consciousness, reflection and existence, and as such beyond moral evaluation, or is it a deficiency within his power to remedy – a failure of his consciousness to project itself beyond its present situation? It is possible to read the passage as an ironic comment upon Roquentin's failure to sustain a project, but the ironic effect is far from unambiguously realised. And although further ambiguities may depend, as we shall see, upon the embodiment of the experience in a fictional character, this fundamental difficulty is implicit in the theory itself – a theory in which an ostensibly descriptive ontology concerned with levels of reflection, affectivity and awareness of the body becomes a field for moral evaluation. 'Impure' reflection, for instance, involving the 'complicity' of consciousness, resulting in the constituting of an Ego and in the near submergence of consciousness in the flesh, is seen to be essentially reprehensible. Yet so elusive is the experience of 'pure' reflection, and so obscure are the means of achieving it, that 'impure' reflection appears to be the only possible mode of reflection, and seems therefore to be outside the jurisdiction of moral imperatives. But yet again, the very postulation of the former leads the reader to recognise in Sartre's work, whether theoretical or fictional, the powerful expression of a certain 'Spleen et Idéal' – of human consciousness aspiring towards purity, self-coincidence and permanence, yet irremediably trammelled by the limitations of its own duality, of the world, time and the flesh.

Transcendence and intentionality

In Roquentin's experience, then, when he ceases to write his biography of the marquis de Rollebon, the facticity of the *pour-soi* – of human consciousness – is revealed through its awareness of its incarnate existence. The experience corresponds closely to Sartre's theoretical analyses of the breakdown of a project and of the instrumentality of the world – a breakdown marked by a transition from awareness of the body *pour moi* to awareness of the body as an independent *en-soi*. This experience, as we saw, is also closely related to Sartre's theories of coenaesthesia and affectivity, to his concepts of *l'objet psychique* and *le corps psychique* and to the distinctions which he establishes between different levels of consciousness and reflection.

A similar correspondence between literary theme and detailed philosophical theory may be seen in two further passages of *La Nausée*. In the second passage which I wish to discuss – the episode in the *Jardin public* – the sequence and the significance of this correspondence are at least superficially easier to establish than in the other two, where the effect of an apparently unstructured 'stream of consciousness' is achieved by abandoning the degree of retrospection implied by the journal form. In the account of the episode in the park Sartre allows Roquentin to return quite explicitly to the convention of the diary: 'Le mot d'Absurdité naît à présent sous ma plume' (*O.r.*, p. 152). But although the tone is no longer one of panic-stricken immediacy and urgency, the control of the intellect over emotional response is still precarious, creating a sense of tension which would be absent from a purely abstract disquisition: '*moi aussi j'étais de trop*. Heureusement je ne le sentais pas, je le comprenais surtout, mais j'étais mal à l'aise parce que j'avais peur de le sentir' (p. 152). Moreover, the implications of the idea of absurdity and the nature of the *en-soi* are still explored, even if in great detail, within a framework of concrete experience. But apart from this exhaustive presentation of the *en-soi* Sartre also examines in this episode the structure of man's modes of consciousness of the world, and of the world's *être-en-soi*.[16] He is concerned not only with absurdity but with ambiguity.

Sartre takes as his starting point the breakdown of the categorising, abstracting function of consciousness. The consequences of this breakdown will involve not only the revelation of the *en-soi*, of brute existence, but the revelation, too, of aspects of consciousness and perception which, though fundamental, are more rarely experienced than the 'normal' sense-giving functions of consciousness. Those functions are, in any event, shown to be gratuitous. First, Roquentin recognises that the tendency to see objects in terms of categories is arbitrary: 'Je pensais l'*appartenance*, je me disais que la mer appartenait à la classe des objets verts ou que le vert faisait partie des qualités de la mer' (p. 150). Objects are seen to be refractory to definition in terms of use or function (a danger signal similar to the intuition which follows the abandoning of the Rollebon project – an intuition which involved, as I pointed out earlier, the experience of facticity): 'Je les prenais dans mes mains, elles me servaient d'outils, je prévoyais leurs résistances. Mais tout ça se passait à la surface' (p. 150). Roquentin realises the inadequacy of general scientific explanation, in terms, for instance, of function, when he attempts to account for the existence of an individual object: 'Je voyais bien qu'on ne pouvait pas passer de sa fonction de racine, de pompe aspirante, à *ça*, à cette peau dure et compacte de phoque, à cet aspect huileux, calleux, entêté. La fonction n'expliquait rien: elle permettait de comprendre en gros ce que c'était qu'une racine, mais pas du tout *celle-ci*' (p. 153). Yet, particularly, the individuality of objects itself dissolves into what Sartre calls 'l'indifférence absolue de l'identité' (*EN*, p. 222) or 'l'indistinction totale de l'être' (p. 227). A further aspect of the breakdown of categories is related to the absence of individuation and differentiation in the *en-soi*, namely, the refusal of the qualities of an object to correspond to essential or ideal concepts of qualities: 'la racine *n'était pas* noire, ce n'était pas du noir qu'il y avait sur ce morceau de bois – c'était. . . autre chose: le noir, comme le cercle, n'existait pas. Je regardais la racine: était-elle *plus que noire* ou noire *à peu près*?' (*O.r.*, p. 154). This particular aspect of Roquentin's *malaise* is closely related to Sartre's theory of sense-perception – a theory which underlines Roquentin's affirmation that to differentiate between the senses is to effect a false categorisation: 'Je ne le *voyais* pas simplement ce noir: la vue, c'est une invention abstraite, une idée nettoyée, simplifiée, une idée d'homme' (p. 155). For the perception of the quality of an object through an 'acte négateur' corresponds to 'un dévoilement total de l'être "par un profil"' (*EN*, p. 237) and that 'profil' is, in the case of a quality, 'entièrement *pénétrée par* le fond, elle le retient en elle comme sa propre densité indifférenciée' (p. 238, my italics). The quality of an object seems, then, to reveal a greater 'densité d'être' (p. 238) than the perceived object (the 'ceci') itself, which appears '*sur* un fond indifférencié' (p. 238, my italics). So while the 'médiation néantisante du pour-soi' is necessary 'pour qu'il y ait des qualités', 'toute qualité de l'être est tout l'être: elle est la présence de son absolue contingence, elle est son irréductibilité d'indifférence' (p. 236). As he looks, then, at the dense but elusive colour of the tree-root, Roquentin senses that he is in the presence of an ambiguous being which attempts, but fails, to struggle out of its amorphous indeterminacy – an obstinately non-human presence which can only be circumscribed, if at all, through a humanising analogy:

Ce noir, là, contre mon pied, ça n'avait pas l'air d'être du noir mais plutôt l'effort confus pour imaginer du noir de quelqu'un qui n'en aurait jamais vu et qui n'aurait pas su s'arrêter, qui aurait imaginé un être ambigu, par-delà les couleurs. Ça *ressemblait* à une couleur mais aussi… à une meurtris-sure ou encore à une sécrétion, à un suint – et à autre chose, à une odeur par exemple, ça se fondait en odeur de terre mouillée, de bois tiède et mouillé, en odeur noire étendue comme un vernis sur ce bois nerveux, en saveur de fibre mâchée, sucrée. (*O.r.*, p. 154–5)

The relationship between the perception of quality and analogical expression will become apparent later; in the meantime it can be noted that before the conclusion of *L'Etre et le Néant* Sartre devotes the last section of his treatise to 'La Qualité comme Révélatrice de l'Etre', in which it is made clear that quality plays a privileged role in the disclosure of the *en-soi*. It is significant that in Roquentin's experience in the *Jardin public* the recognition of the indeterminacy of quality itself is literally central, and transforms his 'malaise' into an 'extase horrible' (p. 155). Even so, the uncanny dissolution of hitherto familiar and comforting qualities, and of the other concepts and categories which normally allow consciousness to humanise 'l'indistinction totale de l'être' (*EN*, p. 227), is only the prelude to the revelation of further rela-tionships between the *pour-soi* and the *en-soi*.

The episode in the *Jardin public* exemplifies two aspects of con-sciousness which are fundamental to the entire structure of Sartre's theory. The first is the purely intuitive nature of Roquentin's ex-perience: understanding is a matter of revelation in which sight and insight are one: 'Et tout d'un coup, d'un seul coup, le voile se déchire, j'ai compris, j'ai *vu*' (*O.r.*, p. 150). The second concerns the uneasy relationship between consciousness and the object of consciousness in Roquentin's awareness of the tree-root: con-sciousness at the same time is and is not that object: '*J'étais* la racine du marronnier. Ou plutôt j'étais tout entier conscience de son existence. Encore détaché d'elle – puisque j'en avais con-science – et pourtant perdu en elle, rien d'autre qu'elle' (pp. 155–6). Equally significant but more specific aspects of Sar-tre's theory are illustrated in the passage by the *fascination* of Roquentin's consciousness with the tree-root and by the nature of his experience of time. The latter is related, both in the novel and in Sartre's theory, to the unveiling of the undifferentiated plenitude of existence beyond the world of objects, and, even-tually, to Roquentin's dawning but imperfect awareness of an elu-sive meaning beyond the brute being of the *en-soi*.

That our most fundamental mode of knowledge is intuitive is taken by Sartre to be axiomatic. 'Il n'est d'autre connaissance qu'intuitive' (*EN*, p. 220); 'l'intuition est la présence de la conscience à la chose' or '[la] présence du pour-soi à l'être' (p. 221).[17] But the idea of intuition as 'presence to' the object involves for Sartre the detachment of consciousness from the object to which it is present: 'La présence enveloppe une négation radicale comme présence à ce qu'on n'est pas' (p. 222). This cumulative definition of consciousness as intuition, presence and negation partly explains Roquentin's attempt to circumscribe his awareness of the tree-root: 'Encore détaché d'elle – puisque j'en avais conscience –' (*O.r.*, p. 156). But it fails to account for Roquentin's earlier affirmation of identity: '*J'étais* la racine du marronnier' (p. 155) and for the qualification of his detachment: 'Encore détaché d'elle – puisque j'en avais conscience – et pourtant perdu en elle, rien d'autre qu'elle' (p. 156). Sartre, however, provides a theoretical explanation for this oscillation between a sense of identity with and separation from an object of consciousness; he does so by arguing that knowledge as intuition is a mode of being: 'Le connaître [. . .] est l'être même du pour-soi en tant qu'il est présence à. . .' (*EN*, pp. 222–3). In other words, consciousness is *nothing but* that to which it is present. But the idea of 'presence', as we saw, involves a negation: consciousness *is not* that to which it is present. Sartre's apparently paradoxical conclusion is that the 'being' of the *pour-soi* can be said to be nothing other than 'une certaine manière de *ne pas être* un être qu'il pose du même coup comme autre que lui' (p. 222). Consciousness is in fact a *non*-being which receives its determination from the massive presence of its object. Hence the insubstantiality and the sense of dependence upon its objects which, for Sartre, afflicts human consciousness; hence, too, the significance of Roquentin's immediate qualification of his affirmation of identity with the substance of the tree-root.

In both *L'Etre et le Néant* and *La Nausée*, Sartre uses the phenomenon of fascination to exemplify the quasi-identity of consciousness with its object. Indeed, for Sartre, fascination seems to represent a fundamental mode of knowledge in its purest form; Roquentin's experience, although extreme, is not idiosyncratic. In *L'Etre et le Néant* Sartre defines the state of fascination (representing 'le fait immédiat du connaître' (p. 226)) as the 'présence *absolue*' of the object to the 'rien' or the 'négation pure' of consciousness (p. 226). Yet this state of fascination cannot be said to be one of fusion with the object, however strong the momentary illusion of such a fusion: 'Combien de temps dura cette fascination? *J'étais* la racine du marronnier. [. . .] Une conscience mal à l'aise et qui pourtant se laissait aller de tout son poids, en porte-à-faux, sur ce morceau de bois inerte' (*O.r.*, p. 155–6). Fusion and identity with the object would involve 'la solidification du pour-soi en en-soi et du coup, la disparition du monde et de l'en-soi comme présence' (*EN*, p. 226). The condition for a state of fascination is rather that the object should occupy the whole field of consciousness, almost saturating it, leaving the remainder of the world as it were in shadow, unperceived. The object 's'enlève avec un relief absolu sur un fond de vide' (p. 226); consciousness is 'négation immédiate de l'objet et rien que cela' (p. 226).

Further, in his analysis of the negating power of consciousness, Sartre distinguishes between two different levels of negation; first, and more fundamentally, 'la négation radicale' (p. 230), in which consciousness is 'present to' (i.e. constituting itself as not being) 'la totalité indifférenciée de l'être' (p. 231); secondly, 'la négation concrète' (p. 231), in which consciousness is present to a specific object against the background of an undifferentiated world into which other objects merge. The phenomenon of fascination is an example of 'négation concrète' in its purest form, when the background of the world is seen simply as a 'fond de vide' (p. 226). The transition from Roquentin's fascinated contemplation of the chestnut-tree root to the revelation of 'le Monde tout nu' (*O.r.*, p. 159) could technically be described as a transition from a 'négation concrète' to a 'négation radicale'.[18]

For a time, then, Roquentin's mesmerised scrutiny of the chestnut-root seems to correspond closely to Sartre's definition of fascination: 'Dans la fascination il n'y a plus rien qu'un objet géant dans un monde désert' (*EN*, p. 226). Moreover, the 'nothingness' of the fascinated consciousness is brought home to Roquentin as he averts his eyes from the all-pervading object: 'Au prix de quel effort ai-je levé les yeux? Et même, les ai-je levés? ne me suis-je pas plutôt anéanti pendant un instant pour renaître l'instant d'après avec la tête renversée et les yeux tournés vers le haut? De fait, je n'ai pas eu conscience d'un passage' (*O.r.*, p. 156). There can be no autonomous 'being' or continuity of consciousness as an 'entity' independently of the objects of which it is conscious.

Roquentin's failure to register the instant of transition in the shift of consciousness from one object to another is significant in that it reveals a further aspect of the negativity of consciousness. It is *not* that to which it is present; but moreover the nature of time is such that the *pour-soi* cannot be seized in the present, any more than the present instant can be isolated or immobilised: 'En tant que Pour-soi, il a son être hors de lui, devant et derrière. [. . .] Il est fuite hors de l'être co-présent et de l'être qu'il était vers l'être qu'il sera' (*EN*, p. 168); 'Il est impossible de saisir le Présent sous forme d'instant car l'instant serait le moment où le Présent *est*' (p. 168); 'le Présent [. . .] est pur glissement le long de l'être, pur néant' (p. 260). This may explain Roquentin's sense of the disintegration of consciousness in time, and his failure to seize the moment of transition.

But this episode has further implications for the significance of time. It seems to anticipate, with considerable rigour, part of the theoretical analysis put forward in the section entitled 'Le Temps du Monde' in the chapter 'La Transcendance' (pp. 255–68). Here, Sartre attempts to trace the ambiguous relationship of the *pour-soi* (essentially temporal in its activity) and the a-temporal *en-soi*, first in terms of a hypothetically immutable and immobile *en-soi*, and secondly in terms of an *en-soi* subject to change. The fundamental character of this relationship is taken to be the fact that the *pour-soi* projects its own temporality upon the external world, but that this temporality can never affect the substance of the essentially a-temporal being-in-itself. It would sometimes appear, indeed, that the temporality of the *pour-soi* is as it were 'infected' by the stagnant a-temporality of the *en-soi* – a situation which seems to be exemplified by certain aspects of Roquentin's experience.

At first, Roquentin's consciousness seems to be overwhelmed by the a-temporality of the *en-soi*; during his fascinated contemplation of the tree-root he is suddenly affected by a sense of immobility and stagnation, by a disappearance of the future dimension – an experience conveyed by Sartre's choice of spatial imagery: 'le temps s'était arrêté: une petite mare noire à mes pieds; il était impossible que quelque chose vînt *après* ce moment-là' (*O.r.*, p. 156). Or the immutability of an object which is refractory to time is suggested by an image which conflates the temporal and the spatial: 'la souche noire *ne passait pas*' (p. 156). Furthermore, when Roquentin wrenches his consciousness away from this temporal stagnation, he experiences, as we saw, no sense of organic continuity and transition; time seems to disintegrate into a succession of discrete instants: 'ne me suis-je pas plutôt anéanti pendant un instant pour renaître l'instant d'après?' (p. 156). Both these experiences are accounted for by Sartre's description of permanence as a characteristic of a static object (such as the tree-root). For

Sartre, the permanence of a perceived object seems to be a compromise between the a-temporal identity of that object and the temporality of the perceiving consciousness; it is a 'pur glissement d'instants en-soi, petits néants séparés les uns des autres et réunis par un rapport de simple extériorité, à la surface d'un être qui conserve une immuabilité atemporelle' (*EN*, p. 256). Roquentin is aware both of the 'glissement' of 'petits néants' ('ne me suis-je pas plutôt anéanti . . .') and of the immutability of the object: ('la souche noire *ne passait pas*').

The perception of movement raises Roquentin's hopes of finding some respite from the pressure of massive existence through a sense of dynamic temporality or of an inner causal relationship between potential and actual states ('un passage de la puissance à l'acte' (*O.r.*, p. 157)). Initially Roquentin hopes to witness meaningful beginnings and ends in the world of existence: 'j'allais enfin surprendre des existences en train de naître' (p. 156). But birth and death, appearance and disappearance are purely external accidents which betoken no internal necessity and which cannot impinge upon the plenitude of the *en-soi*: 'Las et vieux, ils [les arbres] continuaient d'exister, de mauvaise grâce, simplement parce qu'ils étaient trop faibles pour mourir, parce que la mort ne pouvait leur venir que de l'extérieur' (p. 158). In his theoretical analysis, Sartre justifies such an intuition by referring to the law of identity which governs the *en-soi*: 'le principe d'identité, comme loi d'être de l'en-soi, exige que l'abolition et l'apparition soient totalement extérieures à l'en-soi apparu ou aboli: sinon l'en-soi serait à la fois et ne serait pas' (*EN*, pp. 257–8). Equally, the specific 'absence' that precedes or follows the appearance of a particular object to consciousness is again purely external to that object: it is a *néant* which cannot impinge in the slightest upon the fullness of being: 'L'extériorité absolue de l'En-soi par rapport à l'En-soi fait que le néant même qu'est le quasi-avant de l'apparition ou le quasi-après de l'abolition ne saurait même trouver place dans la plénitude de l'être' (p. 258). So, for Roquentin, apparently temporal relationships within the world disintegrate into purely external ones of isolation and juxtaposition: 'Toutes ces agitations menues s'isolaient, se posaient pour elles-mêmes' (*O.r.*, p. 157).

In Sartre's theory, then, the law governing the existence of the *en-soi* must mean that its substance is impervious to change or succession. However, he acknowledges that to human perception the material world does seem to participate in a dynamic temporal dimension, that there do seem to be meaningful beginnings and ends, and that, empirically, 'nothingness' can appear to precede existence: 'la chose peut surgir de son propre néant' (*EN*, p. 258). Indeed, such a 'surgissement' is a 'structure originelle de la perception' (p. 259). But these structures are seen to be highly ambiguous and precarious, and Roquentin's experience of their disintegration is exemplary rather than idiosyncratic in character. This ambiguity is explained by the fact that consciousness perceives the *en-soi* on two different but interdependent levels: that of the individual object ('des ceci') and that of the totality of the world, which is the 'fond de chaque perception singulière' (pp. 229 and 232). The apparently temporal existence of individual objects perceived by the *pour-soi* is underpinned by the 'temporalité universelle' or 'objective' of the world:

C'est seulement dans l'unité d'un monde et sur fond de monde que peut apparaître un *ceci* qui *n'était pas*, que peut être dévoilé ce rapport-d'absence-de-rapport qu'est l'extériorité; le néant d'être qu'est l'antériorité par rapport à un apparu qui 'n'était pas' ne peut venir que rétrospectivement, à un monde, par un Pour-soi qui est son propre néant et sa propre antériorité. (p. 258)

Further, whereas the *pour-soi* may be conscious of the sequence 'néant-apparition' in its perception of a particular object, behind this apparent sequence and behind the world itself lurks a plenitude of being; the *néant* is in fact secondary to that being, and is merely a function of the perceiving consciousness. This proposition is once again given forceful expression in the *Jardin public* episode, where not only does Roquentin fail to 'surprendre des existences en train de naître' (*O.r.*, p. 156), but his experience of the a-temporal fullness of existence is reinforced by an awareness of the secondary status of the *néant*:

Je n'étais pas surpris, je savais bien que c'était le Monde, le Monde tout nu qui se montrait tout d'un coup, et j'étouffais de colère contre ce gros être absurde. On ne pouvait même pas se demander d'où ça sortait, tout ça, ni comment il se faisait qu'il existât un monde, plutôt que rien. Ça n'avait pas de sens, le monde était partout présent, devant, derrière. Il n'y avait rien eu *avant* lui. Rien. Il n'y avait pas eu de moment où il aurait pu ne pas exister. C'est bien ça qui m'irritait: bien sûr il n'y avait *aucune raison* pour qu'elle existât, cette larve coulante. *Mais il n'était pas possible* qu'elle n'existât pas. C'était impensable: pour imaginer le néant, il fallait qu'on se trouve déjà là, en plein monde et les yeux grands ouverts et vivant; le néant ça n'était qu'une idée dans ma tête, une idée existante flottant dans cette immensité: ce néant n'était pas venu *avant* l'existence, c'était une existence comme une autre et apparue après beaucoup d'autres. (*O.r.*, p. 159)

For Roquentin, therefore, as in the theoretical analysis, the 'fascinated' perception of the tree-root ('le "ceci"') and the momentary sense of temporality achieved by the perception of movement against a wider background merges into awareness of a static, ubiquitous, undifferentiated and indifferent mass of being – 'la totalité indifférenciée de l'être' (*EN*, p. 231). From the theoretical passage it is clear that Sartre regards such a transition as being a constant possibility; he asserts that the subject's sense of temporality disintegrates within the act of perception itself:

Mais le caractère *aventureux* de l'événement comme la constitution ek-statique de l'apparition se désagrègent dans la perception même, l'avant et l'après se figent dans son néant-en-soi, l'apparu dans son indifférente identité, le non-être de l'apparu à l'instant antérieur se dévoile comme plénitude indifférente de l'être existant à cet instant, le rapport de causalité se désagrège en pur rapport d'extériorité entre des 'ceci' antérieurs à l'apparu et l'apparu lui-même.   (*EN*, p. 259)

The phenomena of 'surgissement' and 'anéantissement', of objective temporality itself, are therefore, for Sartre, essentially and universally ambiguous structures projected upon the plenitude of being by the 'non-being' of human consciousness.[19] Yet another aspect of this ambiguity is exemplified in Roquentin's final experience in the *Jardin public*. As he leaves the park, the brute and inert massiveness of existence resolves itself again into a series of individual objects, which seem to be groping their way towards an elusive meaning:

Alors le jardin m'a souri. [. . .] Le sourire des arbres, du massif de laurier, ça *voulait dire* quelque chose; c'était ça le véritable secret de l'existence. [. . .] C'était la, sur le tronc du marronnier... c'était *le* marronnier. Les choses, on aurait dit des pensées qui s'arrêtaient en route, qui s'oubliaient, qui oubliaient ce qu'elles avaient voulu penser et qui restaient comme ça, ballottantes, avec un drôle de petit sens qui les dépassait.   (*O.r.*, p. 160)

Although this passage seems to constitute part of the description of the *en-soi*, it can be interpreted as exemplifying a fundamental and apparently paradoxical aspect of human consciousness which is again related to Sartre's theory of time. While Sartre seems to rob the *pour-soi* of all consistency vis-à-vis the plenitude of the *en-soi*, he nevertheless ascribes to it the entire responsibility for conferring significance upon the brute existence of the world, together with the possibility of moving beyond this absurd, concrete existence towards 'abstract' meanings. For Sartre, the 'abstract' is 'le sens de *ceci*' (*EN*, p. 238), the meaning of particular objects in the world. The existing concrete object never possesses its abstract 'meaning' or 'essence' as a present quality; it can only *point towards* this meaning. Sartre takes as his example the complex of qualities of a given object ('vert-rugosité-lumière') and the essence 'green':

> le vert pur vient au 'vert-rugosité-lumière' du fond de l'avenir comme son sens. Nous saisissons ici le sens de ce que nous avons appelé *abstraction*. L'existant ne *possède* pas son essence comme une qualité présente. Il est même négation de l'essence: le vert *n'est jamais* vert. Mais l'essence vient du fond de l'avenir à l'existant, comme un sens qui n'est jamais donné et qui le hante toujours. (p. 243)

The abstract essence or meaning which 'haunts' concrete being can be revealed only through the temporal nature of human consciousness, which can go beyond the present and the brute 'presence' of the *en-soi* to seize its meaning: 'Le Pour-soi est "abstracteur" [. . .] parce qu'il surgit comme présence à l'être avec un avenir' (p. 239). 'L'abstrait est toujours *là* mais *à venir* et c'est dans l'avenir, avec mon avenir que je le saisis' (p. 238). The power of abstraction is also related to the 'potentialising' power of consciousness: it is a *dépassement* of the *en-soi* which can be achieved only 'en tant que le Pour-soi a à être ses propres possibilités' (p. 238). A pure quality is a 'possibility' of the concrete object, but a possibility revealed or realised only by virtue of its being present to a *pour-soi*: 'le vert abstrait est le sens-à-venir du *ceci* concret en tant qu'il se révèle à moi [. . .] à travers les possibilités que je suis; [. . .] l'abstrait hante le concrete comme une possibilité figée dans l'en-soi que le concret a à être' (p. 238).

At an earlier point in Roquentin's experience in the park, when he contemplates the tree-root, his failure to interpret its colour in terms of 'blackness' does not merely demonstrate the artificiality of our normal differentiation of sense-perceptions: 'Ce noir-là [. . .] débordait de loin, la vue, l'odorat et le goût' (*O.r.*, p. 155). It also illustrates a failure of *dépassement* on the part of Roquentin; it is as though the temporal activity of his consciousness, with its powers of sense-giving and abstracting, had been engulfed by the a-temporality of concrete existence. However, his later intuition that objects are struggling towards a 'drôle de petit sens qui les dépassait' suggests that he is again becoming dimly aware of an abstract meaning which 'haunts' their concrete being. But his consciousness has not yet fully recovered its power of abstracting, of 'projecting' meaning; he fails to decipher the 'petit sens' mysteriously offered

33

in the garden's smile. But how far, one may ask, is this failure of *dépassement* on the part of Roquentin intended to be individual, idiosyncratic and perhaps reprehensible? It would seem from the theoretical analyses which we have discussed that such a failure is simply a demonstration of the fragility and ambiguity of the sense-giving functions of consciousness vis-à-vis the stubbornly mean-ingless, a-temporal fullness of the *en-soi*. But Roquentin's intuition that the 'drôle de petit sens' lies beyond the reach not only of his consciousness but of objects themselves recalls a further aspect of Sartre's theory. For the coincidence of an essence (or the 'abstract') with 'la pleine richesse du concret' (*EN*, p. 244) can take place only on the level of a 'structure idéale de l'objet' (p. 244) to which objects constantly point but which they can never reach; such a coincidence therefore remains a 'fusion irréalisable' (p. 244). Moreover (and here the transition in Sartre's theory is abrupt) this fusion is defined as beauty, a value which 'hante le monde comme un irréalisable' (p. 245) and which, as we shall see more fully later, can be 'realised' by consciousness only 'sur le mode imaginaire' (p. 245):[20] 'Il [le beau] est implicitement appré-hendé sur les choses comme une absence; il se dévoile implicite-ment à travers l'*imperfection* du monde' (p. 245). Roquentin's response to the 'drôle de petit sens' suggests, then, that he is moving towards an awareness of the failure of the world to achieve the fusion of existence and essence, of concrete and abstract, which may only be possible in the work of art. He recalls, without appar-ently realising its significance, an earlier experience when such a fusion had seemed possible – the memorable Sunday when the garden had smiled at him before (*O.r.*, p. 50), when 'quelque chose revient en arrière sur les moments épars de ce dimanche et les soude les uns aux autres, leur donne un sens' (p. 68), and when he himself had felt 'heureux comme un héros de roman' (p. 66). And when Roquentin finally seeks a means of transcending the imperfection of the world, his projected solution will be, precisely, an aesthetic one.[21]

The thematic significance of this episode and its elusive 'petit sens' can appear therefore to be twofold: it describes the failure of consciousness to implement its sense-giving aspirations and func-tions; and, correlatively, it exemplifies the refusal of the world to embody the fusion of existence and essence which is beauty. But we shall see later that it also foregrounds the role of writing in enact-ing or transcending that failure and that refusal.

In the *Jardin public* episode as a whole, then, we have seen that

Sartre is concerned to demonstrate not only the contingency of the *en-soi*, but also a number of aspects of the relationship between consciousness and the world: intuitive knowledge, fascinated perception, the manifold implications of temporality, the sense-giving responsibility of consciousness and the frustration of an aesthetic synthesis. But exhaustive though this demonstration may seem to be, Sartre in fact reserves for the third episode (pp. 199–202) a further major aspect of his presentation of consciousness. In this passage it is shown in its spontaneous, transparent, *impersonal*,[22] constantly renewed activity, directed towards the world and depending upon its revelation of the world for its awareness of its own existence.

After Roquentin has returned from his abortive meeting with Anny and has witnessed the disgrace of the Autodidacte in the library, his sense of self disintegrates – 'le Je pâlit' – leaving only a transparent flicker of awareness: 'Lucide, immobile, déserte, la conscience est posée entre les murs; elle se perpétue' (p. 200). But Roquentin's loss of sense of identity is not simply a neurotic response to his isolation; it demonstrates, on the contrary, what is for Sartre a fundamental attribute of consciousness – one which is moreover related to three equally fundamental notions: the 'intentional' nature of consciousness, the pre-reflective cogito, and the intuition of consciousness as an absolute.

In both the early *La Transcendance de l'Ego* and more briefly in *L'Etre et le Néant* (pp. 147–8), Sartre puts forward the thesis that the Ego is not part of the original structure of consciousness. Indeed, given Sartre's emphasis on the nature of consciousness as a lack, an emptiness vis-à-vis the fullness of being, constantly frustrated in its aspirations towards self-coincidence by its temporal dispersion, it would seem to follow that consciousness cannot 'possess' or 'contain' anything so consistent as an identity or Ego. In Sartre's view the Ego shares the attributes of the *en-soi* rather than of the *pour-soi*.[23] However, Sartre cannot deny that we frequently find our experience explicitly associated with an experiencing 'I'. He argues that this 'I', rather than being a part of consciousness, is in fact an object for consciousness in what he calls 'impure' reflection; in reflecting upon consciousness we 'objectify' reflected consciousness in order to make an affirmation of identity – an affirmation which is sought as a refuge from the inconsistency and freedom of the *pour-soi* and which is therefore in *mauvaise foi* (*EN*, pp. 207–9 passim). Moreover, in impure reflection, the Ego is at an intermediary stage between the free, spontaneous *pour-soi* and our being-for-others, in which we are reduced to an object by the consciousness of the other (p. 208).

From this point of view, it is significant that Roquentin's loss of sense of identity follows his ceasing to be an object of consciousness for Anny and the Autodidacte: 'elle [Anny] s'est vidée de moi d'un coup et toutes les autres consciences du monde sont, elles aussi, vides de moi. [. . .] Pour personne, Antoine Roquentin n'existe' (O.r., p. 200). Moreover, his ceasing to 'be-for-another' leads even to the suspension of the self-reflection which normally 'objectifies' his own consciousness in terms of an Ego: 'il y a conscience de la souffrance.[24] [. . .] Mais personne n'est là pour souffrir et se tordre les mains et se prendre soi-même en pitié' (p. 202). He is left with 'des murs, et, entre les murs, une petite transparence vivante et impersonnelle. [. . .] Elle se dilue, elle s'éparpille, elle cherche à se perdre sur le mur brun, le long du réverbère ou là-bas dans la fumée du soir' (pp. 200–1). In this intuition of Roquentin's, Sartre seems to be expressing his own version of Husserl's theory of the 'intentionality' of consciousness: 'Toute conscience est conscience de quelque chose.'[25] Objects are not in consciousness; consciousness is always directed outwards, beyond itself, upon the world. The imagery in which Roquentin's intuition is expressed seems to follow closely the 'reasoning' and vocabulary of Sartre's article on Husserl; the theory of intentionality means that 'la conscience s'est purifiée, elle est claire comme un grand vent, il n'y a plus rien en elle, sauf un mouvement pour se fuir, un glissement hors de soi [. . .] et c'est cette fuite absolue, ce refus d'être substance qui la constituent comme une conscience' (S 1, pp. 32–3). In the same way as Roquentin's consciousness, now impersonal, is 'délaissée entre ces murs', so, for Sartre, our 'intentional' acts of consciousness

ne laissent même pas à un 'nous-mêmes' le loisir de se former derrière eux, mais [. . .] nous jettent au contraire au delà d'eux, dans la poussière sèche du monde, sur la terre rude, parmi les choses; imaginez que nous sommes ainsi rejetés, délaissés par notre nature même dans un monde indifférent, hostile et rétif; vous aurez saisi le sens profond de la découverte que Husserl exprime dans cette fameuse phrase: 'Toute conscience est conscience de quelque chose.' (p. 33)

It would seem that this 'sens profond' is precisely exemplified in Roquentin's experience at this point.[26]

Yet, however impersonal Roquentin's consciousness may now appear to be, there is still awareness of consciousness: 'elle ne s'oublie *jamais*; elle est conscience d'être une conscience qui s'oublie' (*O.r.*, p. 201); 'il y a conscience de tout ça et conscience, hélas! de la conscience' (p. 202). This 'marginal' awareness has, for Sartre, an important theoretical status. It is a form of consciousness which, unlike the level of consciousness implied in impure reflection, does not posit itself explicitly as an object; it simply accompanies consciousness of objects, upon which it depends in order to exist at all: 'elle [la conscience] prend conscience de soi *en tant qu'elle est conscience d'un objet transcendant*. Tout est donc clair et lucide dans la conscience: l'objet est en face d'elle avec son opacité caractéristique, mais elle, elle est purement et simplement conscience d'être conscience de cet objet' (*TE*, p. 24). Or, as Roquentin experiences it: 'Il reste des murs anonymes, une conscience anonyme. Voici ce qu'il y a: des murs, et, entre les murs, une petite transparence vivante et impersonnelle' (*O.r.*, p. 200). Far from its being necessary for one to be reflectively conscious of one's 'self' for consciousness to be said to exist, it is pre-reflective consciousness which takes primacy over reflective consciousness, which in fact makes it possible: 'c'est la conscience non-réflexive qui rend la réflexion possible: il y a un cogito préréflexif qui est la condition du cogito cartésien' (*EN*, p. 20). In losing a sense of self based on impure reflection, Roquentin experiences the pure, free activity of intentionality and pre-reflective awareness, emptied of the 'opacity' of the Ego, but directed beyond itself towards the opacity of the world. In other words, he attains to what is, for Sartre, an absolute: 'un absolu d'existence et non de connaissance' (p. 23), 'le fondement ontologique de la connaissance, l'être premier à qui toutes les autres apparitions apparaissent, l'absolu par rapport à quoi tout phénomène est relatif' (pp. 23–4). Yet this 'absolute' is not without ambiguity, for it is dependent upon the existence of the external world: 'La subjectivité absolue ne peut se constituer qu'en face d'un révélé' (p. 29). Its absolute quality resides in the fact that in perceiving, it constitutes itself as other than that of which it is conscious: 'En tant qu'il est relatif à l'en-soi, l'autre [i.e consciousness] est affecté de facticité; en tant qu'il se fait lui-même, il est un absolu' (p. 712).

This quotation from the conclusion of *L'Etre et le Néant* provides the ultimate clue to the relationship at the level of theory between the three passages from *La Nausée* which I have discussed so far. At the first two climaxes, Sartre is concerned to show the apparent relativity of consciousness: its facticity first in its dependence upon the *en-soi* of the body, secondly in its near-saturation by the *en-soi* of the external world. At the third climax, however, in the most fundamental revelation of the nature of consciousness, it is seen in its pure, spontaneous but still ambiguous activity as an 'absolu non-substantiel' (*EN*, p. 23). And in the presentation of this ultimate intuition lies the explanation of Sartre's literary mode of expression: 'l'absolu est ici non pas le résultat d'une construction logique sur le terrain de la connaissance, mais le sujet de la plus concrète des expériences. Et il n'est point *relatif* à cette expérience, parce qu'il *est* cette expérience' (p. 23). *La Nausée* presents the 'argument' which cannot be encompassed within the relatively abstract structure of *L'Etre et le Néant*.

Writing and meaning

La Nausée, then, dramatises 'la plus concrète des expériences' – whether the experience of the 'absolu non-substantiel' of consciousness, or of its 'relative' dependence on the *en-soi*. But thematically there is much to suggest that such experiences and their ambiguity escape not only translation into analytic modes of language but writing itself. Paraphrase, or exegesis in terms of a theoretical equivalent, leaves a central question: does the act of writing, whether theoretical or fictional and metaphorical, modify rather than formulate the original experience, and, if so, by what yardstick can the modification be measured? Can the experience, and *a fortiori* its meaning, ever be fully recoverable, or does the written word, like Roquentin's *Jardin public*, simply point towards an inaccessible 'drôle de petit sens'? Experience and meaning may be doomed to remain respectively *endeçà* and *audelà*, outside the reach of writing's unhappy medium.

It is perhaps for this reason that in two of the crucial passages of *La Nausée* – Roquentin's reflections after abandoning his biography of Rollebon, and his wanderings through the streets on his last day in Bouville – the act of writing is fictionally suppressed in favour of a supposedly more immediate discourse. In allowing Roquentin to suspend that most concrete and individual form of writing, the diary, is Sartre enacting that questioning of writing which is so dominant as a theme in the novel – a questioning which exposes the false reconstructions and the false teleologies of biography and fiction?[27] Yet the questioning of writing alternates in an unresolved tension with a sometimes panic-stricken dependence upon writing's unique powers of elucidation, whether of the situation, of others and their past, or of the self: 'Le mieux serait d'écrire les événements au jour le jour. Tenir un journal pour y voir clair' (*O.r.*, p. 5); or later: 'Je voudrais voir clair en moi' (p. 10). Or dependence becomes compulsive necessity as Roquentin's interest in the actual history of the marquis de Rollebon wanes: 'C'est au livre que je m'attache, je sens un besoin de plus en plus fort de l'écrire' (p. 19). The act of writing itself seems to have become more essential than the task of elucidating either Roquentin's own life or Rollebon's, which had become, but now ceases to be, the justification of his own. Then, paradoxically, unreflective writing becomes, ostensibly and in a kind of desperation, the hoped-for instrument of enlightenment, as though its spontaneity could guarantee the elusive coincidence of meaning and event: 'J'écris pour tirer au clair certaines circonstances. [. . .] Il faut écrire au courant de la plume; sans chercher les mots' (p. 68). But the threat in turn might be that words should exploit, as it were, that granted autonomy and *become* things or events in their own right, losing their sense-giving distance. And indeed, at the critical moment when Roquentin's project of writing about Rollebon breaks down, this threatened metamorphosis is heralded by the disintegration of both analytic and unreflective writing, and by the questioning of the written document as *témoignage*, as evidence, and as representation.

Further, the 'narrative' of the metamorphosis and breakdown of language does not simply exemplify different modes of discourse: it dramatises their clash. The subversion of written reconstruction is emphasised in the first passage precisely by its juxtaposition with the conventional modes of exposition and argument illustrated when Roquentin quotes the last two sentences of his own historical writing (p. 113). There is first the convention of straightforward 'factual' narrative, which incidentally calls into question the reliability of narrative itself: ' "On avait pris soin de répandre les bruits les plus sinistres." ' There follows the convention of hypothesis and inference from documentary evidence: ' "M. de Rollebon dut se laisser prendre à cette manœuvre puisqu'il écrivit à son neveu [. . .] qu'il venait de rédiger son testament." ' Then, the convention of chronological precision is emphasised: ' "en date du 13 septembre" '. And eventually, the validity of the document as representation is itself questioned: Mme de Genlis' physical description of Rollebon becomes 'irrealising' rather than 'realising': 'ce n'était plus qu'une image en moi, une fiction' (p. 116).[28] With the disappearance of the 'realising' function vanishes the association between representation and unreflective writing exemplified by the Rollebon biography and, with it, Rollebon's significance as a 'structure d'exigence' of the world (*EN*, p. 74): 'Il [. . .] s'était emparé de ma vie pour me *représenter* la sienne. [. . .] Je ne voyais plus ma main qui traçait les lettres sur le papier, ni même la phrase que j'avais écrite – mais, derrière, au delà du papier, je voyais le marquis, qui avait réclamé ce geste' (*O.r.*, p. 117). As we saw earlier, the once purposive gesture implied in such writing lapses into a failure of control: 'Surtout ne pas bouger, *ne pas bouger*. . . Ah!' (p. 117).

Similarly, the breakdown of the reflective ordering of time implied in retrospective writing and its contamination by a glutinous 'écoulement' is foregrounded by a purely mechanical precision of chronology which parodies the day-by-day linearity of the diary form, by a change of tense which mocks the convention of the retrospective mode, and by a notation of gesture incompatible with writing itself: 'Il était trois heures. J'étais assis à ma table' (p. 113); 'Quatre heures sonnent. Voilà une heure que je suis là, bras ballants, sur ma chaise' (p. 116); 'C'est la demie de cinq heures qui sonne. Je me lève, ma chemise froide se colle à ma chair' (p. 120). Such precision becomes the touchstone for a growing awareness of the basic incommensurability between the time of events and the time of discourse – or, *a fortiori*, of writing. The time of events contracts or expands independently of the time of discourse: the swiftness of the knife stabbed into the hand eludes sluggish words. Later, the stagnation of both thought and flesh oozes beyond halting syllables; finally, broken syntax fails to overtake the speed or equal the duration of Roquentin's flight.[29]

Moreover, the status of events themselves as narrative elements is implicitly questioned – particularly if we recall Roquentin's aversion to the 'sentiment de l'aventure [. . .], celui de l'irréversibilité du temps' (p. 69). Narrative no longer seems to control the selection and recording of events: they are arbitrarily self-generating, but lack the dynamism of beginnings and ends. They are reduced to the recurrent micro-events of physical secretion: 'Il y a de l'eau mousseuse dans ma bouche. Je l'avale, elle glisse dans ma gorge, elle me caresse – et la voilà qui renaît dans ma bouche. J'ai dans la bouche à perpétuité une petite mare d'eau blanchâtre – discrète – qui frôle ma langue' (p. 117). 'Adventures' are capriciously imaginary, inconsequential and desultory: the transformation of Roquentin's hand into a crab, and its irrelevant death. The 'sensationnel' (p. 120) is a *fait divers* read in a newspaper. Words themselves lapse into abortive events: 'Il faut que je fini. . .

J'ex. . . Mort. . .' (p. 118). For Sartre, and normally, it would appear, for Roquentin, the sentence is the unit of language as action,[30] but here sentences disintegrate into the materiality of the word and the syllable, and events detach themselves from writing.

This improbable 'entry in a diary', far from enacting the control of language over objects and events, thus exemplifies 'l'esprit traînant parmi les choses' – that definition of the magical proposed by Alain and adopted by Sartre. For him, the magical signifies, as we saw in an earlier analysis,[31] the affective collusion of consciousness with the body, or a 'conscience passivisée'. But it also has linguistic implications: it signifies the transformation of words into things which have the obstinate and proliferating existence of matter; within 'le règne de la magie' 'le mot est cet être étrange: une idée-chose. [. . .] Idées aveuglées, bouchées par la matière, matière possédée par l'esprit et en révolte contre l'esprit' (*S* I, pp. 221–2).[32] The magical, whether affective or linguistic, operates, for Sartre, through an 'action à distance' of which the power is felt, paradoxically, as immediate; as eliminating, through a process of 'participation' in the anthropological sense, the spatial, temporal or sense-giving distance which would be necessary for the efficacy of action or language in a world of rational causality:

> ce visage qui apparaît derrière la vitre, nous ne le prenons pas d'abord comme appartenant à un homme qui devrait pousser la porte et faire trente pas pour arriver jusqu'à nous. Mais au contraire il se donne, passif comme il est, comme agissant à distance. Il est en liaison immédiate par delà la vitre avec notre corps, nous vivons et subissons sa signification et c'est avec notre propre chair que nous la constituons, mais en même temps elle s'impose, elle nie la distance et entre en nous. La conscience plongée dans ce monde magique y entraîne le corps en tant que le corps est croyance. (*ETE*, p. 57)

Roquentin's suspension of writing enacts this loss of rational distance and the plunging of his consciousness into a 'monde magique': when he reads the *fait divers* of rape and murder, the absent child victim is present to his believing body.

For Sartre, language as the medium of the magical is essentially the language of poetry which reveals 'le cœur noir des choses' (*S* II, p. 67)[33] – a medium in which the sentence as practical instrument becomes the '*phrase-objet*' (p. 68), in which the mental operations performed in normal syntax themselves become objectified and non-transitive. It is as though the 'absolu

41

non-substantiel' of the *pour-soi*, having become the 'absolu-relatif' of embodied consciousness, is in turn transformed into an absolute of material autonomy:

> Certains poèmes commencent par 'et'. Cette conjonction n'est plus pour l'esprit la marque d'une opération à effectuer: elle s'étend tout à travers le paragraphe pour lui donner la qualité absolue d'une *suite*. Pour le poète, la phrase a une tonalité, un goût; il goûte à travers elle et pour elles-mêmes les saveurs irritantes de l'objection, de la réserve, de la disjonction; il les porte à l'absolu, il en fait des propriétés réelles de la phrase; celle-ci devient tout entière objection sans être objection *à* rien de précis. (p. 68)

And indeed, compared with the transparent pallor of the two stilted sentences written for his biography of Rollebon, the syntax of Roquentin's later 'unwritten' discourse has within its pattern of repetition its own vividly opaque and arbitrary density. Prepositions convey not a precise topography of action but absolutes of proximity, movement, direction, presence or agency: 'tenir le journal existence contre existence', 'devant moi le long du mur je passe, le long du long mur j'existe, devant le mur', 'ignoble individu à la chair meurtrie meurtrie d'existence à ces murs' (*O.r.*, pp. 120, 121). Conjunctions are absolutely cumulative: 'Et cette mare, c'est encore moi. Et la langue. Et la gorge, c'est moi' (p. 117). Questions confer upon words what Sartre elsewhere calls an 'existence interrogative' (*S* II, p. 69): 'il dit qu'il est dégoûté d'exister est-il dégoûté? fatigué de dégoûté d'exister' (*O.r.*, pp. 121–2).

Such density makes irrelevant the reader's expectation of an immediately accessible meaning, of a 'vouloir dire' ('il serait absurde de croire que Rimbaud a "voulu dire": tout le monde a ses défauts' (*S* II, p. 69)). Moreover, in eclipsing the 'relative existence' of the author, this absolute autonomy of language eclipses the writing subject: 'le poète est absent' (p. 69). Even so, for Sartre, poetic or non-instrumental language does not lose all meaning: rather than provide a self-effacing vehicle of *signification* it acts as the material embodiment of a *sens* 'qu'on ne peut jamais tout à fait entendre' (p. 63).[34] And indeed the discourse attributed to Roquentin emphasises what Sartre elsewhere calls the 'corps sonore' of words (p. 67). In its insistence on aural *leitmotive* it absorbs vestigial meanings into its barely perceptible modulations until sound-patterns achieve the self-referential compulsion of a refrain: 'doux [. . .] tout doux' (*O.r.*, pp. 117, 120, 121), 'douce' (pp. 121, 122), 'doucement' (pp. 118, 120, 122), 'tout doucement'

(p. 119), 'douceurs [. . .] douceur' (p. 122), 'fou [. . .] tout mou
[. . .] tout doux [. . .] roux mou' (pp. 121–2). Here, words are akin
to Sartre's *mot-chose* or *phrase-objet*. Then, when the mirror-
image so pervasive in *La Nausée* captures Roquentin's threatened
consciousness, the minimal survival of a spectral and alienated
reflection which can scarcely visualise or sustain the self is enacted
in his syntax. Thus, an impersonal perception suppresses the verb
'voir', elsewhere so dominant, and the subject oscillates between
the third person and a precarious reflexive *moi*: 'Il est pâle dans la
glace comme un mort, [. . .] Antoine Roquentin n'est pas mort,
m'évanouir' (p. 122).

For Roquentin, then 'l'esprit traîne parmi les choses'. His
discourse none the less stops short, both thematically and linguistically, of Sartre's later definition of poetry: 'Un chant de douleur
[. . .] est une douleur qui *n'existe* plus, qui *est*' (*S* ii, p. 62).
Thematically, when Roquentin is rescued from this experience of
linguistic panic by the melody of the jazz song, he aspires to its
'being': 'Mais, par delà toute cette douceur, inaccessible, toute
proche, si loin hélas, jeune, impitoyable et sereine il y a cette. . .
cette rigueur' (*O.r.*, p. 122). But he lives in a world of existence
and a world of linguistic flux: he is subject to (as much as the
subject of) the unstable distance of a reflection for which meaning
is never fully immanent nor fully transcendent. He is torn between
poetic and discursive language – but also between discourse itself
and vestiges of the 'already written'. These tensions are dramatised
in Roquentin's frequent quotation and self-quotation, whether
parodic or pathetic. The ambiguity of reflection is enacted in the
metamorphosis of his hand, which makes writing impossible, but
also in the self-quotation through 'represented thought' of a consciousness supposedly experiencing – and partly welcoming with
complicity – the disintegration, or near-disintegration, of writing
and thinking: 'il me semble que ma tête s'emplit de fumée. . . et
voilà que ça recommence: "Fumée. . . ne pas penser. . . Je ne
veux pas penser. . . Je pense que je ne veux pas penser. Il ne faut
pas que je pense que je ne veux pas penser. Parce que c'est encore
une pensée." On n'en finira donc jamais?' (p. 119). The 'poet' is
not quite 'absent': the double 'I' of such self-quotation entails the
inescapable distance and self-presence of reflection.

Likewise, the ambiguity of meaning is dramatised. For while
Roquentin, commenting on his quotation from his own writing on
Rollebon, emphasises its semantic futility, and the semantic
futility of all representation, the traces of past writing in his

deliberate misquotations of Descartes' cogito, and even his quotations of his own fragmented syllables, reintroduce the possibility, albeit a transient one, of registering or deliberately modifying meaning. Further, while at one level Roquentin may mistrust 'instrumental' writing and its sense-giving and representational function, at another he is himself the victim of the affective force of writing as he responds helplessly to the newspaper account of the little girl's death. Roquentin's final 'stream of consciousness' suggests that words, like the urgency of his flight, are sucked into a whirlpool which signals the breakdown of the linearity and transcending power of language.[35] Yet, they are pervaded by quotations of the 'already written'. Writing is another form of facticity from which consciousness cannot break away, even in the illusion of 'immediate' discourse. It is both inadequate and contaminating. It can no longer be the instrument of a 'signifying' commentary whereby Roquentin could elucidate his experience of its disabling limits.

The attempt to preserve the fiction of the unwritten is perhaps more radical still when Roquentin wanders through the streets of Bouville on his last day in the town, and it is again set against an explicit act of writing, in which Roquentin records his account of the Autodidacte's expulsion from the public library: 'J'ai demandé du papier et je vais raconter ce qui lui est arrivé' (*O.r.*, p. 190). On this occasion the validity of narrative is not questioned. But after the entry 'Une heure plus tard' (p. 199), the writing subject and even the speaking subject is none the less eclipsed by an apparently pure discourse which, as we saw, seeks to convey the apparently immediate, impersonal presence of consciousness to its intentional objects. The previous refrain of 'j'existe' (pp. 117–22) becomes 'il y a conscience de' (pp. 201, 202); the dense figurative language of the earlier episode with its stagnant time and obsessive echoes becomes a fugitive and anonymous neutrality. Yet language itself subverts the lucid transitivity of consciousness and its flight within time. It turns in upon itself again in quotation of its own voice, detached from its referent: time and again ' "le train part dans deux heures" ' (p. 201). Or it is dragged back into its own past as it quotes from the moment when its own facticity invaded it, denying a new future: 'Ça ne finit jamais. [. . .] On n'en finira donc jamais?' (pp. 118, 119) becomes ' "On n'en finira donc pas?" [. . .] ça ne finira donc pas?' (p. 202). But ambiguity remains. The ability of consciousness to say of itself 'personne ne l'habite plus' (p. 200) or 'la voix dit' (p. 202) betokens that power of negation and that inner distance which constitute the 'absolu non-substantiel' (*EN*, p. 23) of consciousness. But at the same time, the presence of the previously written, of quotation, suggests the inevitable relativising of that absolute, and the inevitable distortion of the 'plus concrète des expériences' and its meaning.

The attempt to convey the immediacy of discourse in both the passages discussed has, then, a double effect. It postulates that immediacy and refuses to offer a 'written', 'signifying' commentary which would elucidate such an experiential immediacy, but it also questions that immediacy by producing vestiges of writing. However, it also suggests that in different modes of reflection and consciousness the survival of discourse itself is threatened, either by the near extinction of the consciousness which reflects ('Antoine Roquentin [. . .] m'évanouir' (p. 122)), or through the momentary eclipse of the self in consciousness. Both passages are therefore linked to Roquentin's final but highly tentative project of attempting to recover the self in a work of art – a project in which the direct, analytic enlightenment earlier hoped for and lost might become a more indirect illumination. The earlier determination to 'voir clair' through a 'classement' of 'les petits faits' (p. 5) expressed on the 'feuillet sans date' which precedes and motivates the writing of the diary becomes, on its last page, a tenuous and presumably unfulfilled hope of justifying his existence through the efficacy of another form of writing: 'Mais il viendrait bien un moment où le livre serait écrit, serait derrière moi et je pense qu'un peu de sa clarté tomberait sur mon passé' (p. 210).[36]

Does such a hope, albeit for a future-in-the-past, suggest that writing might cease to be a regressive aspect of the facticity of consciousness, dragging even supposedly immediate discourse into the past of the 'already written', and that it might become, rather, a stage in a progressive dialectic? Such a dialectic might take as its starting point the inseparable contradictions of consciousness itself (the fact that it 'is what it is not and is not what it is' or the contradiction between facticity and negativity); it might take as the motive force of its operation precisely the negating function of consciousness which makes possible the constitution of both perceived and imagined worlds; and, through the final mediation of writing, it would both negate and preserve those contradictions in a synthesis of consciousness, world and meaning. Does Roquentin intuit the possibility of such a synthesis, even if he does not achieve it?

Within *La Nausée* itself the unresolved tensions between the two poles of such a dialectic and the elusiveness of meaning are most vividly enacted when Roquentin is not only explicitly aware of the refractoriness of pre-linguistic experience to expression and representation, but when the act of writing, far from being supposedly suspended, is made most plainly evident. For in the episode in the *Jardin public* Roquentin affirms that 'je pensais sans mots, *sur* les choses, *avec* les choses' (p. 152), and yet that 'je suis parti, je suis rentré à l'hôtel, et voilà, j'ai écrit' (p. 160). These tensions perhaps account for the fact that in this passage of the narrative the devices deployed in the act of narration and their temporal relationships with the events recounted are at their most complex. It is therefore necessary to distinguish as precisely as possible between these two levels of the writing. The categories of narrative proposed by Gérard Genette in his 'Discours du récit' will be helpful in this connection. For Genette, the *récit* is 'le signifiant, énoncé, discours ou texte narratif lui-même'; the *narration* is the act of narration itself, or 'l'acte narratif producteur' (understood to be the act of the narrator rather than of the author); and the *histoire* is the 'signifié ou contenu narratif' – the events which are the subject of the *récit*, but thought of in the order of their occurrence rather than in the order of their presentation.[37] Among the indices of *narration*, Genette emphasises 'la présence d'un pronom personnel à la première personne qui dénote l'identité du personnage et du narrateur, ou celle d'un verbe au passé qui dénote l'antériorité de l'action racontée sur l'action narrative'.[38] As Genette suggests later, however, the 'antériorité de l'action racontée' is not a decisive indication: the events recounted may be contemporaneous with the act of narrating.[39] We should bear in mind this simultaneous relationship of *histoire* and *narration* in looking at Roquentin's *récit*. Indeed, we shall see that, apart from the antecedent events which the *narration* records and the occasional simultaneity of *histoire* and *narration*, the act of narrating sometimes has its own *histoire*: it generates its own events.

These complexities are particularly, but by no means exclusively, apparent at the beginning and end of Roquentin's account of his experience in the park. (Indeed, they call into question the whole notion of simple beginnings and ends in narrative.) For the *passé composé* 'j'ai écrit' (*O.r.*, p. 160), which concludes Roquentin's *récit* of his experience in the *Jardin public*, expresses the prior occurrence of the recounted action – that is to say, in this case, the act of writing – and, at the same time, the convergence of the *narration* and of the recounted action of writing. Furthermore, the last of the recounted actions (which is, precisely, the act of writing: 'je suis parti, je suis rentré à l'hôtel, et voilà, j'ai écrit' (p. 160)) refers us back to the beginning of the narrating action or of the *narration* – to the heading 'Six heures du soir' (p. 150) which initiates this entry in the diary and Roquentin's *récit* of his afternoon's experiences in the park. This superimposing of end and beginning, of *narration* and of narrated action is, then, complex. It is not, however, ambiguous, and in this it can be distinguished from the *passé composé* which immediately precedes the notation 'Six heures du soir' and which nevertheless forms part of the account of the afternoon's experience: 'Et tout d'un coup, d'un seul coup, le voile se déchire, j'ai compris, j'ai *vu*' (p. 150). For here the transition from the present tense to the *passé composé* prevents us from specifying the time of the act of writing.

However, although in the *passé composé* of 'j'ai écrit' the present time of the act of writing is suggested, it remains implicit. But an earlier sentence refers explicitly to the present and to the presence of the act of writing: 'Le mot d'Absurdité naît à présent sous ma plume' (p. 152): the *narration* seems to generate its own adventures, its own simultaneous *histoire*.

There seems, then, in the order of the *récit*, to be a sequence of three key phrases. First: 'j'ai compris, j'ai *vu*' (p. 150) (a phrase which, incidentally, expresses intuitive and quasi-mystical understanding: 'le voile se déchire, j'ai compris, j'ai *vu*'); this immediately precedes the diary entry offering a narrative explanation of that understanding, and does not refer to the act of writing; secondly: 'Le mot d'Absurdité naît à présent sous ma plume' (p. 152) – a sentence in which the levels of *narration* and simultaneous *histoire* seem to converge in the act of writing ('seem', because the metaphor of the birth of the word will call for further comment); and, finally, 'j'ai écrit' (p. 160) – a phrase which foregrounds, in a curiously absolute and intransitive way, the act of *narration*, and which implicitly initiates and explicitly closes the *récit* of the afternoon's events.

Now the affirmation of understanding, which, as we saw, immediately precedes Roquentin's attempt to account for that understanding, is taken up again shortly after the beginning of the diary entry – after the beginning, therefore, on the level of the *histoire*, of the action summed up in the final phrase 'j'ai écrit': 'je sais ce que je voulais savoir; tout ce qui m'est arrivé depuis le mois de janvier, je l'ai compris' (p. 150). Here, then, intuitive understanding appears to be linked to explicit knowledge. But the relationship between the two modes of awareness becomes more complex as the *récit* proceeds. For while the sentence 'Le mot d'Absurdité naît à présent sous ma plume' (p. 152) implies, at the converging levels of *narration* and simultaneous *histoire*, a linguistically mediated reflection or a knowledge more explicit than the awareness available to immediate intuition, its context evokes, at the level of the antecedent *histoire*, a different mode of understanding. For at this level of recounted events, 'compréhension', far from being reflective, is pre-linguistic: at the moment of intuitive experience, the intuition escapes the grasp even of metaphorical expression: 'je pensais sans mots, *sur* les choses, *avec* les choses. L'absurdité, ce n'était pas une idée dans ma tête, ni un souffle de voix, mais ce long serpent mort à mes pieds, ce serpent de bois. Serpent ou griffe ou racine ou serre de vautour, peu importe' (p. 152). And a little later, the arbitrariness of metaphorical writing as a mode of representation is questioned even more explicitly, first at the level of the antecedent *histoire*, but then through an ambiguous tense which allows represented thought to merge with the level of the *narration*: 'Je me mis à rire parce que je pensais tout d'un coup aux printemps formidables qu'on décrit dans les livres, pleins de craquements, d'éclatements, d'éclosions géantes. [. . .] Et cette racine? Il aurait sans doute fallu que je me la représente comme une griffe vorace, déchirant la terre, lui arrachant sa nourriture?' (pp. 157–8). The contamination of perception itself by modes of representation is recognised: 'impossible de voir les choses de cette façon-là' (p. 158); and, by extension, the ability of metaphor to represent things *en-soi* is itself questioned. For although the traditional function of metaphor is to supplement the deficiencies of discursive language in 'saying what is', and although Roquentin is himself obliged to have recourse to metaphoric language, it is precisely in metaphor that things do not appear 'as they are'. Consciousness creates the illusion of projecting upon them its own structures as *pour-soi*: in metaphor the thing, like consciousness, 'est ce qu'elle n'est pas et n'est pas ce qu'elle est' (*EN*, p. 111). Metaphor humanises things. But for Roquentin, as for Sartre's poet, metaphor also implies the complicity of consciousness with things, 'l'esprit traînant parmi les choses' (*S* i, p. 222). The necessity, the inadequacy and the insidiousness of metaphor are exemplified in Roquentin's personification of things as increasingly dehumanised persons, in the transition from the distance of simile to the would-be absolute proximity of metaphor, and in his own passive complicity with the passive superfluity of objects:

Toutes choses, doucement, tendrement, se laissaient aller à l'existence comme ces femmes lasses qui s'abandonnent au rire et disent: 'C'est bon de rire' d'une voix mouillée, elles s'étalaient, les unes en face des autres, elles se faisaient l'abjecte confidence de leur existence. [. . .] Si l'on existait, il fallait *exister jusque-là*, jusqu'à la moisissure, à la boursouflure, à l'obscénité.   (*O.r.*, p. 151)

Metaphor, then, is ambiguous; furthermore, language as denomination and predication is deficient: 'Oui, j'avais déjà scruté, avec cette inquiétude, des objets innommables, [. . .] et déjà j'avais senti leurs qualités, froides et inertes, se dérober, glisser entre mes doigts' (p. 154). Nor is his attempt to allow words their own initiative any more successful than his earlier intention to 'écrire [. . .] sans chercher les mots' (p. 68): the sentence 'Le mot d'Absurdité naît à présent sous ma plume' fails, as we shall see, to effect a synthesis of experience and concept. The negation involved in perception and reflection, the contradictions of metaphoric expression, the tension between the concrete and the conceptual seem unable to effect the mediations necessary for the synthesis of experience, thought and meaning in the act of writing. And the absence of synthesis seems to be confirmed by the formal organisation of Roquentin's text, by a relationship between *récit*, *narration* and *histoire* in which understanding, expression and meaning often undermine one another through asymmetry and contradiction.

What of the relationship between *récit* and *histoire*? The affirmation of understanding ('j'ai compris, j'ai *vu*' (p. 150)) which precedes the retrospective narrative of the afternoon's events seems to be confirmed, as we saw, at the very beginning of that narrative, on the level of both *intellection* and *compréhension*: 'mon but est atteint: je sais ce que je voulais savoir; tout ce qui m'est arrivé depuis le mois de janvier, je l'ai compris' (p. 150). Yet this reaffirmation that Roquentin understands the meaning of recent events initiates, in the order of the *récit*, a narrative which ends with an avowal of failure – despite the fact that in the order of the *histoire* this reaffirmation of understanding is subsequent to a confession of definitive non-understanding. And, what is more, failure, and the intuition of a meaning which lies forever out of reach, seem to motivate the affirmative narrative. But the narrator does not register the paradox:

Le sourire des arbres, du massif de laurier, ça *voulait dire* quelque chose; c'était ça le véritable secret de l'existence. Je me rappelai qu'un dimanche, il n'y a pas plus de trois semaines, j'avais déjà saisi sur les choses une sorte d'air complice. Etait-ce à moi qu'il s'adressait? Je sentais avec ennui que je n'avais aucun moyen de comprendre. Aucun moyen. Pourtant c'était là, dans l'attente, ça ressemblait à un regard. C'était là, sur le tronc du marronnier. . . c'était *le* marronier. Les choses, on aurait dit des pensées qui s'arrêtaient en route, qui s'oubliaient, qui oubliaient ce qu'elles avaient voulu penser et qui restaient comme ça, ballottantes, avec un drôle de petit sens qui les dépassait. Ça m'agaçait ce petit sens: je ne *pouvais pas* le comprendre, quand bien même je serais resté cent sept ans appuyé à la grille; j'avais appris sur l'existence tout ce que je pouvais savoir. Je suis parti, je suis rentré à l'hôtel, et voilà, j'ai écrit.   (p. 160)

The end of Roquentin's *récit*, then, has an asymmetrical and complex relationship with its beginning. At first, the end seems to echo the beginning: 'ça *voulait dire* quelque chose' (p. 160) seems to refer us back to 'ce que voulait dire "exister"'' (p. 150) – that is, until the 'vouloir' of 'vouloir dire' in the later formulation detaches itself equivocally from the familiar compound and undermines its sense by transforming meaning into abortive will. In addition, the end modifies the theme of sight and insight: the power of vision as revelation ('j'ai compris, j'ai *vu*' (p. 150)) has already been questioned, at the level of both *récit* and *narration*: 'la vue, c'est une invention abstraite, une idée nettoyée, simplifiée, une idée d'homme' (p. 155); now, at the end of the diary entry, the *regard* is attributed by man to things, and becomes a symbol of shared incomprehension. Finally, the *récit* of the afternoon's events ends with the radical questioning not only of the affirmation which precedes it ('j'ai compris' (p. 150)), but of subsequent affirmations which it encompasses: affirmations such as 'Jamais, avant ces derniers jours, je n'avais pressenti ce que voulait dire "exister"'' (p. 150), or 'je comprenais que j'avais trouvé la clé de l'Existence' (pp. 152–3). For as Roquentin leaves the garden the 'véritable secret de l'existence' (p. 160) is something 'que je n'avais aucun moyen de comprendre, [. . .] je ne *pouvais pas* le comprendre' (p. 160).

What happens, then, between the end of the antecedent *histoire* (the final events narrated – the failure of understanding and the return to the hotel (p. 160)), and the beginning of the retrospective *récit* (the affirmation of understanding (p. 150))? On this point, the text remains silent, and the problem of understanding and meaning, as far as the relationship of *récit* and *histoire* within the act of writing is concerned, remains in a state of unresolved and unexplained tension. There is no dialectical synthesis.

Is the relationship of *narration* and *histoire* more fruitful? The fact that they sometimes converge – the fact that the act of writing has its own simultaneous *histoire* which seems to offer, apart from its own adventures, an interpretation of antecedent events – might indeed suggest that a synthesis of writing, experience and meaning is possible. Nowhere is such a convergence more explicit than in the phrase 'le mot d'Absurdité naît à présent sous ma plume' (p. 152). We saw earlier, however, that the emphasis placed here at the level of *narration* on the possibility of reflection and interpretation is at variance with the implications of the antecedent *histoire*. The convergence at this point of the *narration* and its simultaneous *histoire* seems scarcely more productive. The phrase appears at one level to offer a synthesis of writing and explanation, thus affirming the instrumental efficacy of conceptual language, but at the same time the implications of its metaphorical form belie that very instrumentality: the writer is passive vis-à-vis the word 'Absurdité', which has its own autonomy. Furthermore, the temporality of writing undermines in turn the import of the metaphor: at the moment when Roquentin writes the word 'naît' the word 'Absurdité' is already born. Language, whether conceptual or metaphorical, escapes the efforts of the writer to control it. And a little later, again at the level of convergent *narration* and *histoire*, Roquentin is fully conscious of the futility of the struggle to do so: 'Absurdité: encore un mot; je me débats contre des mots' (p. 153). It is true that later still Roquentin's confidence in the power of words seems to increase: he sees a more hopeful relationship between the explanatory function of *narration* and the wordless and horrible ecstasy of his earlier experiences in the park: 'A vrai dire je ne me formulais pas mes découvertes. Mais je crois qu'à présent il me serait facile de les mettre en mots' (p. 155). And his greater confidence seems to be borne out by new-found powers of definition: 'Je veux dire que, par définition, l'existence n'est pas la nécessité. Exister, c'est *être là*, simplement' (p. 155). But both are short-lived, on the levels, equally, of antecedent *histoire* and of *narration*: 'Mais, tout d'un coup, il m'est devenu impossible de penser l'existence de la racine. [. . .] L'existence n'est pas quelque chose qui se laisse penser de loin' (p. 156). The *narration*, ostensibly explanatory, generates its own *histoire* of fluctuating confidence and scepticism in its modes of explanation, in which scepticism and lack of understanding eventually dominate, and in which the approximations of metaphor increasingly eclipse the would-be precision of conceptual language.

At the level of the events recounted, then, Roquentin moves

from apparent understanding to a failure of understanding. At the level of the *narration* and its simultaneous *histoire*, Roquentin moves through a deceptive understanding ('je sais ce que je voulais savoir' (p. 150)) – deceptive because it has *already* been undermined by further events experienced by the time the writing begins – to a dominant lack of understanding which is made explicit towards the end of the writing. Writing, far from consolidating comprehension, seems to undermine it.

One attractive way, however, of satisfying the desire of both Roquentin and the reader for intelligibility, for the reconciliation of writing, meaning and understanding, would be to affirm that Roquentin has understood the impossibility of understanding and formulation, or, in other words, that the 'meaning' of existence is its lack of meaning. This diary entry would thus have fulfilled Roquentin's desire to write in order to make sense of his experiences. But such a solution would have been achieved at the expense of a banal paradox. It would also involve the assimilation of the 'drôle de petit sens', intuited but left uninterpreted by Roquentin, to the absurdity of existence. His narrative, however, differentiates clearly if implicitly between them. Perhaps, then, this differentiation itself might offer some enlightenment – to the reader, if not to Roquentin. This would centre not so much upon the appearance as upon the disappearance of 'le Monde tout nu' (p. 159) – the last event of the recounted *histoire* before the garden smiles mysteriously at Roquentin. Before that disappearance, there *is* no meaning: 'ça n'avait pas de sens' (p. 159); afterwards, objects point towards a 'drôle de petit sens' (p. 160), but one which cannot be understood. Before, the 'meaning' of existence may be its lack of meaning; afterwards, it is the incomprehensible 'drôle de petit sens' which is the 'véritable secret de l'existence' (p. 160). The reader might infer that Roquentin is confronted with two different experiences, one of the lack of meaning of existence, the other of the limitations of the human mind when faced with the indecipherable meaning of existence, and that he is unable to give precedence to one or to the other. But the difficulty here is that at the time of writing Roquentin is led to question the very revelation of 'le Monde tout nu' (p. 159), its very appearance and disappearance – a questioning which follows his perception of the garden's smile, the intuition of the 'drôle de petit sens', the failure of understanding and the resigned decision to write the diary entry which initially affirms the appearance of 'le Monde' and, with it, understanding and revelation: 'Est-ce que je l'ai rêvée, cette énorme présence?' (p. 159), 'Et puis, tout d'un coup, le jardin se vida comme par un grand trou, le monde disparut de la même façon qu'il était venu, ou bien je me réveillai' (pp. 159–60). The reader recalls the words of Roquentin which immediately precede the revelation of Existence: 'Je voudrais tant me laisser aller, m'oublier, dormir' (p. 149).

The relationship between lack of meaning and an intuited but incomprehensible meaning remains, then, ambiguous; the decision to write and the fact of having written, which end *récit*, *narration* and *histoire*, exist notwithstanding the ambiguity of the two experiences and do not resolve it. Indeed, as different modes of writing, discursive or metaphorical, contest each other and themselves, that ambiguity is, if anything, reinforced. The aspiration expressed in the 'feuillet sans date' to 'tenir un journal pour y voir clair' (p. 5) does not seem to have been fulfilled. For if the 'meaning' of Roquentin's successive experiences is not absurdity but ambiguity, no awareness of this is registered or explicitly expressed by Roquentin.

But Roquentin's loss may be the reader's gain. The clue to meaning, for the reader, lies in the 'drôle de petit sens' which Roquentin fails to comprehend but which his writing, without his fully realising it, embodies. I suggested in my earlier analysis of the experience in the *Jardin public* that for the Sartre of *L'Etre et le Néant* 'le sens' is related to abstract meanings, to imagination and to beauty. Sartre's example of the relationship between the concrete qualities of green bark and the 'abstract' word 'green' explains precisely Roquentin's inability to affirm that the root of the chestnut tree is black:

le vert pur vient au 'vert-rugosité-lumière' du fond de l'avenir comme son sens. Nous saisissons ici le sens de ce que nous avons appelé *abstraction*. L'existant ne *possède* pas son essence comme une qualité présente. Il est même négation de l'essence: le vert *n'est jamais* vert. Mais l'essence vient du fond de l'avenir à l'existant, comme un sens qui n'est jamais donné et qui le hante toujours.   (*EN*, p. 243)

We saw too that the coincidence of abstraction, 'sens' and 'la pleine richesse du concret' (p. 244) can only occur within a paradoxical 'fusion irréalisable', a 'structure idéale de l'objet' (p. 244) which Sartre designates as beauty, and which can only be realised 'sur le mode imaginaire' (p. 245). Indeed, we already know from *L'Imaginaire* that such a mode implies a 'sens': the *objet-en-image* or the art-object makes present the 'totality' of the object represented in a way which escapes both perceptual and conceptual modes of consciousness.[40] Thus, the whole of the renaissance is present as the *sens* of Michelangelo's *David* 'par un lien mystique de participation' (*Im.*, pp. 143–4). But this 'presence' has a curious character, for we also know that the image or the art-object makes 'present' a 'derealised' world which transcends the world perceptually present. It is 'une certaine façon qu'a l'objet d'être absent au sein même de sa présence' (p. 98), it is a magical and haunting presence. And this ambiguous quality leads, through one of Sartre's quasi-dialectical reversals, to the contention that *sens* as *présence* is immanent in things themselves, as well as in the *mot-chose* which, in the verbal image, 're-presents' them. Words themselves become thing-like, haunted by the qualities of things and by a meaning which is as opaque and inexhaustible as things. Yet this is a belief which, Sartre perhaps paradoxically thinks, is validated by the practice of the artist and the poet – those creators of 'derealised' worlds. These views are expressed most succinctly in a passage of *Saint Genet*:

Par *signification* il faut entendre une certaine relation conventionnelle qui fait d'un objet présent le substitut d'un objet absent; par *sens*, j'entends la participation d'une réalité présente, dans son être, à l'être d'autres réalités, présentes ou absentes, visibles ou invisibles, et de proche en proche à l'univers. La signification est conférée du dehors à l'objet par une intention signifiante, le sens est une qualité naturelle des choses; la première est un rapport transcendant d'un objet à un autre, le second une transcendance tombée dans l'immanence. L'une peut préparer une intuition, l'orienter mais elle ne saurait la fournir puisque l'objet signifié est, par principe, extérieur au signe; l'autre est par nature intuitif; c'est l'odeur qui imprègne un mouchoir, le parfum qui s'echappe d'un flacon vide et éventé. [. . .] En produisant son premier poème comme un objet, Genet transforme la *signification* des mots en un *sens*.   (*SG*, pp. 340–1)[41]

Now it could be argued that the 'drôle de petit sens' dimly intuited by Roquentin indicates a 'transcendance tombée dans l'immanence'. It is apprehended *upon things*, rather than reflectively understood to be the goal of the 'dévoilant-abstrayant' function of consciousness or the achievement of an aesthetic synthesis (*EN*, p. 244). Despite Roquentin's desire to interpret it, he fails to register the responsibilities and the operations of his own thought: his consciousness remains *irréfléchie*. Flagging thoughts are themselves attributed to things: 'Les choses, on aurait dit des pensées qui s'arrêtaient en route, qui s'oubliaient, qui oubliaient ce qu'elles avaient voulu penser et qui restaient comme ça, ballottantes, avec un drôle de petit sens qui les dépassait' (*O.r.*, p. 160). The *irréfléchi*, if it is to be written, requires figurative language. But within the humanising image, does Roquentin's language hint at a more reflective 'signifying' distance? The word 'dépassait', at once concrete and abstract, colloquial, figurative and technical, registers, thematically, a disjunction of thought and meaning. But it enacts a potential synthesis, beyond the stasis of existence, of *sens* and *signification* – a synthesis which suggests on the one hand movement, increasing distance and elusiveness and, on the other, transcendence. But this is a transcendence deferred and unacknowledged; construed, in the moment which both precedes and concludes writing, as failure.

Nevertheless, in this intuition of a possible but elusive transcendence, Roquentin's mind is dragging less radically among things than in the 'magical' experience of facticity which followed his ceasing to write about Rollebon. Then, thoughts became things; now, things almost become thoughts. It is also less anonymously neutral than the consciousness which wanders through the streets of Bouville after the disgrace of the Autodidacte – a consciousness which fails to write but which is haunted by the 'already written'. Perhaps it is for this reason that when Roquentin leaves the public park, rather than seeking refuge in the non-referential purity of music, as he did on those other occasions, he resorts, although with no stated hope of success, to the potentially sense-giving power of writing. He thereby transforms experience – whether the vision which precedes the disappearance of 'le Monde tout nu' or the intuition of the 'drôle de petit sens' which follows it, into an imaginary mode.[42] But as we know, he has no sense of having achieved the synthesis of non-conceptual language, of conceptual language and of language as aesthetic representation which might constitute the 'fusion irréalisable' of the concrete, the abstract and the beautiful. Thematically the diary is, so to speak, infra-aesthetic, and the *Jardin public* is pre-eminently the symbol of that status: an unlovesome and ambiguous terrain staked out between the brute materiality of nature and an unproductive human effort which never quite transforms that terrain into art. But does Roquentin at least achieve a synthesis of thought and image without being aware – or consistently aware – of his achievement? Elsewhere Sartre suggests, with some relevance to Roquentin's writing, that 'infra-aesthetic' imaginative thought precludes awareness. Here, in a passage of *L'Imaginaire*, is his definition of the relationship between ideation and image:

Les éléments idéatifs d'une conscience imageante sont les mêmes que ceux des consciences auxquelles on réserve ordinairement le nom de pensées. La différence réside essentiellement dans une attitude générale. Ce qu'on appelle ordinairement *pensée* est une conscience qui affirme telle ou telle qualité de son objet mais sans les réaliser sur lui. *L'image* au contraire est une conscience qui vise à produire son objet: elle est donc constituée par une certaine façon de juger et de sentir dont nous ne prenons pas conscience en tant que telles mais que nous appréhendons *sur* l'objet intentionnel comme telle ou telle de ses qualités. (*Im.*, p. 128)

Now in a mode of writing which seeks to conceptualise 'la plus concrète des expériences' neither consciousness as thought nor consciousness as image alone is adequate. It is at the 'reflective' level of the *narration* that Roquentin discovers the inadequacy of the former: 'l'existence n'est pas quelque chose qui se laisse penser de loin' (*O.r.*, p. 156). At the level of the *histoire* the garden's imagined and enigmatic smile is the 'objet intentionnel' upon which Roquentin apprehends his 'façon de juger et de sentir [dont il ne prend pas] conscience': a sense of complicity, of futile mental struggle and of abdication. Yet this unreflective and – from Roquentin's point of view – inadequate 'conscience imagée' obliquely and implicitly 'motivates' the transforming of the rest of his experience into the imaginary mode.

At this point it must be noted that for Sartre imagination is ambiguous, and that his attitude towards it is ambivalent. In *L'Etre et le Néant*, as we saw, the imaginary mode is associated with 'dépassement' and abstraction, and both imagination and abstraction or conceptualisation involve a free negation of the real. In the case of abstraction, the 'négation polymorphe' effected by the *pour-soi* in relation to the concrete object and its qualities may be fused with the 'négation abstraite qui est son sens' to become a 'structure idéale de l'objet' (*EN*, pp. 243–4). In *L'Imaginaire*, too, despite Sartre's view of imaginative thought as 'irréfléchi', as thinking *on* the 'objet intentionnel', as allowing the 'structure matérielle' of the object of consciousness to dominate its 'structure idéale' (*Im.*, p. 151),[43] 'poser une image' is also 'tenir le réel à distance, s'en affranchir, en un mot, le nier' (p. 233). And, again in *L'Imaginaire*, imagination is associated with the 'dépassement' of an experience which closely recalls the suffocating presence of existence before the garden fails to reveal its 'véritable secret' (*O.r.*, p. 160):

S'il était possible de concevoir un instant une conscience qui n'imaginerait pas, il faudrait la concevoir comme totalement engluée dans l'existant et sans possibilité de saisir autre chose que de l'existant. [. . .] Lorsque l'imaginaire n'est pas posé en fait, le dépassement et la néantisation de l'existant sont enlisés dans l'existant, le dépassement et la liberté *sont là* mais ils ne se découvrent pas, l'homme est écrasé dans le monde, transpercé par le réel, il est le plus près de la chose.   (*Im.*, p. 237)

Furthermore, the sudden vanishing of 'le Monde tout nu' before the inscrutable appearance of the 'drôle de petit sens' exemplifies the 'nihilating' power of imagination and its reciprocal relation to the world:

Le glissement du monde au sein du néant [. . .] ne peut se faire que par la position de *quelque chose* qui est néant par rapport au monde et par rapport à quoi le monde est néant. Nous définissons par là, évidemment, la constitution de l'imaginaire. C'est l'apparition de l'imaginaire devant la conscience qui permet de saisir la néantisation du monde comme sa condition essentielle et comme sa structure première. [. . .] Tout imaginaire paraît 'sur fond de monde', mais réciproquement toute appréhension du réel comme monde implique un dépassement caché vers l'imaginaire. Toute conscience imageante maintient le monde comme fond néantisé de l'imaginaire et réciproquement toute conscience du monde appelle et motive une conscience imageante comme saisie du *sens* particulier de la situation.   (*Im.*, pp. 237–8)

The paradox of Roquentin's writing, however, is that after he has given up the attempt to decipher the 'véritable secret' of existence, he tries to recreate in a 'conscience imageante' the fact of being 'enlisé dans l'existant' (p. 237). And within that attempted recreation, at the level of the recounted experience, a further relationship between existence, thought and imagination is implicitly postulated – a relationship which, within its very instability, enacts the paradox. It is given theoretical grounding in *L'Imaginaire*:

Les choses se donnent d'abord comme des présences. Si nous partons du savoir, nous voyons naître l'image comme un effort de la pensée pour prendre contact avec les présences. Cette naissance coïncide avec une dégradation du savoir qui ne vise plus les rapports comme tels mais comme *qualités* substantielles des choses. Ces savoirs imageants vides [. . .] passent et disparaissent sans se réaliser en images, non sans nous avoir mis, pourtant, au bord de l'image proprement dite. Le sujet ne sait pas trop ensuite s'il a eu affaire à une 'image éclair' à une 'aurore d'image' ou à un concept.   (pp. 91–2)

At the levels of both *histoire* and *narration* Roquentin experiences a 'dégradation du savoir' (whether of an intuitive understanding – 'j'ai compris, j'ai *vu*' (*O.r.*, p. 150) – or of a more reflective knowledge – 'je sais ce que je voulais savoir' (p. 150)). We saw earlier that he apprehends the presence of things no longer in terms of the relations between them but in terms of their material and uncannily indeterminate qualities, which it appears the image alone can capture and which, for Sartre, are pre-eminently 'révélatrices de l'être' (*EN*, pp. 690–708). Sartre sees in each apprehension of quality an attempt to 'percer le manchon de néant du "il y a" et pour pénétrer jusqu'à l'en-soi pur' (p. 695). And yet, we can only apprehend 'la qualité comme *symbole* d'un être qui nous échappe totalement, encore qu'il soit totalement là, devant nous' (p. 695, my italics). At the level of Roquentin's intuition of quality as a symbol of being 'nous voyons naître l'image' in an experience in which presence, relation, quality, image and concept are unstably related, and in which the written image seeks, precisely, to convey the birth of an image: 'La qualité la plus simple, la plus indécomposable avait du trop en elle-même, par rapport à elle-même, en son cœur. Ce noir, là, contre mon pied, ça n'avait pas l'air d'être du noir mais plutôt l'effort confus pour imaginer du noir de quelqu'un qui n'en aurait jamais vu et qui n'aurait pas su s'arrêter, qui aurait imaginé un être ambigu, par-delà les couleurs' (*O.r.*, pp. 154–5). Then the attempt to penetrate to the pure *en-soi* generates, at the level of the writing, an at first hesitant search for analogy: 'Ça *ressemblait* à une couleur mais aussi. . . à une meurtrissure ou encore à une sécrétion, à un suint' (p. 155). However, after the tentative *points de suspension*, the image, no longer nascent, dominates in the synaesthetic 'correspondances', the inverted mysticism, the 'extase horrible' (p. 155) in which Roquentin seeks to disclose the elusive yet pervasive being of the chestnut-tree root.[44]

Indeed, if there is in Roquentin's writing and in his experience a 'dépassement vers l'imaginaire', there are times when it does appear to be a 'dépassement caché' (*Im.*, p. 238) or even, as we have just seen, an inverted 'dépassement'. For within his attempt to evoke his 'enlisement' in existence, at the level of the *histoire* he experiences imagination itself as yet another mode of 'enlisement': 'Je me laissai aller en arrière et je fermai les paupières. Mais les images, aussitôt alertées, bondirent et vinrent remplir d'existences mes yeux clos: l'existence est un plein que l'homme ne peut quitter' (*O.r.*, p. 158).

Yet, still within the *histoire*, those images precede the disappearance of 'le Monde tout nu' and the dim sense of covert meaning. But Roquentin is unable to register a significant transition: there again, the text is silent. The relationships of vision, pre-linguistic comprehension, negation, imagination, writing and meaning reach no synthesis in full understanding, and the text remains *lacunaire*. The major tensions lie between the lines: between the decision to write in a mood of scepticism and the beginning of writing in a mood of confidence which becomes, with writing, increasingly sceptical; between experience and the writing of experience. And these are tensions which the act of writing cannot resolve: it cannot, it would seem, become the 'mediation' of a dialectical synthesis.

But what of the act of reading? For 'l'opération d'écrire implique celle de lire comme son corrélatif dialectique' (*S* II, p. 93). The ostensibly 'infra-aesthetic' character of Roquentin's writing does not lie in its attempts to conceptualise, classify or transcribe, nor in its ostentatious efforts to 'se méfier de la littérature' (*O.r.*, p. 68). It lies in the fact that the diary – and Roquentin's diary in particular – is a solipsistic form. Later, Sartre will maintain that 'il n'est pas vrai qu'on écrive pour soi-même: ce serait le pire échec' (*S* II, p. 93). One justification of Roquentin's eventual but abortive desire to write a novel, as distinct from a diary, might be its recognition of the role of the reader. But that role, as Roquentin sees it, is limited to the reception of a didactic effect, or to the justifying of the author's own life:

Une histoire, par exemple, comme il ne peut pas en arriver, une aventure. Il faudrait qu'elle soit belle et dure comme de l'acier et qu'elle fasse honte aux gens de leur existence. [. . .] Et il y aurait des gens qui liraient ce roman et qui diraient: 'C'est Antoine Roquentin qui l'a écrit, c'était un type roux qui traînait dans les cafés', et ils penseraient à ma vie comme je pense à celle de cette négresse: comme à quelque chose de précieux et d'à moitié légendaire.
(*O.r.*, p. 210)

Roquentin seems to anticipate the view that 'il n'y a d'art que pour et par autrui' (*S* II, p. 93), but despite his sympathy for the author and the singer of the jazz song, he emphasises the 'par' rather than the 'pour': his aspiration is ultimately a narcissistic one. For Sartre, the role of the reader is both essential and active. The writer himself can never fully read his work nor constitute it as an object or as meaning; it is for the reader to attempt a synthesis of 'dévoilement' and production, 'la synthèse de la perception et de la création' through the work (pp. 91–4). And indeed, it is also for the reader to accomplish the synthesis of *signification* and of *sens* which eludes Roquentin's writing. Already, in *L'Imaginaire*, Sartre suggests that the reading of a novel is precisely an example of such a synthesis, which reconciles, also, the *mot-signe* and the *mot-chose*:

Lorsque je lis 'cette belle personne', sans doute et avant tout, ces mots *signifient* une certaine jeune femme, héroïne de roman. Mais ils *représentent* dans une certaine mesure la beauté de la jeune femme; ils jouent le rôle de ce *quelque chose* qui est une belle jeune femme. [. . .] Il ne s'agit donc plus tout à fait ici d'un savoir imageant vide: le mot joue souvent le rôle de représentant sans quitter celui de signe et nous avons affaire, dans la lecture, a une conscience hybride, mi-signifiante et mi-imageante.

(*Im.*, p. 91)[45]

And despite the controversial and apparently rigid distinction between *signification* and *sens* established in the first part of *Qu'est-ce que la littérature?*, in the second part their complementarity – even in committed literature – is indicated. Its locus is none other than those silent gaps between the lines which we noted both in Roquentin's writing about his experience in the public park and in those suspensions of the act of writing which contest its power as transcription, expression or convention. For in disrupting the verisimilitude of Roquentin's diary and hence of Sartre's novel they frustrate the securities of reading as an 'opération mécanique' (*S* II, p. 94) and frustrate the reader's readiness to settle for an accessible and superficial meaning. Rather, Sartre's reader 'projettera au delà des mots une forme synthétique dont chaque phrase ne sera plus qu'une fonction partielle [. . .]. Ainsi, dès le départ, le sens n'est pas contenu dans les mots puisque c'est lui, au contraire, qui permet de comprendre la signification de chacun d'eux; et l'objet littéraire, quoiqu'il se réalise *à travers* le langage, n'est jamais donné *dans* le langage; il est, au contraire, par nature, silence et contestation de la parole' (p. 94). Meaning arises from 'ce que l'auteur ne dit pas' (p. 95) and, as in the silences of Roquentin's text, both the silence and the meaning go unrecognised by the author: 'Car si le silence dont je parle est bien en effet le but visé par l'auteur, du moins celui-ci ne l'a-t-il jamais connu' (p. 95). But the *sens* of the text, which is the reflective responsibility of the reader, can never be definitive: 'pendant qu'il lit et qu'il crée, il sait qu'il pourrait toujours aller plus loin dans sa lecture, créer plus profondément; et, par là, l'œuvre lui paraît inépuisable et opaque comme les choses' (p. 96). The prose work, ostensibly so transparent for the 'committed' Sartre, also mysteriously generates that elusive *sens* which haunts the *mot-chose* of the poet and which, for Roquentin, haunts things themselves.

Roquentin's writing, apart from the solipsism which distinguishes his diary from Sartre's novel, enacts, then, the dilemma of all writers, and the silent spaces between his lines are the spaces of all literary language. It enacts, too, the problem of the relationship between theoretical and literary writing. Theory relies on the *mot-signe*, but a theory which seeks to explore and account for the infinitesimal and unbridgeable spaces of negation between the *pour-soi* and the *en-soi* and of reflection within the activity of consciousness itself must also exploit 'ce *rien*, ce non-savoir silencieux que l'objet littéraire doit communiquer au lecteur' (*S* VIII, p. 437).

2
LES MOUCHES: EMOTION AND REFLECTION

The interpretation of Sartre's dramatic writing in the light of his philosophy has long been regarded as a legitimate, if not exclusively valid, method of approach. The themes of his plays have revealed increasing depths of complexity as critics have related them to Sartre's theoretical analyses of freedom, identity and action, of human conflict and inauthenticity. Conversely, the plays themselves have led some critics to pinpoint apparent ambiguities and paradoxes in Sartre's thought. Francis Jeanson, for example, suggests that Sartre's heroes tend to substitute theatrical gesture for effective action; he sees in this propensity a symptom of a fundamental tension between Sartre's theory of freedom and his recommendation of commitment. Others have sought to analyse the formal qualities of Sartre's plays in the light of this theory. Frederic Will, for instance, notes their apparent avoidance of traditional characterisation, and explains it in terms of Sartre's rejection of deterministic psychology and of the concept of the Self as a definable, consistent entity.[1]

But there is one aspect of Sartre's theory of consciousness which seems to have been largely neglected in discussion of his dramatic work; namely, his analysis of emotional behaviour and emotional attitudes.[2] I refer here not simply to the emotions involved in personal relationships: love, desire, pity, shame; they are obviously rich in dramatic potential, they have been fully exploited in Sartre's plays, and they have given rise to exhaustive critical comment. I refer also to Sartre's analyses of emotional responses to a given *situation* – a situation possibly but not of necessity associated with personal relationships. The implications of these analyses for the dramatic representation of emotion in the plays are seen more clearly if they are looked at in conjunction with specific aspects of Sartre's theory of reflection. Although these theories of emotion and reflection may at first appear to be less inherently dramatic than those associated with *l'être-pour-autrui*, my present purpose

62

is to show that a closer examination of them may lead us to elaborate upon or to modify existing interpretations of the plays, and to clarify, or at least to account for, certain ambiguities. They may also help us to evaluate the success with which Sartre has resolved problems of dramatic structure and expression posed by his theories of emotion and reflection. This transition from theoretical and thematic to aesthetic concerns seems in itself to reflect a development implicit in Sartre's thinking, in which certain aspects of his analysis of emotion can be seen to be related to his theories of imagination and poetic creativity. These theories are considered in their own right in other chapters: apart from their intrinsic interest, they raise fundamental questions concerning Sartre's view of the committed function of literature. These issues can be explicitly touched upon only very briefly within the scope of my present argument, but aspects of their significance will emerge in an analysis of one of Sartre's more problematic plays, *Les Mouches*.[3]

Sartre's theories of emotion and reflection are formulated before *L'Etre et le Néant* in *La Transcendance de l'Ego: esquisse d'une description phénoménologique* (1936–7) and in *Esquisse d'une théorie des émotions* (1939). Although three years separate the publication of these two short essays, the available evidence suggests that they were elaborated at approximately the same time in 1934.[4] The *Esquisse*, though second to appear, does in fact provide a more convenient starting-point for a consideration of the theory. For Sartre moves from an examination of *unreflective* emotional *behaviour* in the *Esquisse* to an analysis of emotional *states*, involving different levels of reflection and introducing the notion of the Psyche, in *La Transcendance de l'Ego*. In *L'Etre et le Néant* Sartre reformulates these views on reflection and emotion, and develops his description of anguish as the sole example of emotion possible in 'pure' reflection.

But there are certain assumptions concerning emotional behaviour and attitudes which are fundamental to all these analyses. For Sartre, emotion as much as perception is a means of apprehending the world; emotion is a sense-giving activity, and a purposive way of dealing with the world. Such an assumption seems to run counter to common sense, for emotion is usually associated with a sense of uncontrolled passivity, rather than with purposive activity. How then does Sartre sustain and justify his purposive definition of emotion in the *Esquisse*?

Perception, for Sartre, is perception of a world of things-to-be-done; we see the world as making different demands upon us, as offering us different paths towards our different goals. We live in an instrumental relation to the world, in which objects are tools for the achieving of our aims. Our activity in this world is of an unreflective kind; that is to say, we are primarily aware of the world of objects and although we are secondarily or marginally aware of ourselves as acting, we do not make our acting selves objects of our thought in a reflective way.

Living in this 'instrumental' world, we are however inevitably aware of obstacles which interfere with our goals, and it is here that the definition of emotion as a means of dealing with the world finds its place:

Lorsque les chemins tracés deviennent trop difficiles ou lorsque nous ne voyons pas de chemin, nous ne pouvons plus demeurer dans un monde si urgent et si difficile. Toutes les voies sont barrées, il faut pourtant agir. Alors nous essayons de changer le monde, c'est-à-dire de le vivre comme si les rapports des choses à leurs potentialités n'étaient pas réglés par des processus déterministes mais par la magie. (*ETE*, p. 41)

Emotion, then, substitutes a 'magical' world for the instrumental world; it is 'une transformation du monde' (p. 41), but it is an ineffective transformation to which we resort when practical action is seen to be impossible, and in which we deceive ourselves. Sartre's most extreme and striking example of this phenomenon is his analysis of fainting as a response to a situation of grave danger: one faints in order to annihilate a danger even if one can only do so by annihilating consciousness itself:

faute de pouvoir éviter le danger par les voies normales et les enchaîne-ments déterministes, je l'ai nié. J'ai voulu l'anéantir. L'urgence du danger a servi de motif pour une intention annihilante qui a commandé une condu-ite magique. Et, par le fait, je l'ai anéanti autant qu'il était en mon pouvoir. Ce sont là les limites de mon action magique sur le monde: je peux le supprimer comme objet de conscience mais je ne le puis qu'en supprimant la conscience elle-même. (pp. 43–4)

Thus, for Sartre, the apparently most involuntary act of fainting is in fact purposive and unreflectively chosen. Similarly, flight is 'une conduite magique qui consiste à nier l'objet dangereux avec tout notre corps' (p. 44). Emotion, then, is a purposive transformation of the world. But in any analysis of emotion one must obviously dis-tinguish between true emotional behaviour and the assuming of an outward show of joyous or sad responses in a situation where such behaviour seems appropriate. The distinguishing factors for Sartre seem to be the role of the body in emotional responses, and the fact that we *believe* in the world transformed by our emotion: we suffer and live our affective projections as though they were, objectively, qualities of the world: 'La conscience ne se borne pas à projeter des significations affectives sur le monde qui l'entoure: elle *vit* le monde nouveau qu'elle vient de constituer' (p. 51). These two factors are closely related: physical responses (flight, trembling, fainting, physiological characteristics of anger and joy) help to constitute the magical world in which we then believe. For emotional behaviour '[revient] à constituer un monde magique en utilisant notre corps comme moyen d'incantation' (p. 48). In true emotion, then, we believe in the world we have created as though it were independent of us: 'il faut que nous soyons envoûtés, débordés, par notre propre émotion' (p. 50). Although it is usually assumed that Sartre's theory of emotion applies most convincingly to 'negative' emotions,[5] his analysis of joy affords perhaps one of the clearest examples of the transformation of the world and of the role of the body in sustaining our belief in that transformed world. In the instance of joy it is evident that we do not seek to transform an impossibly difficult world: it is rather that we seek to possess immediately an object of desire which is not yet within our grasp, or to possess immediately, in its totality, an object of desire which will in fact only yield itself gradually, if at all. The physical symptoms of joy are, as it were, symbolic of immediate and total possession:

La joie est une conduite magique qui tend à réaliser par incantation la possession de l'objet désiré comme totalité instantanée. Cette conduite est accompagnée de la certitude que la possession sera réalisée tôt ou tard, mais elle cherche à anticiper sur cette possession. [. . .] Danser, chanter de joie, représentent des conduites symboliquement approximatives, des incantations. A travers elle, l'objet – qu'on ne saurait posséder réellement que par des conduites prudentes et malgré tout difficiles – est possédé d'un coup et symboliquement. (pp. 47–8)

But whether we experience positive or negative emotion, our belief in the world we ourselves constitute accounts for the fact that, although emotion is an *activity* directed at the transformation of the world, it is experienced as something which we undergo: we seem to be passive in relation to it. In emotion, as Sartre says, we are caught in our own trap. Moreover, we perpetuate the trap in which we are caught, and we assume that the trap is laid for us by the objects of the world:

Ainsi donc comme la conscience vit le monde magique où elle s'est jetée, elle tend à perpétuer ce monde où elle se captive: l'émotion tend à se perpétuer. C'est en ce sens qu'on peut la dire subie: la conscience s'émeut sur son émotion, elle renchérit. Plus on fuit, plus on a peur. Le monde magique se dessine, prend forme, puis se resserre sur la conscience et l'étreint: elle ne peut pas vouloir y échapper, elle peut chercher à fuir l'objet magique, mais le fuir, c'est lui donner une réalité magique plus forte encore. Et ce caractère même de *captivité*, la conscience ne le réalise pas en elle-même, elle le saisit sur les objets, les objets sont captivants, enchaînants, ils se sont emparés de la conscience. La libération doit venir d'une réflexion purifiante ou d'une disparition totale de la situation émouvante.   (p. 53)

In *Esquisse d'une théorie des émotions*, then, Sartre suggests that what he calls purifying reflection can alone release us from the illusion that an emotional response has its source in an objective quality of the world rather than being primarily an activity of our consciousness. Conversely, both in unreflective emotion and in impure reflection emotion is wrongly thought to be caused by an agency in relation to which we seem to be passive: 'je suis en colère *parce qu'il* est haïssable' (p. 61) is the response of impure reflection or 'la réflexion complice', while purifying reflection will reverse the terms: 'je le trouve haïssable *parce que* je suis en colère' (p. 60). These arguments are developed further in *La Transcendance de l'Ego* and *L'Etre et le Néant*, where Sartre also differentiates between unreflective emotional acts of consciousness and emotional states – a distinction which is in turn central to the psychology of his plays.[6]

We have already seen that according to Sartre's definition of unreflective emotion, I am primarily aware not of myself as hating, but of an object in the world as objectively hateful. In unreflective emotion I do not posit my consciousness as an object for reflection. Sartre, however, envisages a situation in which consciousness seeks to reflect upon itself in its own spontaneous, free activity. But the reflected consciousness which is posited by reflecting consciousness cannot be grasped in the same way as an external transcendent object might be, or it would lose, precisely, its active, transparent spontaneity. It remains a quasi-object (*EN*, p. 201). This attempt of consciousness to grasp itself in its free, intuitive activity Sartre terms 'pure reflection': it is both the original and ideal form of reflection, but it would none the less seem to be a highly elusive operation, and Sartre, as we saw in Chapter 1, is more than usually elliptical about the means of achieving it. However, the important point for my discussion here is that since in an emotional response we usually conceal from ourselves the free spontaneity of our consciousness, in that we regard our affective projections as objective qualities of the world, emotional consciousness and pure reflection are in general incompatible. (The question of whether unreflective emotion can indeed reveal actual qualities of the world will remain to be considered later.) There would seem to be only one emotional activity of consciousness which can be sustained in pure reflection, and that is the emotion of anguish: in anguish we are precisely aware of ourselves as free agents, with all the weight of responsibility that such freedom implies. Emotion is more frequently associated with 'la réflexion impure' or 'la réflexion complice'. In impure reflection consciousness, reflecting upon itself, attempts to seize itself as an object – an *en-soi* 'susceptible d'être déterminé, qualifié' (p. 207) – instead of trying to grasp itself in its constant movement towards its own possible futures. Reflecting consciousness posits reflected consciousness as a series of definable qualities and states – the quality of being given to anger, the state of hating (*TE*, pp. 44–54; *EN*, pp. 208–9). The ideal synthesis of these qualities and states is the Psyche, or the Ego. This synthesis of past acts of consciousness is effected in order to make an affirmation of identity or selfhood possible. This is, of course, a supreme example of *mauvaise foi*, for Sartre regards identity as being fundamentally and inevitably beyond the reach of human consciousness. Moreover, in impure reflection we regard the qualities and states which supposedly constitute our Ego as being causally efficacious: a specific angry response is determined by my tendency to be angry – a tendency in turn deduced from my past acts.[7] For the temporality of impure reflection ('la temporalité psychique' (*EN*, p. 206)) differs fundamentally from that of pure reflection ('la temporalité originelle' or 'l'historicité' (p. 205)). Within the 'non-substantialité originelle' of its temporality, pure reflection discovers

les possibles *en tant que possibles*, allégés par la liberté du pour-soi, elle dévoile le présent comme transcendant, et si le passé lui apparaît comme en-soi, encore est-ce sur le fondement de la présence. Enfin, elle découvre le pour-soi dans sa totalité détotalisée en tant que l'individualité incomparable qu'elle *est elle-même* sur le mode d'avoir à l'être; elle le découvre comme le 'réfléchi', par excellence, l'être qui n'est jamais que comme *soi* et qui est toujours ce 'soi' à distance de lui-même, dans l'avenir, dans le passé, dans le monde. La réflexion saisit donc la temporalité en tant qu'elle se dévoile comme le mode d'être unique et incomparable d'une ipséité, c'est-à-dire comme historicité. (pp. 204–5)

But the 'temporalité psychique' of impure reflection is a time of external rather than internal relationships, unlike the flow of individual historicity 'qui s'appelle du fond de l'avenir' (p. 206); and although it resembles the time in which the objects of the external world have their being for us, it is paradoxically illustrated by our emotional experiences:

> Ainsi, la conscience réflexive de l'homme-dans-le-monde se trouve, dans son existence quotidienne, en face d'objets psychiques, qui sont ce qu'ils sont, qui paraissent sur la trame continue de notre temporalité comme des dessins et des motifs sur une tapisserie et qui se succèdent à la façon des choses du monde dans le temps universel, c'est-à-dire en se remplaçant sans entretenir entre eux d'autres relations que des relations purement externes de succession. On parle d'une joie que j'*ai* ou que j'*ai eue*, on dit que c'est *ma* joie comme si j'en étais le support et qu'elle se détachait de moi comme les modes finis chez Spinoza se détachent sur le fond de l'attribut. On dit même que *j'éprouve* cette joie, comme si elle venait s'imprimer comme un sceau sur le tissu de ma temporalisation ou, mieux encore, comme si la présence en moi de ces sentiments, de ces idées, de ces états était une sorte de *visitation*. (p. 205)

Further, in impure reflection and in the attempted constitution of the Ego, consciousness abdicates its spontaneity and its free orientation towards the future in favour of the primacy of the past; in favour, that is to say, of a false determinism:

> du fait que le psychique est en-soi, son présent ne saurait être fuite ni son avenir possibilité pure. Il y a, dans ces formes d'écoulement, une priorité essentielle du Passé, qui est ce que le Pour-soi *était* et qui suppose déjà la transformation du Pour-soi en En-soi. Le réflexif projette un psychique pourvu des trois dimensions temporelles, mais il constitue ces trois dimensions uniquement avec ce que le réfléchi *était*. (p. 212)

So, while in unreflective emotion a response which is a spontaneous act of consciousness is seen as having its source in the external world, in impure reflection emotion is seen to be caused by an emotional disposition or state – again, something in fact *external* to the spontaneous consciousness which creates the response. (As we have seen, for Sartre emotional states and qualities and their synthesis in the Ego are not modes of consciousness but *objects* of consciousness.) In both unreflective emotion and impure reflective emotion we deceive ourselves to a greater or lesser extent. Only in pure reflection does consciousness at any given moment recognise its absolute freedom, its causal independence of the past, and hence its responsibility. Only in pure reflection do we realise that an emotion is not caused by an external quality of the world or a falsely constituted quality of the Ego but that our conscious evaluation of our situation in the world motivates the emotional response. Emotion, then, both unreflective and in impure reflection, is essentially related to *mauvaise foi*; the only emotional response in which we are purged of *mauvaise foi* is that of anguish, in which we recognise our freedom.

It is of course in terms of a conflict between bad faith and the realisation of freedom that *Les Mouches* is usually and justifiably interpreted. The Argive people have abdicated their freedom by surrendering to the ethos of remorse imposed upon them by Egisthe. Electre alone stands out against this ethos and the religious super-stition which supports it; her sustained intention to seek revenge on Clytemnestre and Egisthe, thereby restoring freedom to Argos, is her *raison d'être*. Oreste, at first negatively free, seeks identity; the murder of his mother and the king seems to offer a possible means of achieving this by securing for him his rightful place in the city of Argos. But instead his act reveals to him his true, funda-mental freedom and responsibility, which are incompatible with achieving selfhood as king of the Argives; he refuses Jupiter's offer of the throne and leaves the city. As for Electre, the murder so suddenly robs her of her *raison d'être* that she fails to accept the revelation of freedom with its inevitable anguish and seeks false refuge from that awareness in remorse.

This generally accepted view of the play's theme is no doubt a valid one, but I shall try to show that its significance lies less in the *fact* of Electre's abdication of freedom than in the implications, both moral and dramatic, of the emotional mode of her abdication of freedom. In my discussion of Oreste, I shall be concerned less with the fact of his discovery and implementation of freedom than with the dramatic problems involved in the presentation of purifying reflection and anguish, and with the possible ambiguity of effect resulting from these problems. This emphasis on interpretation in the light of emotion and reflection may help to account for the apparent dramatic patchiness of *Les Mouches* – a patchiness usually explained in terms of the inadequacy of the motivation attributed to the characters: Electre's over-sudden change of heart, or Oreste's decision to leave Argos after his initial intention to win his place as the Argive leader. But the discussion of Sartre's character-motiv-ation in traditional terms is itself inadequate to deal with a presenta-tion of behaviour designed precisely to modify traditional concepts of character and motivation. The point is to decide whether Sartre's play works dramatically, or can work, on its own terms; or whether a sense of less than total satisfaction arises from the tension between Sartre's attempt to present a relatively new view of human behaviour and the relatively traditional form which he chooses to adopt.

However, the significance of the emotional and reflective modes of Electre's and Oreste's responses must first be established. Those of Electre initially appear to be more varied and more complex; as the play develops we witness the transition from her hatred of her mother and the king to the brief expression of joy at the 'Fête des Morts' and to the mingled fear and joy released by her brother's act of murder. This response is in turn transformed into desperate fear, and into revulsion against Oreste before her final experience of remorse.

If we return to consider the state of hatred which initially defines Electre's situation and personality, it can be seen to correspond closely to Sartre's definition of emotion in impure reflection. For Electre is not primarily and unreflectively aware of Clytemnestre and Egisthe as having-to-be-eliminated (as Sartre might have put it); such an unreflective awareness should find its issue in action. She is reflectively aware of her state of hating them, and she depends upon that state for a definition of her selfhood: it is an emotional state which falsely constitutes the Ego. It is for this reason that her situation is at first envied by Oreste, in words which underline the autonomy of an emotional state in impure reflection and which emphasise the passivity of consciousness in relation to that state: 'Il est beau, l'homme [. . .] qui se donne un beau jour à l'amour, à la haine [. . .]. Qui suis-je et qu'ai-je à donner, moi? J'existe à peine' (II, i, 4, p. 67). Electre, too, realises the value of her emotional state (without, of course, realising the inauthenticity of that value) when her hatred leaves her for the first time: 'tu m'as fait oublier ma haine; j'ai ouvert mes mains et j'ai laissé glisser à mes pieds mon seul trésor' (II, i, 4, p. 63). But the implications of Electre's state of hatred and of impure reflection are perhaps even more significant in relation to her attitude towards action. We saw that for Sartre a *state* of emotion in impure reflection is really a substitute for spontaneous unreflective consciousness of something which must be done but which is impossibly difficult to do in reality. Electre regards her hatred as motivating her desire to kill Egisthe and Clytemnestre, thereby (if we follow Sartre's theory) inauthentically introducing a false determinism into her behaviour. But the inauthenticity is twofold: hatred is also a substitute for the impossibly difficult act. For, paradoxically, the hatred which motivates the desire to kill guarantees Electre's failure to fulfil that desire; to do so would destroy the state of hatred: 'mon seul trésor'. This paradox explains the ambiguous response of excited but fearful anticipation with which she greets the immediate prospect of the murder: the possibility that the merely imagined will become real. It explains too her later rejection of responsibility for the act. In fact, then, for Electre the sustaining of her state of hatred takes precedence over the desire for action which would seem to be motivated by that state. In other words, the past takes precedence over a free future. The state of hatred is a refuge from the dispersal in time of unreflective, spontaneous consciousness.

Yet, before realising that the young Philèbe is in fact her brother and before realising the imminent possibility of the deaths of the king and queen, Electre ceases to hate: 'j'ai ouvert mes mains et j'ai laissé glisser à mes pieds mon seul trésor' (II, i, 4, p. 63). In Sartrean terms, her consciousness moves from a level of impure reflection to one of unreflective emotion. For the first time Electre is vividly aware of another future more positively desirable than the persistence of her hatred or the hypothetical deaths of the objects of her hatred. Oreste has brought with him the image of peaceful, sunlit, unremorseful towns. But Electre rejects the possibility of patiently and actively creating that future. She chooses instead to enact the immediate realisation of that future through the emotional response of joy: 'je ris, c'est vrai, pour la première fois de ma vie, je ris, je suis heureuse' (II, i, 3, p. 57). Indeed, Electre's joyful enactment in the present of a hypothetical future is a perfect transposition of Sartre's analysis of the unreflective emotion of joy. It occurs when the possibility of the realisation of desire is glimpsed, but when, in fact, much remains to be done before that realisation can become actual. It substitutes magical means – gesture, invocation, incantation – for practical action.[8] It has an absolute urgency: 'La joie est une conduite magique qui tend à réaliser par incantation la possession de l'objet désiré comme totalité instantanée' (*ETE*, p. 47). As she dances, Electre's body becomes her means of incantation. As Sartre puts it in the *Esquisse*, 'Danser, chanter de joie, représentent des conduites symboliquement approximatives, des incantations. [. . .] Pour l'instant [on] possède l'objet par magie, la danse en mime la possession' (*ETE*, p. 48). In Electre's words, 'je danse pour la joie, je danse pour la paix des hommes, je danse pour le bonheur et pour la vie' (II, i, 3, p. 59). Electre, then, is caught in her own emotional trap:

la conscience est victime de son propre piège. Précisément parce qu'elle vit le nouvel aspect du monde en *y croyant*, elle est prise à sa propre croyance, exactement comme dans le rêve, l'hystérie. La conscience de l'émotion est captive, mais il ne faut pas entendre par là qu'un existant quelconque extérieur à elle l'aurait enchaînée. Elle est captive d'elle-même, en ce sens qu'elle ne domine pas cette croyance, qu'elle s'efforce de vivre, et cela, précisément parce qu'elle la vit, parce qu'elle s'absorbe à la vivre.

(*ETE*, pp. 52–3)

'Voyez son air d'extase' exclaim the people of Argos as Electre dances (II, i, 3, p. 59). But she is not only caught within her own trap: she seeks to capture others. She must transmit faith in her own emotional world to the Argive people; her dance is not only rapt, spontaneous private gesture but also exemplary spectacle. It is ritual theatre within the play.[9] Moreover, for the effective persuasion of others, Electre must create a sacred context for her ritual act, and the boundaries between incantation, magic and sacred ritual become extremely tenuous:

O mes chers morts, Iphigénie, ma sœur aînée, Agamemnon, mon père et mon seul roi, écoutez ma prière. Si je suis sacrilège, si j'offense vos mânes douloureux, faites un signe, faites-moi vite un signe, afin que je le sache. Mais si vous m'approuvez, mes chéris, alors taisez-vous, je vous en prie, que pas une feuille ne bouge, pas un brin d'herbe, que pas un bruit ne vienne troubler ma danse sacrée. (II, i, 3, p. 59)

Electre herself fails to break away from the trammels of the sacred which men invoke to justify their action: so much for the 'free' Electre who apparently represents the autonomy of man in her stand against Jupiter (I, iii).

Moreover, in the same way as the Argive people see remorse as an absolute value, so Electre now sees well-being, peace and happiness as essential absolutes to which one abandons oneself passively rather than as the precarious goals of man's practical creative action.[10] Such absolutes are, in fact, figments created in bad faith as an escape from the *fadeur* of existence revealed in a true realisation of freedom. So Electre, apparently the embodiment of freedom in her revolt against institutionalised remorse and superstition, is herself in bad faith – first simply through the emotional nature of her response, secondly in assuming that peace and happiness exist as stable absolutes, and finally by believing in the trappings of the sacred and by exploiting them for the persuasion of others. This episode, then, may be interpreted as an example of bad faith, rather than in terms of a manifestation of freedom or an exhortation to freedom. But it can certainly be read or witnessed with a sense of ambiguity, and with a response of fascination and involvement. It could indeed be argued that this ambiguity derives from an equivocal attitude on the part of Sartre, or, at least, from his sense of the duality and asymmetry of the sacred. In *L'Etre et le Néant*, in the context of his discussion of language as a form of seduction, of affective communication, Sartre attempts to establish a distinction between the sacred and the magical. In such communication,

la pensée a besoin du concours d'une liberté aliénante pour se constituer comme objet. C'est pourquoi ce premier aspect du langage – en tant que c'est moi qui l'utilise pour l'autre – est *sacré*. L'objet sacré, en effet, est un objet du monde qui indique une transcendance par delà le monde. Le langage me révèle la liberté de celui qui m'écoute en silence, c'est-à-dire sa transcendance.   (*EN*, p. 442)

Electre, then, paradoxically recognises the freedom of the Argive people in seeking to fascinate them, but as she does so, thereby becoming an object for them, the sacred is transformed into the magical: 'le langage demeure pour autrui simple propriété d'un objet magique – et objet magique lui-meme: il est une action à distance dont autrui connaît exactement l'effet.[11] Ainsi, le mot est *sacré* quand c'est moi qui l'utilise, et *magique* quand l'autre l'entend' (p. 442). This elliptical distinction is clarified to some extent in the *Esquisse d'une théorie des émotions*, and with particular relevance to Electre's emotional incantation, to its double status as would-be action and as 'passion':

Nous pouvons dès à présent faire remarquer que la catégorie 'magique' régit les rapports interpsychiques des hommes en société et plus précisément notre perception d'autrui. Le magique, c'est l' 'esprit traînant parmi les choses' comme dit Alain, c'est-à-dire une synthèse irrationnelle de spontanéité et de passivité. C'est une activité inerte, une conscience passivisée. Or c'est précisément sous cette forme que nous apparaît autrui, et cela non pas à cause de notre position par rapport à lui, non pas par l'effet de nos passions, mais par nécessité d'essence. En effet la conscience ne peut être objet transcendant qu'en subissant la modification de passivité.   (*ETE*, p. 56)

In the case of Electre the 'nécessité d'essence' of passivity and of the magical is reinforced by the emotional mode of her experience. A further ambiguity arises from Sartre's attitude to the theatrical enactment of emotional experience. Electre's spectacular, exemplary, would-be cathartic ceremonial dance corresponds curiously to Sartre's definition of the value of the theatre in 'Forgers of Myths', an article published in 1946.[12] There Sartre maintains that the theatre should be a collective, religious phenomenon of mythic significance; its value should derive precisely from the embodiment of its social and religious functions in a ritual form; and it should exact, for its exemplary effect, a distanced but fascinated admiration from the spectators of this ritual. If Electre's ceremonial enactment of her joy is in bad faith, the same charge might be levelled at Sartre's institutionalising and exploiting of such ritual enactments in the theatre.

Conflicting moods of moral questioning and aesthetic fascination may, then, characterise our response to Electre's ritual dance. Her final withdrawal into remorse, on the other hand, seems to be a relatively unequivocal manifestation of bad faith. It also unequivocally exemplifies Sartre's theory. The role of impure reflective emotion in the constitution of the Self is defined by negative implication: as Electre's hate dies with the death of Egisthe, her sense of self disintegrates. Other emotional states must be created to fill the void; first, love of Oreste: 'Il faut que je pense que je t'aime' (II, ii, 8, p. 91); then, hatred: 'Ha! je te hais' (III, i, p. 104); and, finally, remorse (III, iii). Sartre is also able to show the transition from an unreflective emotional response – initial horror and fear *of* the remorse promised by the gloatingly menacing Erinnyes (III, i) – to the final acceptance of the *state* of remorse: a refuge which also involves, in Electre's plea to Jupiter, the acceptance of falsely absolute moral values (III, iii). Further, the image of darkness closing in upon Electre despite the dawn, suggests the encroaching passivity and opacity threatening a consciousness which denies its free creativity (II, viii, p. 91). For as Oreste points out, she imagines her moral situation to be determined by an external agency when she has in fact created it: 'ses souffrances viennent d'elle, c'est elle seule qui peut s'en délivrer' (III, ii, p. 105). Her imagination bodies forth this false sense of fatality in the compelling figures of the Erinnyes.[13] They symbolise what Sartre calls the phenomenon of belief in one's own emotional projections: they exist because Electre believes in them and needs to believe in them. As Oreste insists, 'C'est ta faiblesse qui fait leur force' (III, i, p. 103). Their symbolic significance is underlined by their parody of Electre's earlier joyful dance when she had attempted to win the faith of the Argive people: '*Elles dansent très lentement comme pour la fasciner*' (III, i, p. 104). This implicit ironic recall is reinforced, too, by the repetition of Jupiter's timely intervention.

These later episodes, then, allusively exemplify several aspects of Sartre's theory of emotion and bad faith, but they by no means represent an abrupt change of attitude on the part of Electre. Her behaviour here is simply another *conduite d'évasion*, perhaps more extreme, but of the same order as her earlier hatred and joy. Electre is consistent in her escape from the reality of her situation and in her ability to symbolise that escape in phenomena of belief.

However, consistency in Sartrean terms and consistency in traditional terms refer to quite different scales of value. For Sartre psychological consistency is, if anything, reprehensible;[14] for the traditional theatre-goer it is positively reassuring. In presenting the character of Electre, however, Sartre tries to have his cake and eat it: he tries to involve the traditional spectator in the mythical magic of Electre's world by largely traditional means, but to induce him also to regard Electre as morally negative. His relative success, however, in ensuring involvement means that the moral effect is ambiguous. At certain moments he leads us to respond positively to her situation by exploiting the trappings of traditional motivation, in which mental and emotional states are seen as potential and justifiable sources of action, or by involving us poetically, through gesture and image, in the compact intensity of Electre's emotions of hatred, joy and horror. He only retrospectively undermines our belief in the validity of our involvement – if, indeed, he does so at all. Even at moments when an apparently gratuitous change of mood – from brooding hatred to radiant joy – might disconcert or alienate the spectator, Sartre deflects such a response by creating a particularly intense dramatic atmosphere. Electre's dance at the 'Fête des Morts' sustains such an atmosphere with purely traditional means: on the narrative and dramatic level through conflict and suspense, mythical distancing and anticlimax; in terms of spectacle through the clash of life-denying and life-enhancing ritual atmospheres and through the effect of an embryonic play within a play; stylistically, through the adroit modulation of spontaneity and stylisation, lyricism and rhetoric, sustained invocation and – perhaps less traditionally – bathetic parody. During Electre's final recourse to remorse similar but more diffused techniques of persuasion are exploited not only to convince us intellectually of its plausibility, but to involve us dramatically and emotionally.

The success of such devices has, however, the effect of undermining the balance of the play: the positive density of the morally negative Electre threatens to overshadow the Sartrean hero, the *homme sans qualités*, Oreste. In order to sustain his authenticity Oreste must remain, precisely, *un homme sans qualités*, otherwise he would be seen to be, like Electre, in a state of impure reflection and bad faith. It follows from this that Sartre has set himself a difficult dramatic problem. The *showing* of an absence of qualities requires a renewal of dramatic technique; within the traditional framework sustained by Sartre we can only be *told* of Oreste's lack of qualities and register this information neutrally, or with a rather insipid sense of pathos: 'Qui suis-je et qu'ai-je à donner, moi? J'existe à peine' (II, i, 4, p. 67). But Oreste must be seen not only to lack the qualities which, in bad faith, constitute our Ego; he must also be seen to be capable of exercising the pure reflection with which we recognise our freedom, and to experience the emotion which inevitably accompanies pure reflection and which is alone compatible with it – namely, anguish. The presentation of pure reflection and of anguish again requires new forms of expression. The difficulty involved in the formulation of such experience is visible, for instance, in *L'Etre et le Néant*; there, Sartre is able to discuss, in discursive terms, the theoretical implications and structures of pure reflection, but gives up the attempt to circumscribe the experience. It seems, in quasi-mystical fashion, susceptible to definition only in terms of what it is not, or of being evoked through oblique, analogical modes. In the more leisurely context of a relatively experimental novel like *La Nausée* Sartre is able to explore, precisely, the problem of formulation, but he fails to do so in the less contemplative context of traditional dramatic expression. The experience of anguish, too, is refractory to such expression; traditional linguistic forms, adapted to traditional psychological concepts, might simply reduce this precarious emotion to the level of an 'impure' state. Oreste's anguish, thus formulated, might be taken to be fear. Theoretically, following Kierkegaard and Heidegger (*EN*, p. 66), Sartre distinguishes between anguish and fear. Anguish is a reflective awareness of the fact that no situation or motive constrains me to act or prevents me from choosing to act in a certain way. Fear, on the other hand, is directed outwards towards a threatening object or situation in the outside world, in such a way that 'je suis donné à moi-même comme une chose, je suis passif par rapport à ces possibilités, elles viennent à moi du dehors' (p. 67). Anguish is incompatible with a stable sense of self: 'L'angoisse, en effet, est la reconnaissance d'une possibilité comme *ma* possibilité, c'est-à-dire qu'elle se constitue lorsque la conscience se voit coupée de son essence par le néant ou séparée du futur par sa liberté même' (p. 73). As a structure of consciousness anguish, and the freedom which it reveals, can never be posited as an object *of* consciousness. It seems refractory to traditional dramatic or symbolic representation. We see Oreste's pure reflection and hypothetical anguish set against Electre's vividly embodied joy and fear either as an emotional neutrality which can only be baldly stated, or as a relatively wooden stoic resolve, or, more seriously, as finding expression in dubious and explicitly didactic rhetoric. Sartre's difficulties are particularly apparent in four central scenes of the play. The first constitutes the play's basic *revirement*, exemplified in Jupiter's sign to Oreste and Oreste's immediate realisation of its hollowness and of his own positive freedom (II, i, 4, pp. 69–70); the second is the ostensible climax of the action: the murder of Egisthe (II, ii, 6, pp. 87–8); the third involves Oreste's struggle to convince Electre of her freedom and responsibility (III, i); the fourth is the final scene of Oreste's departure from Argos (III, vi).

Jupiter's urbane and frivolous sign, produced with the showmanship of spurious power, is obviously and effectively an anticlimax. In Oreste's crucial rejection of such 'divine revelation' Sartre is allusively portraying a moment of purifying reflection, a realisation of positive freedom, as an 'intuition fulgurante et sans relief', 'une connaissance débordée par elle-même et sans explication' (*EN*, p. 202), or, rather, as I remarked in Chapter 1 (p. 14, n. 10) a 'reconnaissance' (p. 202). For consciousness, in its revealing of itself as the source of revelation, is a form of apodictic recognition of its own activity rather than a form of knowledge of the self: 'dans le dévoilement réflexif, il y a position d'un être qui était déjà dévoilement dans son être' (p. 202). Further, in the doubt which immediately precedes Oreste's 'reconnaissance' ('Alors. . . c'est *ça* le Bien?' (II, i, 4, p. 70)), Sartre expresses one of the paradoxes of pure reflection. For despite its status as an 'intuition fulgurante', it cannot be limited to an 'instant infinitésimal' (*EN*, p. 202). In *L'Etre et le Néant*, the act of doubting which is essential to Descartes' cogito is invoked in order to establish the 'historicity' of pure reflection – a historicity spatialised, perhaps, in the image of Oreste's future path and underlined by his farewell to his youth: 'Se découvrir doutant, c'est déjà être en avant de soi-même dans le futur qui recèle le but, la cessation et la signification de ce doute, en arrière de soi dans le passé qui recèle les motivations constituantes du doute et ses phases, hors de soi dans le monde comme présence à l'objet dont on doute' (p. 203).[15]

In presenting Oreste's first intuition of positive freedom, Sartre resists the temptation of heroic rhetoric, but he falls, instead, into unintentional and almost bathetic anticlimax: 'Filer doux. Tout doux. Dire toujours "Pardon" et "Merci". . . c'est ça?' (II, i, 4, p. 70). Freedom is lamely defined only in terms of what it is not, and disorientation only in terms of a conventional image of emptiness: 'Ah! quel vide immense, à perte de vue. . .' (p. 70). But then Sartre seems to overcompensate for this colourless expression in Oreste's savage imagery of sexual wounding, possession and butchery as he foresees his new role of the 'voleur de remords' of Argos (II, i, 4, p. 72). But for Sartre the language of possession is the language of a desire to *be* (*EN*, p. 689): has Oreste already lapsed into a new desire for immediate self-definition, or is his freedom betrayed by poetry?

Sartre is anxious, too, not to present the murder of Egisthe as a conventionally heroic act. Egisthe, who is weary of life and a willing victim, messily takes too long to die: 'Tu n'en finiras donc pas, de mourir?' (II, ii, 6, p. 88). But neither can it be a spectacularly impassioned act of hatred: such motivation is reserved for Electre. Rather, Sartre, faithful to his view that our acts reveal our intentions (*EN*, p. 564), has to suggest in Oreste a new awareness of solidarity with the people of Argos. The effect, however, is one of unimpassioned and paternalistic didacticism: 'il est juste de leur rendre le sentiment de leur dignité' (II, ii, 6, p. 88). And after the assassination Oreste's assertion of the value of freedom and of the necessary experience of anguish, although more morally positive in theory, is nevertheless eclipsed dramatically and imaginatively by the density of Electre's emotion and by her conflict with the Erinnyes and with Jupiter.

But the greatest sense of unease and dissatisfaction is probably felt during Oreste's speech of farewell at the moment of his final departure from Argos. This sense is not adequately explained in terms of the internal thematic or philosophical inconsistency which some critics have postulated, maintaining that Oreste's departure runs counter to his apparent solidarity with the Argive people and that it is incompatible with a theory of commitment. For even if one sets aside the constraints of the myth and the fact that, as we saw earlier, the criterion of consistency is not one that can be applied with particular relevance to Sartre, Oreste's departure has been plausibly 'motivated' in traditional terms: the role of king of the Argives is too negatively associated with abdication to the false power of Jupiter (III, ii, p. 108). The 'message' of the play can certainly accommodate Oreste's awareness of isolation, anguish and a precarious future – an awareness which must accompany the realisation of freedom and the exercise of pure reflection. His decision to leave is perfectly compatible with his refusal of a facile identity as leader of the Argive people, and with the suggestion that they must now realise and assume their own freedom. Furthermore, Sartre has yet to try to reconcile the ethical priority of pure reflection – the primary concern of *Les Mouches* – with an ethic of sustained commitment. For the Sartre of 1943, concrete relationships with others (as distinct from the ontological implications for the *pour-soi* of the fact of the existence of others) are based upon the 'faits psychiques' of the Ego. These constructs of impure reflection, unlike the certain intuition of its own activity which is available to the *pour-soi*, are accessible both to the self and others, but only as 'objets probables de mon intention réflexive' (*EN*, p. 218): 'c'est au niveau du fait psychique que s'établissent les rapports concrets entre les hommes, revendications, jalousies, rancunes, suggestions, luttes, ruses' (p. 205).[16] Sartre has not yet elaborated a theoretical basis for a dialectic of individual consciousness, social alienation and progressive collective freedom, or for passing from the solitary 'historicity' of pure reflection to positive historical action: such a transition is not the central concern of *Les Mouches*. The internal difficulty is a stylistic and formal one: Sartre is tempted by the necessities of dramatic climax to have recourse to perfunctory rhetoric and traditional symbolism. However, the philosophically central but dramatically tenuous experience of pure reflection cannot be declaimed, nor can the free emotion of anguish be defined in rhetorical statement; the possible function of such techniques in sustaining the interest of the traditional spectator is not compatible with the philosophical experience. In attributing to Oreste the language of myth-makers, Sartre confers upon his hero's intuition the dubious definition of a state in impure reflection, a limiting of freedom. Oreste seems to belie his status as an *homme sans qualités* and to define himself as a magical and exemplary object for the people of Argos. Furthermore, his departure should suggest a breaking away from a determining past towards an open but uncertain future. We are *told* that it does: 'tout est neuf ici, tout est à commencer. Pour moi aussi la vie commence' (III, vi, p. 120). But the weight of suggestion at this moment of climax draws the spectator back towards the past, in the retelling of the legend of the rats of Scyros and in the recalling of other persistent but irrelevant associations of the Orestes myth.

What, then, is the final balance of response to the moral and aesthetic effect of the play? Within the play emotional responses should, it appears, be seen to be morally negative; our earlier examination of Sartre's theory reinforces this view. But the dramatic and pathetic intensity of the play's effect is largely sustained by the morally negative character who, through her capacity for emotional *mauvaise foi*, is also capable of imagining, of creating worlds of joy and horror, of creating a poetic, incantatory language which transcends the world of reality. Our positive response to this dramatic intensity as readers or spectators may obscure the play's moral significance. Yet, should our emotional involvement be regarded, on subsequent reflection, simply as a temporary response to traditional techniques? Do we feel that the author expects us and leads us to re-evaluate this response in retrospect? It is far from clear that he does, and it cannot be assumed that Sartre is simply using adventitious imaginative and poetic techniques to involve the spectator in an emotional trap from which he should later extricate himself. We have already seen that Sartre attributes to Electre, in her dance of joy, the creating of a dramatic atmosphere which in its ritual, hieratic, mythical effect corresponds closely to his own definition of the purpose of dramatic expression: 'un grand phénomène collectif et religieux' (*TS*, p. 62). Moreover, Sartre's own attitude towards the closely related faculties of emotion, imagination and poetic creativity are ambivalent. He rightly distinguishes between 'feelings', or the general affective aspect of experience, and emotions proper, and is consistent in maintaining that the affective responses which accompany our perceptions reveal actual qualities and structures of the world; it is disconcerting to find, however, in a final *revirement* of the *Esquisse d'une théorie des émotions*, that those specific emotions hitherto regarded as reprehensible 'conduites *d'évasion*' (*ETE*, p. 43) also constitute an 'intuition de l'absolu' (p. 54), an authentic intuition of absolute qualities of joy and horror in the world.[17] Emotion also involves a transcending of reality through the imagination; imagination is defined in *L'Imaginaire* both as a 'savoir dégradé' (*Im.*, p. 82) and as a fundamental aspect of the free creativity of man's consciousness (pp. 236–7). The language of poetry – 'l'émotion [. . .] devenue chose' (*S* ii, p. 69) is, like emotion itself, a 'conduite d'échec' (*ETE*, p. 21; *S* ii, p. 86): it is a symptom of man's failure to use language as a means to a practical end in the world. Yet the failure represented by poetic expression, which itself represents the failure of 'pure' reflection, paradoxically has its own absolute and cathartic value: 'L'échec seul, en arrêtant comme un écran la série infinie de ses projets, rend [l'homme] à lui-même, dans sa pureté' (*S* II, p. 86). Here, again in the unexpected context of *Qu'est-ce que la littérature?*, we find a description and justification of the poetic figure of Electre: in the world of poetry, 'l'action, détachée de ses buts qui s'estompent, devient prouesse ou danse' (*S* II, p. 85).

Awareness of Sartre's ambivalent attitude to the world of emotion, imagination and poetry may mitigate an uneasy sense that in responding emotionally rather than reflectively to Sartre's plays one is not his ideal spectator. But does he expect his spectator or his reader to be capable of pure reflection, capable of freeing himself from the inauthenticity of his emotional states, his Ego, his 'objectified' past and his constituted values in readiness for the new departures that Sartre wishes to recommend? Far from it: 'Ce que l'écrivain réclame du lecteur ce n'est pas l'application d'une liberté abstraite, mais le don de toute sa personne, avec ses passions, ses préventions, ses sympathies, son tempérament sexuel, son échelle de valeurs' (p. 100). Moreover, the emotional response is now associated with psychological freedom: 'l'on voit des gens réputés pour leur dureté verser des larmes au récit d'infortunes imaginaires; ils étaient devenus pour un moment ce qu'ils auraient été s'ils n'avaient passé leur vie à se masquer leur liberté' (p. 101). There seems in fact to be a fundamental tension between Sartre's theoretical analysis of emotion as a form of *mauvaise foi* and his claim that an emotional response to a work of art can be an affirmation rather than a concealment of one's freedom. And the tension is not resolved by Sartre's argument that the emotions aroused by an aesthetic object are free because they are not conditioned by external reality, or because the belief and the passivity inherent in an emotional response are a chosen belief and a chosen passivity (pp. 100–1). In other less polemical contexts Sartre still maintains that, in any case, our responses can never be totally conditioned by external reality, and that they are all chosen, whether reflectively or unreflectively. Nor is a solution offered at this stage by Sartre's perfunctory reference to the function of aesthetic distance (p. 99).

Might it not, indeed, be more appropriate to speak of a radical reversal, rather than of a fundamental tension, between the earlier largely negative view of emotion and the later, more positive, evaluation of an emotional response to a work of art? Sartre's evolving attitude to the relationship between emotion, imagination and art would seem to suggest such a reversal. We saw earlier that he seeks to exploit the imaginary and the mythical in order to elicit an emotional and aesthetic response. But a response to what end? In *Qu'est-ce que la littérature?* (1947) we find that the end should be a moral one. The work of art should help us to realise mutually our metaphysical and political freedom: 'au fond de l'impératif esthétique nous discernons l'impératif moral' (*S* II, p. 111). This assertion runs quite counter to an earlier definition of the relationship between aesthetic experience and moral action: in the conclusion of *L'Imaginaire* (1940), Sartre writes:

La contemplation esthétique est un rêve provoqué et le passage au réel est un authentique réveil. On a souvent parlé de la 'déception' qui accompagnait le retour à la réalité. Mais cela n'expliquerait pas que ce malaise existe, par exemple, après l'audition d'une pièce réaliste et cruelle, en ce cas, en effet, la réalité devrait être saisie comme rassurante. En fait ce malaise est tout simplement celui du dormeur qui s'éveille: une conscience fascinée, bloquée dans l'imaginaire est soudain libérée par l'arrêt brusque de la pièce, de la symphonie et reprend soudain contact avec l'existence. Il n'en faut pas plus pour provoquer l'écœurement nauséeux qui caractérise la conscience réalisante.

De ces quelques remarques on peut déjà conclure que le réel n'est jamais beau. La beauté est une valeur qui ne saurait jamais s'appliquer qu'à l'imaginaire et qui comporte la néantisation du monde dans sa structure essentielle. C'est pourquoi il est stupide de confondre la morale et l'esthétique.   (*Im.*, p. 245)

Given this apparent reversal, it is perhaps significant that *Les Mouches* stands almost midway, both chronologically and, as it were, theoretically, between *L'Imaginaire* and *Qu'est-ce que la littérature?* Where the play is aesthetically satisfying, it is morally ambiguous or negative; where Sartre does attempt to express an unambiguous moral 'message' in conventional dramatic form, it fails to convince on either level. Such attempts, and such failures, become less frequent as Sartre's theatre develops. In fact, despite the categorical statements of *Qu'est-ce que la littérature?*, the reversal is neither complete nor permanent. As, in *Le Diable et le Bon Dieu*, we watch Goetz's charismatic gestures, or as we share the hysterical and obsessive seclusion of Frantz von Gerlach's imaginary world in *Les Séquestrés d'Altona*, we may not be immediately seized by a free and generous urge to change the real world: we may rather remain caught in fascinated contemplation. For the dramatic vitality of Sartre's 'committed' plays lies in his presentation of problematic heroes who, like Electre, Goetz and Frantz, create their own private worlds of magical significance – the seekers of absolutes, guilt-ridden, passion-ridden, obsessed. In

Sartre's theory of emotion and in its dramatic embodiment, but also throughout his work, the conclusions of the reflective moralist and the sensibility of the artist are often at odds; these conflicting claims may resist dramatic synthesis, or they may enrich the texture of a work precisely through the dramatic tensions which they generate. The best of Sartre's plays engage our aesthetic commitment in releasing both complex emotions and reflective awareness: they can be morally unambiguous only in synopsis.

3

HUIS CLOS:
DISTANCE AND AMBIGUITY

A number of critics of Sartre's *Huis clos*[1] have maintained that the dictum 'l'enfer, c'est les Autres'[2] expresses a universalising thesis which attempts to define human relationships in totally pessimistic terms. Internal evidence, however, seems to show that the play's thesis and the modes of behaviour to which it refers are, far from being universal, highly specific and remediable.

If we could accept 'l'enfer, c'est les Autres' at face value, *Huis clos* would be an unambiguous thesis play. One reading (or misreading) of *Huis clos* seeks, however, to reconcile the view that Garcin's dictum is the central negative message of the play with the claim that the play as a whole is inadvertently ambiguous. The claim is based on an attempt to apply retrospectively to *Huis clos* the criteria of Sartre's 1960 Sorbonne lecture 'Théâtre épique et théâtre dramatique'.[3] The definition of epic theatre to which Sartre refers in opposing it to traditional dramatic or bourgeois theatre is that of Brecht. (Epic, in this context, carries no connotations of heroism or grandeur: epic theatre emphasises reflectively narrative rather than dramatic modes and exploits alienation effects in order to induce a critical social awareness in the spectator.) The relevance of Sartre's lecture to the inadvertent ambiguity of *Huis clos* lies, it is argued, in the conflict between, on the one hand, Sartre's contention that playwrights should fight the psychological bourgeois theatre by using the techniques of both 'participation' (i.e. dramatic) and 'epic' theatre, and, on the other hand, his practice of combining the traditional psychological play with the epic Everyman play. It is suggested that Sartre's plays, including *Huis clos*, would have a much more unified impact if he had kept any one play within any one mode.[4]

There are two fallacies in this argument: the first lies in the assimilation of the epic play and the Everyman play, which is warranted neither by Brechtian theory nor by Brechtian practice.[5] The second fallacy is to assume that alienation or distancing effects are possible only within the epic mode: the thrust of Sartre's argument in 'Théâtre épique et théâtre dramatique' is, precisely, that they can be manipulated in other dramatic contexts. Sartre had outlined his own theory of aesthetic distance in *L'Imaginaire* of 1940, and, despite his admiration for Brecht, it is still basically to this theory that he refers in 1960. There are other continuities which will be relevant to my argument and which justify reference to Sartre's 1960 lecture for the interpretation of a play written in 1943: the first is the anti-bourgeois stance which persists from *La Nausée* (1938) to *L'Idiot de la famille* (1971–2); the second is the view that the theatre should arouse the spectator's critical consciousness of a *specific* situation – a principle which informs *Les Mouches* (1943) and is still present in *Les Séquestrés d'Altona* (1959); the third, more basic still, is the axiom that human consciousness, knowledge and action (action on the individual, collective or historical levels) are fundamentally unstable and ambiguous. My argument will be that *Huis clos* is intentionally and effectively specific, critical and ambiguous, rather than universalising and inadvertently ambiguous. I will adduce as external evidence Sartre's view of the bourgeois as spectator and man, and his evaluation of Brecht insofar as it clarifies his own theory of critical distancing; internal evidence will suggest that techniques of parody and subversion in *Huis clos* create distancing effects which induce a critical *prise de conscience*.

What, according to Sartre, does the bourgeois seek in the theatre? In Sartre's view, the theatre should offer an image of man's acts as being capable of changing the world (*TS*, p. 122): what the bourgeois desires is 'l'action de l'auteur construisant des événements' (p. 120) – that is to say, the well-made play (p. 123).[6] He seeks a presentation of his own self in which he can participate, and an image rather than a critique of his own ideology (p. 120). Sartre defines that ideology as a 'naturalisme pessimiste': 'qu'il y ait une nature humaine, [. . .] que cette nature soit mauvaise, [. . .] et qu'elle soit immuable' (p. 121). Within this immutability, effective action, as distinct from adaptation, is seen to be undesirable and impossible: between the rising and the falling of the curtain 'ça s'agite mais ça ne doit pas *agir*' (p. 122), action is replaced by passion, and psychological explanation focuses on causes rather than ends:

c'est toujours par le passé, par le déterminisme, qu'on explique les choses. [. . .] Le but de ce théâtre est d'ôter aux actes leur fin, donc leur signification, de remplacer les forces de l'action par ce qu'il y a de plus imperméable et de plus faux dans [. . .] la passion – prise comme ils l'entendent, c'est-à-dire quelque chose qui ne comprend rien aux autres ni à soi-même et qui s'en va toujours se perdre en cherchant à se sauver.

(p. 125)

Furthermore, in bourgeois theatre the relationship between objects and action is vitiated in that objects are superfluous accessories rather than integrated into, or created by, action or work.[7]

Closer examination of these definitions – tendentious though they may be – may suggest an interpretation of *Huis clos* as a straightforwardly bourgeois play, since it apparently presents human nature as 'mauvaise' and 'immuable', characters who try to explain their behaviour in terms of causes rather than ends (Estelle: 'J'étais orpheline et pauvre' (v, p. 145)), acts which are robbed of their meaning, and objects which have lost their instrumentality. (The 'bronze de Barbedienne' *seems* to be the epitome of the superfluous accessory, and so does the paper-knife, for there are no pages to be cut. It cannot even be used as a dagger, for the 'victim' is already dead.) It is a play not of action but of passionate attitudes as defined by Sartre, even to the hyperbolic vocabulary of salvation and damnation:'quelque chose qui ne comprend rien aux autres ni à soi-même et qui s'en va toujours se perdre en cherchant à se sauver' (*TS*, p. 125). Garcin's cry to Inès: 'si tu me crois, tu me sauves' (v, p. 178) is based on a misapprehension of her personality and of his own needs: in seeking his salvation in her, 'il se perd'. Is it the case, then, that Sartre has inadvertently written a bourgeois play? Or is he seeking to show that to be a bourgeois involves being condemned to a living death, and thereby simply substituting a pessimistic view of a particular class for a pessimistic view of human nature? A further alternative may, however, be suggested: namely, that Sartre holds up a seemingly familiar and yet distorting mirror to his bourgeois audience in order to subvert its accepted ideas and attitudes of determinism, immutability, pessimism and passion. Such a subversive intention, one could argue, suggests an affinity with Brecht – an unconscious affinity in Sartre's earlier development, but one which is later marked by conscious awareness of a degree of theoretical convergence.

The theoretical convergences are indeed striking. Theatre should undermine a fatalistic ethos and involve a critical *prise de conscience*; it should stress that what may seem natural and inevitable is relative and open to modification:[8] these emphases pre-date Sartre's knowledge of Brecht, to whom he made his first published reference in 1955,[9] and they are exemplified already in *Les*

86

Mouches. Again, independently of each other, Sartre and Brecht reject conflicts of character in favour of portraying moral decisions, conflicting rights and interrelated inner and social contradictions. Both reject, together with the belief in an immutable human nature, the notion of Everyman, and they take a similarly negative view of any deterministic relationship between character and action.[10] Moreover, the elements which Sartre consciously emphasises in his reading of Brecht are no less interesting: first, the ambiguity of his characters: '[. . .] ses personnages sont toujours ambigus: il met en lumière leurs contradictions qui sont celles de leur époque et tente de montrer, en même temps, comment ils font leur destin';[11] secondly, ambiguity of theme, in a phrase which recalls strongly the language of *Huis clos*: 'c'est qu'il n'y a pas de salut individuel: il faut que la Société se change toute entière; [. . .] il [le dramaturge] nous découvre ce que nous sommes: victimes et complices à la fois';[12] and finally, ambiguity of emotional response – a response of 'malaise' or disquiet: 'Ce malaise ne disparaît pas quand le rideau tombe; il grandit, au contraire, il rejoint notre malaise quotidien, ignoré, vécu dans la mauvaise foi, dans la fuite et c'est lui qui l'éclaire. La "purification" s'appelle aujourd'hui d'un autre nom: c'est la prise de conscience' (*TS*, p. 84).

However, although Sartre here acknowledges Brecht's relevance, his own choice of vocabulary betrays potential reservations: the shift from the relative clarity of Brechtian contradiction, alienation and critical consciousness to the less well-defined sphere of ambiguity, complicity and disquiet is a tell-tale one. It suggests why, despite some ideological and theoretical convergence, Sartre's dramatic methods and distancing techniques are quite different from those of Brecht, and why they remain intentionally so. Sartre's practical objections to epic theatre are far-reaching: its emphasis on reason at the expense of emotion is, he feels, appropriate only to a 'public déjà politisé',[13] and not, therefore, to the French bourgeois audience. Moreover, certain types of alienation technique – for instance, the attribution of masks to some characters (those, such as the palace guards in *The Caucasian Chalk Circle*, who are to be regarded as ideologically 'negative') and not to others – effect a selective de-humanisation, and express a reprehensible moral prejudgement which reduces human objects of criticism to the level of 'insects' (pp. 145–6). More fundamentally, the basic alienation effects of epic theatre result in explanation at the expense of comprehension, and in the elimination of subjectivity: 'Dans l'épique, [. . .] on explique ce qu'on ne comprend pas' (p. 149).

We may note, in parenthesis, that although this aphorism seems to express characteristically biased dismissiveness on the part of Sartre, it in fact refers extremely allusively to two apparently conflicting traditions in German thought of which Sartre was well aware: those of 'Erklären' or 'explication' and 'Verstehen' or 'compréhension'. The former adopts methods of psychological or social explanation based on mechanistic or biological models: as a gross generalisation the example in psychological analysis would be Freud, and in social analysis classical Marxism. The opposed tradition of 'Verstehen' seeks to understand social and psychological phenomena in terms of distinctively human intentions and meanings apprehended either through empathy and intuition or by rational reconstruction. It is exemplified in sociology by Max Weber, in social psychology by Max Scheler (whose work Sartre had certainly read and to whom I shall have occasion to refer later), and in psychology by Karl Jaspers, whose *Allgemeine Psychopathologie* (1913) Sartre helped to translate in 1927 and 1928.

How, then, does Sartre, having rejected epic alienation effects, reconcile his own theory of aesthetic distancing with a measure of empathy, or, more characteristically, of complicity, in order to create a critical *malaise* in the bourgeois spectator? Sartre's evaluation of Brecht leads him to ask a question which is central to his own aesthetic criticism and dramatic practice: 'Faut-il que [. . .] la pièce soit représentée à titre d'objet ou à titre d'image?' (*TS*, p. 144). The question may, however, be rephrased: 'Faut-il que l'homme soit représenté dans la pièce à titre de quasi-objet ou à titre d'image?', for in Sartre's view men seek their own image in art because they can never *be* objects either for themselves or – and this should be stressed – for other people (p. 117). The function of the work of art is to create a desired 'subjectivité extérieure', but as a purely imaginary object, an 'irréel' (p. 116) upon which we cannot act. No action of ours can affect an *objet-en-image*: we are simply led to collude to a greater or lesser extent with the work of art as readers or spectators. As we saw earlier, the bourgeois, according to Sartre, seeks in the work of art an image of himself with which he can identify himself emotionally, rather than a representation of himself as a quasi-object – an image 'aussi proche [que possible] de la façon dont lui se voit dans une glace et aussi loin que possible de la façon dont un autre le voit' (p. 120). But while Brecht's aim is to create a form in which, through alienation effects, the spectator may see himself 'de la façon dont un autre le voit', Sartre seems to follow the method of adapting or subverting the forms of bourgeois participation theatre in order to create an unstable and ambiguous relationship between complicity – itself an ambiguous response – and a critical disquiet, thereby creating a 'théâtre qui ne soit pas bourgeois'.

The challenge offered by such a method would seem to be a particularly arduous one in a play like *Huis clos* in which the dramatic interest lies precisely in the tension between the characters' desire for an acceptable self-image and their rejection of their status as quasi-objects in the eyes of others. In *Huis clos* Sartre meets the challenge, I would argue, by adopting, or alluding to, the conventional dramatic modes which his hypothetical bourgeois spectator would recognise, and by gradually subverting them. As the curtain rises on *Huis clos*, the first visual impact of the Second Empire drawing-room would or should be familiar to the bourgeois spectator,[14] although the recognition of a certain non-naturalistic stylisation may also create a sense of unease. Moreover, Sartre is at pains to draw attention immediately to two crucial periods in the history of the bourgeoisie; first, that of its consolidation – Garcin to the *garçon d'étage*:

Une situation fausse dans une salle à manger Louis-Philippe, ça ne vous dit rien?

and secondly, that of its apogee:

Le Garçon. Vous verrez: dans un salon Second Empire, ça n'est pas mal non plus. (i, pp. 127–8)

For Sartre, the bourgeois dramatist of the reign of Louis-Philippe is Scribe, while Sardou exemplifies Second Empire theatre; both are responsible, in his view, for 'cet imbroglio superficiel [. . .] qui n'avait pas de valeur humaine'.[15] But for the bourgeois audience whom Sartre seems to presume to be familiar with the *drame bourgeois* of Sardou, Augier and Dumas *fils*, the Second Empire drawing-room betokens at least a veneer of moral and social stability. Other perspectives are of course possible: Zola in *La Curée* and *Pot-Bouille* shows savagely what might lie beneath the bourgeois veneer. But in the Second Empire *drame bourgeois* 'des situations fausses' tend to be resolved in order, harmony and rectitude, often with a touch of *attendrissement*; it presents a world in which naturalism guarantees the natural order, in which drawing-room comedy and social satire do not ultimately disturb the human dignity of the righteous, in which a *frisson* of melodrama, kept within the bounds of taste and of the well-made play, maintains the clarity of moral values, a world in which the 'eternal' triangle is eternally resolved.[16]

It is intriguingly disturbing, then, to find security and order transformed into infernal torment and a living death. The more so, because the author, ostensibly giving the bourgeois audience what it wants ('l'action de l'auteur construisant des événements' (*TS*, p. 120)), goes further and reduces his characters to passive puppets of diabolical contrivance:

Estelle les regarde tous deux avec stupeur. Mais pourquoi, *pourquoi* nous a-t-on réunis?   (v, p. 142)

Naturalistic detail undermines the dignity of human nature as the comedy of discrepancy turns against itself – Garcin to the *garçon d'étage*:

Et pourquoi m'a-t-on ôté ma brosse à dents?
Le Garçon. Et voilà. Voilà la dignité humaine qui vous revient. C'est formidable.   (i, p. 128)

Drawing-room comedy becomes black comedy in which the audience's laughter is constantly stifled by the repeated laughter of the characters – *grinçant*, sardonic or hysterical laughter which creates rather than relieves tension and subverts old clichés: 'c'est à mourir de rire!' (v, pp. 165, 177). This is a drawing-room in which the politenesses of social exchange are rapidly and radically undermined, and in which servants do not answer the bell. The eternal triangle remains eternally unresolved: 'Eh bien, continuons' (v, p. 182). The play which evolves in this setting is a parody of a well-made play in exposition, revelation of character, *péripétie*, climax and *dénouement*. The exposition, in which the informed servant is asked to enlighten the uninformed guest, mocks the repeated stereotyped exposition which each well-made play seeks to present as unique:

Le Garçon. [. . .] Qu'est ce que vous voulez, tous les clients posent la même question. Ils s'amènent: 'Où sont les pals?' [. . .] Et puis, dès qu'on les a rassurés, voilà la brosse à dents.   (i, p. 129)

But the repetitiveness is itself undermined when the next guest fails to ask the expected question:

Le Garçon, déçu. D'ordinaire les clients aiment à se renseigner. . . Je n'insiste pas. D'ailleurs, pour la brosse à dents, la sonnette et le bronze de Barbedienne, monsieur est au courant et il vous répondra aussi bien que moi.   (ii, p. 134)

The revelations of character made as parodic extensions of formal introductions are at first false revelations and lead not to the illusion of a 'human nature' but to the questioning of the concept of character itself. The *péripétie* – the sudden opening of the door – leads to *no* change in the situation; the climax – Estelle's attempted murder of Inès – is an anticlimax, as the victim is already dead. There is no *dénouement*: 'Eh bien, continuons.' The world of melodrama – of extreme action, over-simplified moral attributes and exaggerated emotion – is, strictly speaking, absent: the past world of betrayal, perversion, suicide, adultery and infanticide is an *objet-en-image*, impervious to action, which can be referred to only verbally by the characters and is thus doubly distanced from the spectator; well-defined moral characteristics have the status only of images – desired, feared or rejected – in the consciousness of others. The function of rhetoric is subverted: the language which refers to absent melodrama is flat and unrhetorical. Rhetoric, which incidentally draws attention to its own repetitiveness and staleness, is reserved for the problematic creation of the unstable image of the self or of the other. Even then, the lack of congruence between word and quality inherent, but never consciously exposed, in melodrama and the *drame bourgeois*, becomes a conscious element in the rhetorical device, revealing the hollowness of sentimentality and wish-fulfilment – Inès to Estelle: 'Mon eau vive, mon cristal. [. . .] Viens! Tu seras ce que tu voudras: eau vive, eau sale, tu te retrouveras au fond de mes yeux telle que tu te désires' (v, pp. 167–8).

Through these subversive shifts of emphasis an unambiguously emotional response of horror to the melodramatic world of the characters' past actions is undermined, while no stable emotional response is possible to the present shifting relationships of power and vulnerability, initiative and passivity, to the whirl of torturing, suffering, pleading, placating, torturing. Even when words are used as weapons, they, no more than the actual weapon Estelle tries to use, cannot truly designate their victim as victim: the weapon 'lâche' misses its target, as the ostensible victim is incapable of suffering unequivocally: '*Garcin*. Je veux souffrir pour de bon. Plutôt cent morsures, plutôt le fouet, le vitriol, que cette souffrance de tête, ce fantôme de souffrance, qui frôle, qui caresse et qui ne fait jamais assez mal' (v, p. 177). Not only do the emotional relationships and those of power and vulnerability shift too rapidly to provide even brief moments of stability, but emotion and will are themselves inherently equivocal. As Sartre asserts in *L'Etre et le Néant*, the will and the passions are not *things* which have 'la permanence et l'existence "en-soi" d'une propriété'; he sets out to undermine 'l'opinion commune [qui] conçoit la vie morale comme une lutte entre une volonté-chose et des passions-substances'. Undermined too is the notion of a simple opposition of moral values which tends to be associated with such a view: 'Il y a là comme une sorte de manichéisme psychologique absolument insoutenable' (*EN*, pp. 520–1). And, indeed, the instability of emotion and will in *Huis clos* creates instability of moral judgement at the level of interpretation, and the impossibility of resolution at the thematic level: 'Eh bien, continuons.' Furthermore, the import of the play's central image is offered only to be eventually subverted, for this Hell is ultimately a *tolerable* Hell where, as we saw, suffering is never quite intense enough. It is a Hell which is preferable to a world either of isolation or of action: when the door opens, none of the victims will leave. And, as we have also seen, the dramatic context of the central image is subverted too: traditional modes are alluded to in parodic forms which undermine the stability of traditional responses. One may provisionally conclude, then, that these techniques of subversion and, hence, of distancing, generate a sense of instability and disquiet. But does this sense in turn create the critical *prise de conscience* which is Sartre's aim: the bourgeois spectator's *prise de conscience* of his own image?

Huis clos presents not a single but a triple image of the bourgeoisie: the bourgeois intellectual (Garcin), the 'petite bourgeoise' (Inès, *employée des postes*), and the 'grande bourgeoise' (Estelle). (Hitherto, any recognition of the play's allusions to the bourgeoisie has focused on the character of Estelle.)[17] That the three characters fail to recognise themselves or each other as members of the same class is comprehensible in a Sartrean context: in *L'Etre et le Néant* the bourgeoisie, essentially heterogeneous, is distinguished by its 'nuances innombrables et retorses' from the proletariat, and is further described as having 'une conscience qui ne reconnaît pas son appartenance à une classe'.[18] But it is also noteworthy that all three characters are in some degree marginal to their class – a marginal position which accounts for their own sense of instability and vulnerability, and hence, the instability of our response. Garcin, 'publiciste et homme de lettres' (iii, p. 135), first defines himself *against* the bourgeois setting of the play – which he immediately recognises for what it is – in the bourgeois intellectual's ostensible questioning of his own class. Of the 'fauteuil Second Empire': 'Et moi, qu'est-ce que vous voulez que j'en fasse? Savez-vous qui j'étais? Bah! ça n'a aucune importance. Après tout, je vivais toujours dans des meubles que je n'aimais pas et des situations fausses; j'adorais ça' (i, p. 127). The 'situation fausse' exemplifies precisely the superficiality of Garcin's deviance from the typical values of his class, as well as the failure, characteristic of the intellectual, to substitute positive action for evasive reflection. His *contestation* takes the form of a purely verbal *prise de position*: pacifism, against the bourgeois principle of patriotism. As such, it falls far short of a genuinely militant commitment and is soon reabsorbed into the bourgeois domain of abstract principles through collusion with Estelle: 'Trouvez-vous que ce soit une faute de vivre selon ses principes?' (v. p. 145). That his theoretical commitment and his principles are empty is shown by the discrepancy between humanitarian theory and a mirage of solidarity on the one hand, and his cruelty towards his lower-class wife on the other – this being justified, in his view, by the rise in status conferred by her marriage: 'Je l'ai tirée du ruisseau' (v, pp. 145, 155). But the 'situation fausse' was sustained by his own complicity: 'j'adorais ça'. It is Garcin, significantly, who immediately recognises the 'bronze de Barbedienne' for what it is, in a curious response of nightmare fascination and eventual acceptance (i, p. 129; v, p. 181): a super-fluous object perpetrated by the Second Empire bronze-caster, Barbedienne, whose speciality was the production *en série* of reduced models of well-known sculpture. A 'bronze de Bar-bedienne' may be taken as a symbol both of bourgeois philistinism and of infinite and potentially nightmarish repetition.

Garcin, then, is marginal by virtue of his inauthentic *contestation* of the values of his class: Inès is so by virtue of her position on the lowest level of the bureaucratic hierarchy. She is distinct in class, as an *employé salarié* in the state bureaucracy, from the proletariat;[19] she is distinct in position within her class from the leisured, propertied bourgeoise, Estelle, and from the bourgeois intel-lectual. Estelle is allowed to draw attention inadvertently to the disparity as she describes for Inès the bureaucratic structure of Hell: 'Pensez à la quantité de gens qui. . . qui s'absentent chaque jour. Ils viennent ici par milliers et n'ont affaire qu'à des subalternes, qu'à des employés sans instruction. Comment voulez-vous qu'il n'y ait pas d'erreur. Mais ne souriez pas' (v, p. 144). From Inès' marginal *petit bourgeois* position within her class evolves a particularly characteristic set of psychological responses. She is one of the embodiments in Sartre's work of *ressentiment*, the socially condi-tioned complex of emotional attitudes defined by Max Scheler in *Das Ressentiment im Aufbau der Moralen*,[20] to which Sartre refers in *L'Etre et le Néant*: '[. . .] le sens et la fonction de ce que Scheler

93

appelle "l'homme du ressentiment" c'est le Non' (*EN*, p. 85). Scheler gives the word a precise social context: '*Ressentiment* must be strongest in a society like ours, where approximately equal rights, [. . .] publicly recognised, go hand in hand with wide factual differences in power, property and education. While each has the "right" to compare himself with everyone else, he cannot do so in fact'.[21] And further, *ressentiment*, which is the result of a decay of the feeling of social identity in an unstable society, is most characteristic of 'the disappearing class of artisans, in the petty bourgeoisie and among small officials'.[22] It is 'chiefly confined to those who *serve* and are *dominated*'.[23] According to Scheler, *ressentiment* involves the repression and subterranean working of revenge, hatred, *Schadenfreude*, malice, the impulse to detract, vindictiveness and spite. But these are not yet *ressentiment*: they lead to it

only if there occurs neither a moral self-conquest (such as *genuine* forgiveness in the case of revenge) nor an act or some other adequate expression of emotion [. . .], and if this restraint is caused by a pronounced awareness of impotence, [. . .] coupled with the feeling that one is unable to act them out – either because of weakness, physical or mental, or because of fear.[24]

These feelings are reflected with curious rigour in Inès. The first, which she elucidates herself, is her past fear (iii, pp. 135–6); her sexuality as a Lesbian reinforces her sense of social inferiority and impotence; her emotions can find no outlet in action, nor could they overtly in her past life; she is not capable of moral self-conquest, but only of a despairing recognition of her moral negativity; her impulse to detract extended even to the object of her ostensible love: 'Florence était une petite sotte et je ne la regrette pas' (iii, p. 134). Her malice as she destroyed Florence's own image of her husband was insidious, subterranean: 'Je me suis glissée en elle, elle l'a vu par mes yeux' (v, p. 157). She embodies even, in Schelerian terms, the ontological core of *ressentiment*: her envy of Garcin and Estelle becomes the existential envy which, in Scheler's view, seeks to destroy the identity of the other:

existential envy, which is directed against the other person's very *nature*, is the strongest source of *ressentiment*. It is as if it whispers continually: 'I can forgive everything, but not that you *are* – that you are *what* you are – that I am not what you are – indeed that I am not *you*.' This form of envy strips the opponent of his very existence, for this existence as such is felt to be a 'pressure', a 'reproach', and an unbearable humiliation.[25]

Hence the ferocity with which Inès seeks to destroy the self-image of others. She exemplifies, too, the hollowness of *ressentiment* pride in the affirmation of her own identity ('Moi, je me sens toujours de l'intérieur' (v, p. 149) and its gradual undermining ('Je me sens vide' (v, p. 161) – a hollowness implicit in Scheler's definition: 'Pride results from an experienced *diminution* of naïve self-confidence. It is a way of "holding on" to one's value, of seizing and "preserving" it deliberately'.[26] And in the context of *ressentiment*, Inès's despairing resignation cannot be, as it has been so often, mistaken for lucidity. For in *ressentiment*, hatred and envy turn against their own bearer, in self-hatred and self-torment: 'Je suis méchante.' 'Je suis pourrie.' 'Puisqu'il faut souffrir, autant que ce soit par toi. Assieds-toi. Approche-toi' (v, pp. 157, 162, 149). Nor is her resignation courageous. It is left to the bourgeois intellectual to expose the myth of Inès' lucidity and courage:

Garcin. Tu sais ce que c'est que le mal, la honte, la peur. Il y a eu des jours où tu t'es vue jusqu'au cœur – et ça te cassait bras et jambes. Et le lendemain, tu ne savais plus que penser, tu n'arrivais plus à déchiffrer la révélation de la veille. Oui, tu connais le prix du mal. Et si tu dis que je suis un lâche, c'est en connaissance de cause, hein?

Inès. Oui. (v, p. 178)

And if self-denigration and the acknowledgement of cowardice are to be regarded as a guarantee of lucidity, Estelle is as lucid as Inès:

Estelle. Je suis lâche! je suis lâche! [. . .] Vous savez que je suis une ordure.
(v, pp. 160, 165)

But although the bourgeois intellectual, the *petite fonctionnaire* and the *grande bourgeoise* are at one in their cowardice, Estelle is sharply differentiated from the others by her sense of property, as befits her position in her class.[27] Whereas Garcin 'se foutait de l'argent, de l'amour' (v, p. 179), and Inès has no property, Estelle substitutes the sense of property for the sense of love:

Estelle. Bien sûr que je ne l'aimais pas. [. . .]
Inès. Alors laisse-les. Qu'est-ce que cela peut te faire?
Estelle. Il était à moi. (v, p. 164)

Inès recognises and parodies the substitution: 'Tout ce qui t'appartient est ici. Veux-tu le coupe-papier? Le bronze de Barbedienne? Le canapé bleu est à toi. Et moi, mon petit, moi je suis à toi pour toujours' (v, p. 165). But the *grande bourgeoise* woman of property – or the woman, rather, of her husband's property – is also defined

95

by being the property of another. She defines herself by her complicity in acknowledging the power of her husband's material possessions: 'Il était riche et bon, j'ai accepté', or by the inauthentic offering of her body to Garcin: 'Prends ma bouche; je suis à toi tout entière' (v, pp. 145, 181).

What, then, can we conclude from the mutual torture of these three bourgeois in their bourgeois drawing-room? That Hell is the refusal of the critical *prise de conscience* which Sartre seeks to induce in his bourgeois audience: an ambiguous refusal, because those who indulge in it are both 'victims' and 'complices'. That the *prise de conscience* should be a specific one – by the bourgeois intellectual of his own inauthenticity, by the *petite bourgeoise* of her *ressentiment*, by the *grande bourgeoise* of her sense of possessing and of being possessed. And what of the response of disquiet – the ambiguous interplay of empathy, complicity and distance which, for Sartre, is necessary to his audience's *prise de conscience*? Perhaps we should equate it, as Sartre indeed invites us to do,[28] with what he describes in *L'Etre et le Néant* as the catharsis of purifying reflection (p. 206) – a reflection which will purge us of bad faith and redeem our vitiated relationships with others, but which is itself vulnerable and unstable. Does Sartre suggest that it is particularly so for the bourgeois? In a comment on the bourgeois audience of *Les Séquestrés d'Altona* – the play which he sees as closest in spirit to *Huis clos* – he seems to suggest that it is: 'La distanciation ne doit pas détruire l'*Einfühlung* [. . .]. Pour faire comprendre au public ce que c'est que de revenir d'une guerre et de se rappeler qu'on y a été un bourreau, il faut que le public puisse s'identifier au héros en question. Il faut qu'il puisse *se haïr en lui*'.[29] Empathy, then, becomes self-hatred – an emotion which, for Sartre, can only be in bad faith, the antithesis of purifying reflection. And as the audience is buffetted between empathy, detachment, complicity, disquiet and self-hatred, ambiguity is sustained in a typical but far from inadvertent Sartrean *tourniquet*.

4

LES MAINS SALES:
WORDS AND DEEDS

In 1943, in *L'Etre et le Néant*, Sartre elaborates a theory of action, will and motivation. In 1944, in a lecture on 'Le Style dramatique', he puts forward specific views on language and action, and on language as action in the theatre, which in some ways confirm and in some ways subvert, apparently unwittingly, the arguments of *L'Etre et le Néant*. In 1948 he publishes a play – *Les Mains sales* – which questions, more radically still, the already partly conflicting positions set out in the philosophical treatise and the literary lecture. The analysis which follows attempts to explore the unacknowledged shifts of emphasis revealed in these three texts, and to show how *Les Mains sales* offers both an enactment of and a commentary upon the relationship between speech-acts and action, and between representation and meaning.[1]

In 'Le Style dramatique' Sartre bases his theory of language in the theatre on the contention that action should replace psychology as a paramount dramatic concern. It should do so, in the first instance, by virtue of its status as an enterprise:

L'acte, en effet, est ce qui, par définition, échappe à la psychologie; c'est une entreprise libre d'abord, c'est-à-dire que [. . .] si la liberté existe, elle doit au moins être dans la composition même d'un acte qui est une entreprise, qui a une fin, qui est projetée, qui est concertée; c'est donc là ce qui d'abord nous apparaît dans le théâtre: des gens poursuivant une entreprise et faisant des actes pour la réaliser. (*TS*, p. 29)

The representation of an enterprise freely undertaken is set against psychological explanation which, by implication, refers to those aspects of the self which attenuate freedom. Secondly, and elliptically, Sartre argues that the moral context of action (a context which, incidentally, seems to preclude the experience of hesitation or indecision) overrides the psychological investigation of the 'inner life':

D'autre part, ces actes nous transportent toujours ailleurs que sur le plan psychologique parce qu'il y a une vie morale: chaque acte comprend ses propres fins, et son système d'unification; quelqu'un qui fait un acte est persuadé qu'il a raison de le faire; par conséquent, nous nous trouvons en fait non pas sur le terrain du fait mais sur le terrain du droit puisque chaque individu qui agit, dans une pièce, du fait qu'il a une entreprise et que cette entreprise doit être menée à bien, la justifie par des raisons, se donne des raisons de l'entreprendre.

De ce seul fait, nous sommes maintenant sur le terrain réel du théâtre, où il ne s'agit pas de savoir ce qu'il y a dans les consciences mais de considérer les droits qui se heurtent.   (*TS*, p. 30)

It is not, however, only action as an expression of 'la vie morale' which suppresses psychology. Speech itself does so: 'Quant à la psychologie, il n'y en a pas: les personnages sont trop occupés à se déclarer ce qu'ils ont à dire' (p. 30). One's inference here might be that the function of language is not so much to express or analyse the self as to articulate the 'rights' which serve, in turn, as a motive or justification for action. The relationship between words and action is, however, closer than this – and crucially so in its implications for Sartre's dramatic practice:

Un mot est un acte, c'est une manière d'agir parmi d'autres manières d'agir [. . .]. Un mot au théâtre doit être ou serment ou engagement ou refus ou jugement moral ou défense des droits ou contestation des droits des autres, donc éloquence, ou moyen de réaliser l'entreprise, c'est-à-dire menace, mensonge, etc., mais en aucun cas il ne doit sortir de ce rôle magique, primitif et sacré.   (*TS*, pp. 33–4)

In short, for Sartre the language of the theatre should be essentially performative – or, more precisely, it should consist in the performance of illocutionary acts.[2] That performance, as we shall see, goes beyond the normal, even trivial, sense in which dialogue furthers the action of a play.

In moving rapidly and elliptically to this conclusion, the passages quoted beg a number of central questions. Sartre's implicit definition of psychology is perhaps the most readily clarified. For him, as we saw in earlier chapters, psychology concerns the analysis of the Ego, a relatively static entity constructed by a consciousness which, engaged in impure reflection, has thereby to some extent abdicated its freedom. The states and qualities which constitute the Ego are quasi-objects for the 'intentional acts' of consciousness. They do not constitute a pre-existing core of personality which might 'cause', motivate or explain such intentional acts. Sartre, then, by giving priority to action over psychology in 'Le

Style dramatique', seems to assert that in the theatre the dynamism of free and active consciousness should take precedence over the stasis of the Ego – a precedence which, as we saw, finds ostensible expression in *Les Mouches*.

The implications of Sartre's emphasis on action itself are not, however, so easily unfolded. The essentially 'goal-directed' character of the enterprise as described in 'Le Style dramatique' does, it is true, reflect the theory of action set out in *L'Etre et le Néant*. Conventionally, the motivation of an act might be thought to include determining external constraints, specific traits of character or unconscious drives. Sartre, however, refuses to consider the *motifs* and *mobiles* of an act in terms of preconditions, predisposing tendencies or, indeed, causes. The *motif* is an aspect of the agent's situation, but, far from determining his actions, that aspect is only revealed in and through his project of acting in order to change that situation. In other words, the agent's 'motivating' definition of his situation is only revealed by virtue of the fact that he has already chosen his goals and his possibilities – that is to say, his *mobile*.[3] Explicit awareness of the *motif* involves implicit, unreflective consciousness of one's project: *motif* and *mobile* are therefore correlative: 'le motif, le mobile et la fin sont les trois termes indissolubles du jaillissement d'une conscience vivante et libre qui se projette vers ses possibilités et se fait définir par ces possibilités' (*EN*, pp. 525–6). Further, the value and meaning ascribed to past *motifs* and *mobiles*, or newly assigned to present ones, are revealed and decided only in the act itself:

je n'en décide, précisément, que par l'acte même par lequel je me pro-jette vers mes fins. La reprise des mobiles anciens – ou leur rejet ou leur appré-ciation neuve – ne se distingue pas du projet par quoi je m'assigne des fins nouvelles et par quoi, à la lumière de ces fins, je me saisis comme décou-vrant un motif d'appui dans le monde. Mobiles passés, motifs passés, motifs et mobiles présents, fins futures s'organisent en une indissoluble unité par le surgissement même d'une liberté qui est, par delà les motifs, les mobiles et les fins.   (p. 527)

Or, in other words, my intentions and my motivation are structures of the act itself.

However, in 'Le Style dramatique' the description of 'free' action as an enterprise 'qui a une fin, qui est projetée, qui est con-certée' (*TS*, p. 29) creates a significantly different emphasis. The word 'concertée' – which here implies premeditation – attenuates or distorts the sense of spontaneous choice which is in principle so central to Sartre's theory of action – so central that he can maintain in *L'Etre et le Néant* that 'la délibération volontaire est toujours truquée' (*EN*, p. 527). In deliberating – and, by implication, pre-meditating – consciousness ceases to be unreflectively engaged in its chosen project, with its complex of *motifs* and *mobiles*: 'la structure de l'acte volontaire, au contraire, exige l'apparition d'une conscience réflexive qui saisit le mobile comme quasi-objet, ou même qui l'intentionne comme objet psychique à travers la conscience réfléchie' (p. 528). In other words, in voluntary deliberation the *mobile* is posited as a structure of the Ego. Further, since explicit awareness of the *motif* is no longer grasped through implicit, unreflective consciousness of the *mobile*, but through reflected consciousness, the synthesis of *motif* and *mobile* postulated in spontaneous action is split in what can only be the mode of impure reflection. In other words, through the 'entreprise concertée' the psychological elements associated with impure reflection and the Ego – which Sartre had in principle wished to extirpate from the theatre – make their reappearance.

Furthermore, Sartre's transition in 'Le Style dramatique' from the sphere of action to 'la vie morale' and to 'le terrain du droit' (*TS*, p. 30) creates further inconsistencies. For the Sartre of 'Le Style dramatique', the individual's tendency to seek prior or retrospective justification for his actions is morally justifiable, but the Sartre of *L'Etre et le Néant* takes a different view. There, Sartre sees 'authentic' action as a 'pure transcendance qui porte sa justification dans son existence même, puisque son être est choix', while it is from the point of view of other people that an action is an '*objet donné* d'appréciation morale' (*EN*, p. 611). Hence self-justification and self-judgement are mutually implicating modes of 'la conscience de mauvaise foi qui a pour idéal de se juger, c'est-à-dire de prendre sur soi le point de vue de l'autre' (p. 611). (It is, of course, in its own 'pure' reflection that consciousness discovers the moral implications of its own actions.) Moreover, the fact that in the theatre action occurs 'non pas sur le terrain du fait mais sur le terrain du droit' (*TS*, p. 30) suggests that Sartre, while on the one hand emphasising the 'free' act, is on the other hand concerned with the agent's determination to conceal the facticity of his freedom from himself by asserting his rights and through them defining his social role – thereby attenuating or denying his freedom:

parmi les mille manières qu'a le pour-soi d'essayer de s'arracher à sa contingence originelle, il en est une qui consiste à tenter de se faire reconnaître par autrui comme existence de droit. Nous ne tenons à nos droits individuels que dans le cadre d'un vaste projet qui tendrait à nous conférer l'existence à partir de la fonction que nous remplissons.   (*EN*, p. 565)

And theoretically, for Sartre, such an attempt to give freedom a foundation is incompatible with freedom itself: 'Une liberté qui se produirait elle-même à l'existence perdrait son sens même de liberté' (p. 565).

The threat of impure reflection, and of the *mauvaise foi* associated with self-justification and the assertion of rights, is elided, then, in 'Le Style dramatique'. Yet Sartre does not recognise these inconsistencies. There is no suggestion that the emphasis in his lecture on deliberation and a conflict of rights is seen to undermine the theory of action and consciousness of *L'Etre et le Néant* or to be at odds with the clash between 'psychology' (Electre) and metaphysical liberty (Oreste) in *Les Mouches*. (There, Electre, who reflects and deliberates, fails to act, while Oreste abandons an apparently predisposing complex of traditionally recognisable motives – love for his sister, desire for identification with Argos – for a 'free' act, grasped in pure reflection, which reveals a new structure of *motifs*, *mobiles* and values.) Indeed, the stress on will and rights as the positive, legitimate and 'anti-psychological' moral concern of the playwright is reaffirmed in 1946 in 'Forgers of Myths'.[4] Now, moreover, although Sartre confirms some aspects of the relationship between will, passion and choice analysed in *L'Etre et le Néant*, certain crucial distinctions are suppressed: in 'Forgers of Myths' Anouilh's Antigone 'représente une volonté nue, un choix pur et libre; on ne peut distinguer en elle la passion de l'action' (*TS*, p. 57). The definition of emotion and passion as purposive modes of consciousness is familiar both from *Esquisse d'une théorie des émotions* and from *L'Etre et le Néant*. (They are, it is true, only recognised as such in pure reflection: in impure reflection the agent considers his passion, as the etymology of the word suggests, to be suffered or undergone.) However, in keeping with Sartre's distinction between conscious and reflective choices, both works affirm that emotional modes of action are not voluntary, although they are chosen: indeed, they are chosen only when voluntary and instrumental modes are apparently impossible.[5] Further, in *L'Etre et le Néant* will and passion are alternative means of achieving the same end: rather than fully constituting in themselves a 'choix pur et libre' they are secondary to the choice of 'un projet plus profond' (*EN*, p. 528).

In Sartre's essays on the theatre, then, the distinction between the chosen and the willed is not maintained. Other problems may be seen to arise from his linking of will, passion and the assertion of rights – an association validated, he suggests, by the practice of the Greek tragedians. The irrelevance of 'psychology' is underlined, in his view, by the fact that for them 'la passion n'était jamais un simple orage affectif mais toujours, fondamentalement, l'affirmation d'un droit' (*TS*, p. 59). But as his argument continues, it becomes apparent that this passionate and highly voluntaristic assertion of rights is implicitly associated with a more traditional view of psychological motivation on Sartre's part. More seriously, such assertions are seen to refer to a pre-existing system of values at variance with the definition in *L'Etre et le Néant* of value as the unrealisable goal of human activity: a play will offer through its characters 'des expressions d'une volonté inébranlable qui sont l'affirmation de systèmes de valeurs et de droits, tels que les droits des citoyens, les droits de famille, la morale individuelle, la morale collective, le droit de tuer, le droit de révéler à des êtres humains leur condition pitoyable' (*TS*, pp. 59–60). This recommendation of a 'représentation de conflits de droits' does not, however, allude, as one might expect, to a possible source of dramatic conflict in the struggle between the awareness of value as 'unrealisable' and the opportunistic exploitation of existing systems of value – a struggle arguably represented in *Les Mouches* on the one hand by Oreste and on the other by Egisthe and Jupiter. Nor can the apparent 'bad faith' of affirming that values are 'given' be eliminated by associating them with the Sartrean notion of 'situation'. For the Sartre of *L'Etre et le Néant* 'situation et motivation ne font qu'un' (*EN*, p. 568). That is to say, *motif*, *mobile* and situation are integrated into an act which, rather than following from a prior system of values, itself decides the fragile values which are 'ce vers quoi un être dépasse son être' or 'le sens et l'au-delà de tout dépassement' (p. 137). Further, the prior definition of the meaning of an act through the assumption that its ends pre-exist it in the world – that '[les fins] viennent de Dieu, de la nature, de "ma" nature, de la société' (p. 516) (an assumption which can be inferred from the affirmation of rights referred to earlier) is seen in *L'Etre et le Néant* as a futile attempt to 'étouffer la liberté sous le poids de l'être' (p. 516).

Does Sartre, then, in what he presents as the legitimate themes and functions of the theatre, unsettle the theories of *L'Etre et le Néant*? Or are the inner contradictions of his dramatic theory generated by a tension between his rejection of the 'natural attitude' of traditional psychology and the demands of a dramatic efficacy which rehabilitates an intensified version of 'everyday' experience? Has Sartre intuitively learned from *Les Mouches* that the exemplifying of metaphysical freedom, pure reflection and anguish raises insuperable technical difficulties? Or that the presentation of spontaneous choice, in the absence of reflection and deliberation, may appear to be merely arbitrary caprice? This last conclusion is one which he is at pains to forestall in *L'Etre et le Néant* through the theory of the fundamental project. To present this 'projet plus profond' (*EN*, p. 528) in its relation to secondary projects might, however, create the equally unwelcome suggestion of a deterministic relation between the former and the latter.

The implying of positive though not unambiguous values through the strongly negative tenor of *Huis clos* might indeed suggest that Sartre had learned the lessons of *Les Mouches*, but such a development none the less begs a further question: why, in his early essays on the theatre, does Sartre suppress the element of bad faith which seems, if we accept the arguments of *L'Etre et le Néant*, to be inherent in the exercise of will, the affirmation of rights and the implied predefinition of values? There is perhaps a purely pragmatic explanation in that the increasingly 'committed' Sartre might wish to ensure communication with his audience by enacting the problems of empirical freedom rather than of abstract metaphysical freedom, and by presenting the exercise of the will not as a 'délibération truquée' but as an assertion of autonomy. The parallel aim of inducing a critical *prise de conscience* might involve both, on the one hand, a degree of subversive 'defamiliarisation', whether judicious or savage, and, on the other, a tactical recognition of the spectator's 'everyday' expectations: 'Nous revendiquons le *véritable* réalisme car nous savons qu'il est impossible, dans la vie de tous les jours, de distinguer le fait du droit, le réel de l'idéal, la psychologie de la morale' (*TS*, p. 61). But it should still be recalled that for Sartre our everyday concerns involve the exercise of 'impure' reflection, while a critical *prise de conscience* is related to 'la réflexion pure'.[6]

Whether or not these inconsistencies can be legitimated or rationalised, they are certainly dramatically functional. The exercise of the will in 'impure' reflection can, for instance, be seen to be the source of dramatically interesting error. For, as I mentioned in Chapter 1 (p. 14, n. 10), only unreflective or 'purely' reflective consciousness can offer us certain rather than probable evidence concerning our aims and projects. Such error may itself create moral complexities, for although it derives from impure reflection it may, curiously, be committed 'de bonne ou de mauvaise foi' (*EN*, p. 550) – a revealing and unusual crevice which threatens to breach Sartre's established position in *L'Etre et le Néant*, where impure reflection is normally associated with bad faith. This breach, however, allows him to explain the occasional 'inefficacité profonde de l'acte volontaire dirigé sur soi' (p. 550), and the fact that the agent may sometimes take voluntary decisions which run counter to his chosen fundamental project. (Indeed, if they *do* run counter to his project, it can only be *because* they are voluntary rather than spontaneous and *irréfléchies*.) Here Sartre differentiates sharply between errors about the objective situation and errors concerning the self – a distinction which will be particularly relevant to the situation of Hoederer and Hugo in *Les Mains sales*:

Il faut se garder, en effet, d'appeler erreur sur soi les erreurs d'appréciation touchant la situation objective – erreurs qui peuvent entraîner dans le monde des conséquences absolument opposées à celles qu'on voulait atteindre, sans cependant qu'il y ait eu méconnaissance des fins proposées. L'attitude réflexive, au contraire, entraîne mille possibilités d'erreur, non pas dans la mesure où elle saisit le pur mobile – c'est-à-dire la conscience réfléchie – comme un quasi-objet, mais en tant qu'elle vise à constituer à travers cette conscience réfléchie de véritables objets psychiques qui, eux, sont des objets seulement probables [. . .] et qui peuvent même être des objets faux. Il m'est donc possible en fonction d'erreurs sur moi-même, de m'imposer réflexivement, c'est-à-dire sur le plan volontaire, des projets qui contredisent à mon projet initial, sans toutefois modifier fondamentalement le projet initial. (p. 550)

This passage underlines and helps to explain the problematic nature of 'psychology' and 'character' – whether in life or in drama – for Sartre. It also suggests how it becomes possible for the theatre audience to pass moral judgement on the varying degrees of error or insight displayed by the characters (*TS*, pp. 30–1). But judgement, for Sartre, involves distance. In a sense, traditional theatre ensures the form of distance which is implied by the inaccessibility of the stage action, and 'il faut en prendre son parti et la présenter dans sa pureté, en jouer même' (p. 28). But how can the playwright further ensure that the more deliberate, reflective exploitation of distance (involving non-naturalistic and perhaps 'defamiliarising' techniques) may coexist with that evocation of the everyday which, according to Sartre, is essential to the concern of contemporary theatre with 'les droits actuels, les milieux actuels' (p. 32)? Sartre's reply in 'Le Style dramatique' is less complex than his analysis of epic and bourgeois theatre in 'Théâtre épique et théâtre dramatique', but he introduces one crucial element which becomes central to his own practice: namely, the notion of verbal acts. For the utterances which Sartre enumerates ('serment ou engagement ou refus ou jugement moral ou défense des droits ou contestation des droits des autres [. . .] ou [. . .] menace, mensonge' (p. 34)) are ones from which a specific result may follow. In the terms of speech-act theory, as illocutionary acts they perform an act *in* saying something (for instance: promising, warning, greeting, commanding) as opposed to the performance of the purely locutionary act *of* saying something. They may further imply the possibility of perlocutionary effects. Those utterances *in* which a speaker does something are also utterances *through* which he may achieve certain intended effects in the hearer: for instance, in performing the act of arguing (illocution) the speaker may convince his interlocutor (perlocution). For Sartre, verbal actions, like physical actions, are above all instrumental: they are actions which transcend the *donné* towards a chosen end (*EN*, pp. 597–9). Their function is not primarily to express prior elements within the individual. There is, indeed, a symmetry between the elision of this function and the view that action, in general, although 'situated', is not convincingly explained by reference to prior and abstract motives.

Language as action, then, Sartre argues, supplants naturalistic psychology in the theatre by substituting modes of persuasion or of *engagement* for the description or expression of inner states. However, in 'Le Style dramatique', a highly compressed transition then redefines language in a way which seems covertly to call into question its everyday status and suggests that its speech-acts short-circuit familiar modes of practical action: as a means of achieving one's goals it should never relinquish its magical, primitive and sacred role (*TS*, p. 34).

How effectively can moral judgement, theatrical distance, language as action and language as magic be interrelated, in Sartre's view? As we have seen in earlier chapters, there are several ways in which Sartre's allusions to the 'magical' function of language can be construed – not all of them compatible with the ostensibly correlative function of eliminating traditional psychology in the theatre, nor with the apparently instrumental character of illocutionary acts. According to one interpretation, the magical effects of language may be closely related to emotional expression: their interrelationship, as we saw, informed the moral and dramatic ambiguities of *Les Mouches*. But such magical effects would be, strictly speaking, ineffective: they would, in theory, undermine the purely instrumental function of language. For Sartre, emotional expression, by substituting magical for practical means, attempts but fails to transform a refractory world. Can 'magical' language, then, count as action? And what is the status of the language of commitment and of persuasion?

Sartre provides no clear-cut answers, but a more fruitful interpretation would invoke the more complex relationship between emotion, language and action which he develops briefly within his theory of *l'être-pour-autrui*. There, language is seen to be fundamentally constituted in our being-for-others: 'le langage n'est pas un phénomène surajouté à l'être-pour-autrui: il *est* originellement l'être-pour-autrui, c'est-à-dire le fait qu'une subjectivité s'éprouve comme objet pour l'autre' (*EN*, p. 440). And since love is the exemplary mode of being-for-others, so the language of love is the paradigmatic language: it is the essential mode in which the subject seeks to captivate and assimilate the freedom of the other in order to effect the impossible project of founding his own freedom. Language, in this analysis, is experiential and affective rather than cognitive, not only in its attempt to fascinate the other, but insofar as, for the speaker, the source of meaning lies beyond himself, in the other: 'Autrui est toujours là, présent et éprouvé comme ce qui donne au langage son sens. Chaque expression, chaque geste, chaque mot est, de mon côté, épreuve concrète de la réalité aliénante d'autrui' (p. 441). It is this aspect of language for the speaker which, as I suggested in analysing *Les Mouches*, constitutes its sacred nature: 'L'objet sacré, en effet, est un objet du monde qui indique une transcendance par delà le monde. Le langage me révèle la liberté de celui qui m'écoute en silence, c'est-à-dire sa transcendance' (p. 442). However, language, sacred for the speaker, becomes for the listener a magical object which operates at a distance, short-circuiting that distance by 'irrational' means rather than working through instrumental, practical action. As such, far from revealing the free, spontaneous transcendence of the speaker-as-consciousness, it can only indicate obliquely a series of relationships between attitudes and other attitudes, expressions and other expressions, words and other words – fragmented relationships which are maintained in an illusory synthesis by the relatively inert 'cohésion magique' of the Ego or Psyche (pp. 213–17).[7] Already, in *La Transcendance de l'Ego*, Sartre offers a description of the role of the 'magical object' in non-verbal communication:

this effects a transition between his account in *Esquisse d'une théorie des émotions* of the magical properties of the social world, and the highly compressed reference to sacred and magical language in *L'Etre et le Néant*. He also already emphasises the status of the magical object as one of the 'aspects dégradés de la spontanéité consciente'. Here, as elsewhere, Sartre uses the term 'dégradé' in a sense analogous to the scientific notion of the degradation or dissipation of energy:

> Une mimique expressive et fine peut nous livrer l'"Erlebnis' de notre interlocuteur avec tout son sens, toutes ses nuances, toute sa fraîcheur. Mais elle nous la livre *dégradée*, c'est-à-dire *passive*. Nous sommes ainsi entourés d'objets magiques qui gardent comme un souvenir de la spontanéité de la conscience, tout en étant des objets du monde. Voilà pourquoi l'homme est toujours un sorcier pour l'homme. En effet, cette liaison poétique de deux passivités dont l'une crée l'autre spontanément, c'est le fonds même de la sorcellerie, c'est le sens profond de la 'participation'.
>
> (*TE*, p. 64)

This description, in linking the power of expression with an Ego-based psychology, suggests that such expression and communication attenuates, through a form of entropy, the spontaneity of consciousness and its dynamic capacity for action. Such a view, one might infer, might equally apply to the calculated rhetoric of persuasion, and to its 'performative' efficacy. But further, in its allusion to the role-playing aspects of communication ('une mimique expressive et fine'), Sartre's description is also relevant to the world of the theatre. For there, it could be argued, both actor and spectator experience a 'liaison poétique', paradoxically combining both spontaneity and passivity, through the medium of the role played. Now although in 'Le Style dramatique' Sartre does not differentiate between the magical, participatory role of language as it might 'fictively' operate between the characters of a play (between, for instance, Electre's incantation and the people of Argos) and as it might affect the spectator, he nevertheless sees its implications for the interplay of distance and identification characteristic of the aptly named 'participation' theatre. There, the element of 'action à distance' (another legitimate play on words in the 'magical' context of the theatre) is accentuated by the fact that the audience cannot intervene in the action in order to modify it. (From this point of view Sartre deplores the device of intermingling actors and audience, and applauds the double distancing effects of the play within a play.) None the less, the spectator in participation theatre is passively fascinated by, and caught up in, the apparent inevitability or the 'spontanéité dégradée' of the unfolding action.

In the theatre, then, language as action has been covertly transformed into language as 'action at a distance'. But Sartre's invoking of the magical effects of dramatic language creates more problems than it solves. The sense of 'envoûtement' and of inevitability which such language generates might seem to undermine the directly transitive results presupposed in Sartre's enumeration of speech-acts as a form of *engagement* in 'Le Style dramatique', and extensively described in *Qu'est-ce que la littérature?*. Furthermore, the 'degraded spontaneity' implied in his theory of magical effects entails an Ego-based structure incompatible with the elimination of psychology in a 'speech-act' theatre. It could indeed be argued that Sartre's thinking on language, as on so many other themes, oscillates between the polarisation or the reconciliation of apparent opposites, or that it is quite simply inconsistent, or that it is particularly sensitive to the contradictions and tensions inherent in our experience and use of language.

Indeed, the attempt in 'Le Style dramatique' to reconcile the aesthetic, magical action of language with its practical, everyday functions mirrors a number of further theories sketched in *L'Etre et le Néant*. There, for instance, Sartre establishes but does not develop a direct analogy between our existence 'within' language and our bodily existence (*EN*, p. 442). Such an analogy would yield, first, a view of language as pure instrument, a 'transparent' and unreflective means of attaining our practical ends – an instrument of which the structures would be 'passé sous silence' (p. 395). In addition, however, my body (as we saw in Chapter 1) and, by analogy, language, is seen to be part of my facticity, as being capable of 'magically' generating its own passivity. Further, it is a fundamental source of my alienation. Other aspects of the relationship between expression as communication and expression as alienation, and between individual discourse and the structure and evolution of language are explored in Sartre's account of the world of pre-existing techniques in which individual activity finds its place. Here the stress is at first strongly on the free, goal-directed, constructive act of the speaker or writer, whether in relation to the 'lieux communs' of discourse or to the rules of language. As we shall see, Sartre later takes a more negative view of the 'lieu commun' as the literal locus of ideology and of what might be called our 'social facticity'. But at this early stage 'ces phrases perdent leur caractère banal et conventionnel si on se place au point de vue de l'auteur

[. . .]. L'unité verbale étant la phrase signifiante, celle-ci est un acte constructif qui ne se conçoit que par une transcendance qui dépasse et néantise le donné vers une fin' (p. 597). Nor do linguistic laws, any more than the 'lieu commun', limit the creativity of specific utterances: 'Ainsi est-ce à l'intérieur du projet libre de la phrase que s'organisent les lois du langage' (p. 599). However, such rules, together with other aspects of the situation of the *pour-soi*, are at the same time part of the 'condition' or the 'donné' which constitute the limits of its freedom, and are, as such, the source of an 'objectification aliénante' (p. 608) of my situation by other people.

For Sartre, then, language operates at a number of different levels: as the instrument of unreflective action, as the medium of a magical 'action à distance' and of passive fascination, as creative freedom and as alienation. And within his theory, a certain ambivalence is visible: at times Sartre seems to consider all language to be magical (p. 442), at others magical language seems to be at variance with everyday usage. Now it is his emphasis on the communicative and transitive linguistic act, reinforced as it is in *Qu'est-ce que la littérature?*, which is usually taken to be dominant until a much later stage in the development of his thought. But we shall see that the 'magical' aspects of language and the struggle between the inertia of the 'lieu commun' on the one hand and linguistic instrumentality and creativity on the other are both thematically and stylistically crucial to his dramatic effects. And these, in turn, suggest a view of committed literature in practice which is far more complex than the theory of *Qu'est-ce que la littérature?* would seem to allow. Indeed, the specifically stylistic problems created by a tension between the magical and the everyday are posed as early as 'Le Style dramatique' in terms of the creation of theatrical distance: 'Comment trouver un langage dramatique en parlant aux spectateurs de leurs droits actuels, dans des milieux actuels, qui soit à la fois quotidien et qui réalise la distance?' (*TS*, p. 32). Sartre's answer is first to suggest the use of 'les mots de tout le monde', but with an emphasis on rhythm 'tel [. . .] qu'on les élève précisément à cette dignité que doit avoir le langage au théâtre' (p. 33).

Further, the rhythm itself should be dependent upon a use of ellipsis: 'cette ellipse [. . .] doit être rendue sensible par les ruptures de mouvement, c'est-à-dire que, précisément, il doit toujours manquer dans un texte une partie qui exprimerait complètement la pensée de l'acteur' (p. 34). Finally, the language, however 'everyday', should give an impression of irreversibility and inevitability correlative to the spectator's 'distance absolue' from the stage events: it should, 'en utilisant les mots les plus banals, les plus usés, rendre exactement cette dureté et cette nécessité qui doit être précisément l'intouchabilité de l'acteur' (p. 35). This impression should be reinforced, even in plays involving a contemporary setting, by a non-naturalistic mode of diction.

Sartre's plays are often thought to owe their success not so much to verbal subtlety as to long-tried (and sometimes meretricious?) effects associated with the threat of violent physical action and its attendant suspense; their shortcomings are held to arise from a tendency to excessive verbalising and rationalisation on the part of agents or victims. In theatrical terms *Les Mains sales* is usually, if patronisingly, placed firmly on the side of success. Within the 'flashback' and its emphasis on the inevitability of the central act of assassination it offers, for the box-office, melodramatic answers to simple questions. When and how (and only secondarily, why) will Hugo kill Hoederer? How will Hugo conceal his intentions? Within the 'present' action, will Olga save Hugo from the consequences of his action and of the Party's change of policy? Will Hugo save himself? For the 'thinking' spectator, the stereotyped characterisation may be ignored as he catches a hint of the 'problem play' in the themes of means and ends, and of prospective and retrospective self-justification – satisfying ambiguities within reassuringly perennial areas of moral concern. He may identify emotionally with the respectable pathos of hesitant middle-class commitment, find rational exhilaration, at a safe distance, in the gambles and ironies of pragmatism, or feel morally superior to the casuists of the Party Line. Stylistically, the varied social origins of the characters ensure an adequate, if sometimes contrived, range of linguistic registers, while static rhetoric is never allowed to hold back the speed of the action.[8]

However, dramatically and linguistically, *Les Mains sales* is more complex than such responses would suggest – complex in ways which illustrate, complicate and subvert Sartre's theories of style, action and motivation in the theatre. What, for instance, in terms of a theory of will, is the significance of the fact that Hugo's intention to kill Hoederer, when based upon deliberation, fails, and that it only succeeds when 'motivated' by apparently unreflective emotion? (Here Sartre introduces a variation on the pattern of *Les Mouches*, where, for Oreste, intention and action coincide through pure reflection, while, for Electre, emotion precludes apparently desired action.) What is the significance of the fact that, for Hugo, words are means of representing his experience to himself, either through the narration of past events or, during the 'represented' action of the flashback, through the attempt to categorise this experience as comedy, farce, or tragedy?

At the most obvious level, as far as Sartre's theory of motivation, will and emotion is concerned, *Les Mains sales* seems to conform in part at least to the more complex arguments of *L'Etre et le Néant* as well as to the relatively simplified inconsistencies of 'Le Style dramatique'. Hugo clearly enacts the possibility of the agent's voluntary and reflective error concerning his own projects which, as we saw earlier, Sartre distinguishes sharply from the intuitive certainty of unreflective or 'purely' reflective consciousness. Hugo mistakes the reflectively adopted goal of political commitment for the more fundamental project of self-realisation, which he fails to differentiate from the construction of a spurious Ego:

> L'attitude réflexive [. . .] entraîne mille possibilités d'erreur, non pas dans la mesure où elle saisit le pur mobile – c'est-à-dire la conscience réfléchie – comme un quasi-objet, mais en tant qu'elle vise à constituer à travers cette conscience réfléchie de véritables objets psychiques qui, eux, sont des objets seulement probables, [. . .] et qui peuvent même être des objets faux. (*EN*, p. 550)

For Hoederer, on the other hand, the reflective construction of the Ego is not a potentially dominant 'possible secondaire' (p. 549); his own political goals are integrated into a more creative circuit of situation and project. For him, too, words are primarily acts, rather than modes of reflective self-representation. He is none the less vulnerable to error, but in less self-deceptive ways than Hugo – for the fact that the situation and its contingencies can never be fully known always entails the risk of objective error, as Hoederer is well aware. (The initial failure of his plans is as dependent on contingency as their eventual success after his death.) 'Il faut se garder [. . .] d'appeler erreur sur soi les erreurs d'appréciation touchant la situation objective – erreurs qui peuvent entraîner dans le monde des conséquences absolument opposées à celles qu'on voulait atteindre, sans cependant qu'il y ait eu méconnaissance des fins proposées' (p. 550). It is the absence of 'erreur sur soi' in Hoederer which Hugo envies, mistakenly taking it for a form of psychological 'solidity' which he himself lacks, and which he equally mistakenly desires.

For Hugo, then, the false goal of political commitment, reflectively and erroneously conceived as a 'motive' for killing Hoederer, cannot lead to action when that act itself would destroy the only partly acknowledged possibility of more fruitful self-realisation through the friendship of Hoederer. But Hugo's emotional response to apparent betrayal as he finds Jessica in Hoederer's arms suggests, too, that the 'volitional' aspect of Hugo's original intention to kill was superficial, while the spontaneity of the emotional response and of the actual shooting suggests that the Ego was not reflectively engaged in the act itself. Hence the impossibility for Hugo of saying, after the death of Hoederer, 'j'ai fait ce que j'ai voulu' (p. 528). Hence, too, his resentment of the apparent contingency of the emotion and the act, and his realisation that the self was, precisely, not engaged: 'Ce n'est pas moi qui ai tué, c'est le hasard. [. . .] *Moi*, là-dedans, qu'est-ce que je deviens?' (VII, p. 245). Hugo therefore needs to re-establish his sense of self, first through the representation of experience noted above. The futility of such a tendency to associate will, responsibility and representation is, of course, crucial to the action (or to the delayed action) of the play, and to Hugo's narrative 'framing' of that action. Sartre, with one of his rare concessions to common sense, gives this futility a theoretical basis in *L'Etre et le Néant*:

Le sens commun conviendra avec nous, en effet, que l'être dit *libre* est celui qui peut *réaliser* ses projets. Mais pour que l'acte puisse comporter une *réalisation*, il convient que la simple projection d'une fin possible se distingue *a priori* de la réalisation de cette fin. S'il suffit de concevoir pour réaliser, me voilà plongé dans un monde semblable à celui du rêve, où le possible ne se distingue plus aucunement du réel. Je suis condamné dès lors à voir le monde se modifier au gré des changements *de* ma conscience, je ne puis pas pratiquer, par rapport à ma conception, la 'mise entre parenthèses' et la suspension de jugement qui distinguera une simple fiction d'un choix réel. L'objet apparaissant dès qu'il est simplement conçu, ne sera plus ni choisi ni seulement souhaité. La distinction entre le simple *souhait*, la *représentation* que je pourrais choisir et *le choix* étant abolie, la liberté disparaît avec elle. Nous sommes libres lorsque le terme ultime par quoi nous nous faisons annoncer ce que nous sommes est une *fin*, c'est-à-dire non pas un existant réel, comme celui qui, dans la supposition que nous avons faite, viendrait combler notre souhait, mais un objet qui n'existe pas encore. Mais dès lors cette *fin* ne saurait être transcendante que si elle est séparée de nous en même temps qu'accessible. Seul un ensemble d'existants réels peut nous séparer de cette fin – de même que cette fin ne peut être conçue que comme état à-venir des existants réels qui m'en séparent.

(*EN*, pp. 562–3)

In the light of Sartre's analysis here, it can be argued that Hugo fails to distinguish between wishing and choosing, between the illusion of choice and choice itself, or between imagined action and the practical action which presupposes a resistant world. Indeed, in anticipation, Hugo allows the 'fiction' of his desired *political* assassination of Hoederer to masquerade as a 'real' choice, thereby denying his own freedom and precluding the realisation of his ostensible goal. And in retrospect he persistently thinks of the reality of experience as a fiction which none the less escapes the bounds of narration or of definition (whether as comedy, tragedy or farce). It is Hoederer who acknowledges the resistance of 'existants réels' (for instance, the political opposition of Karsky and the Prince) which separate him from his goals, and who therefore exemplifies the apparently paradoxical relationship between freedom and *engagement*:

l'ordre même des existants est indispensable à la liberté elle-même. C'est par eux qu'elle est séparée et rejointe par rapport à la fin qu'elle poursuit et qui lui annonce ce qu'elle est. En sorte que les résistances que la liberté dévoile dans l'existant, loin d'être un danger pour la liberté, ne font que lui permettre de surgir comme liberté. Il ne peut y avoir de pour-soi libre que comme engagé dans un monde résistant. (p. 563)

Conversely, it is Hugo's failure to take into account the relationship between 'resistant' reality and freedom which leads to the irony of his cry as he gives way to the impulse to shoot Hoederer: 'Et puis vous m'avez délivré' (vi, iv, p. 242). It is ironic because he will later realise that, far from being the result of his (Hugo's) 'free' choice, the death of Hoederer will appear rather as a contingent event. Hence Hugo's need to construct retrospectively a responsible and voluntaristic self by claiming to have killed for political motives, by refusing to relegate his act to the 'inferior' status of a *crime passionnel*, and by rejecting, through a form of suicide, the possibility of being 'recuperated' for the Party's purposes. *L'Etre et le Néant* offers a relevant gloss on Hugo's final cry 'Non récupérable' (vii, p. 260), in which he attempts to enact two irreconcilable intentions. At one level he seeks to assert in retrospect a 'willed' and therefore reflective motivation for the killing of Hoederer through the immediate and self-destructive exercise of the will in the present. Such a retrospective assertion of motive is, of course, futile, since it attempts to short-circuit or reverse the passage of time which is essential to practical action and which is implicated in its precarious contingency. At another level Hugo seeks to achieve *in extremis* through the 'récupération' of the self a forever elusive totality within the *pour-soi*. And it is the very exercise of the will

113

which makes such an achievement impossible. Sartre's theoretical argument takes up the relationship between *motif, mobile,* project and act already referred to earlier and continues:

si le *résultat* de la réflexion est d'élargir la faille qui sépare le pour-soi de lui-même, tel n'est pas, pour autant, son *but.* Le but de la scissiparité réflexive est [. . .] de *récupérer* le réfléchi, de manière à constituer cette totalité irréalisable 'En-soi-pour-soi' qui est la valeur fondamentale posée par le pour-soi dans le surgissement même de son être. Si donc la volonté est par essence réflexive, son but n'est pas tant de décider quelle fin est à atteindre puisque de toutes façons, les jeux sont faits, l'intention profonde de la volonté porte plutôt sur *la manière* d'atteindre cette fin déjà posée. Le pour-soi qui existe sur le mode volontaire veut se récupérer lui-même en tant qu'il décide et agit. Il ne veut pas seulement être porté vers une fin, ni être celui qui se choisit comme porté vers telle fin: il veut encore se récupérer lui-même en tant que projet spontané vers telle ou telle fin. L'idéal de la volonté, c'est d'être un 'en-soi-pour-soi' en tant que projet vers une certaine fin: c'est évidemment un idéal réflexif et c'est le sens de la satisfaction qui accompagne un jugement tel que 'J'ai fait ce que j'ai voulu'. (*EN*, p. 528)

The very attempt to *will* the unity of consciousness and being ensures, then, a reflective widening of the fissure within consciousness. Hence the all-or-nothing coincidence of would-be self-affirmation and self-destruction in Hugo's final verbal act: the illusion of momentary unity cannot be sustained, and the possibility of disillusion is intolerable. Hugo's 'Non récupérable' therefore exemplifies an identity of contradictory propositions, or a complicated oxymoron, if we take that term in Vico's sense: 'to deny of something that it is what it is'.[9] For Hugo denies at the political level what he takes himself to be at the ontological level: that is to say, 'récupérable'. The negation is intended to be a simultaneous affirmation. But the affirmation is illusory, and the illusion is reinforced, both despite and because of Hugo's will, by the act of denial.

Les Mains sales ends, then, with a complex and concise rhetorical figure. And indeed the whole play could be said to be a play on words or about words, a play which exemplifies but also exceeds Sartre's definition of 'speech-act' drama. For it involves a whole spectrum of illocutionary acts and of intended perlocutionary acts, among them those enumerated in 'Le Style dramatique': the illocutionary 'serment', 'engagement', 'refus', 'jugement moral'; or the would-be perlocutionary 'défense des droits', 'contestation des droits des autres', 'menace' and 'mensonge' (*TS*, p. 34). Hugo, for instance, persuades his party colleagues to allow him to kill Hoederer, promises to do so, asserts his rights, offers definitions, pleads his case, declares his intentions, threatens, lies, narrates, names. Hoederer judges, commands, argues, persuades, predicts, offers to give his word. All plays could, of course, trivially be said to involve illocutionary or perlocutionary acts, but the dramatic effects of *Les Mains sales* depend crucially upon the relationship between speech-acts and action, or between action and subsequent narration, or upon the delayed and tangential results of persuasion. Furthermore, the play offers not only physical action, linguistic action, and linguistic commentary upon physical action – which creates its own complexities – but a metalinguistic commentary, whether explicit or implied, upon its own speech-acts. It dramatises and invites reflection upon the 'infelicities' which may disrupt the intended efficacy of such acts, the possibly conflicting illocutionary acts which a single utterance may perform, the scope of language to represent, define, obfuscate, frustrate or destroy, the instability of patterns of inference established through ellipsis, the dead weight of cultural codes, the power of context, whether properly linguistic or 'situational' to confer, extend, limit or subvert meaning, either from the point of view of the play's 'fictive' interlocutors or from the point of view of the audience. And while the entire discourse of the play is fictive, much of it is fictive to the second degree.[10]

The first speech-act represented in the play is the act of informing, in the radio announcement 'Les armées allemandes battent en retraite sur toute la largeur du front. Les armées soviétiques se sont emparées de Kischnar à quarante kilomètres de la frontière illyrienne' (I, i, p. 11). Its import and its medium, and its historical context, if not its setting, would be familiar to the French audience of 1948. But the straightforwardness of its content and its reassuring familiarity are soon undermined, as purely referential information dissolves into the more sinister familiarity of political rhetoric: 'Illyriens, nous savons qu'on vous a contraints de prendre les armes contre l'U.R.S.S., nous connaissons les sentiments profondément démocratiques de la population illyrienne et nous. . .' (I, i, p. 12). Here the apostrophe implies an assumption and an assertion of leadership camouflaged as a plea for communication and reciprocity. But the responsibility of leadership is belied by the unidentified 'nous' and the evasive 'on', while spurious intimacy fades into condescension and into the dehumanising impersonality

115

of 'la population illyrienne'. Such propagandist rhetoric may well create a sense of distanced scepticism or cynicism in the spectator. But this second response is, in turn, prevented from remaining stable. Any confirmation in the response of the stage-listener, Olga, is withheld: as she turns off the radio, the predictable staleness of the rhetoric is underlined, but the 'jeu de scène' ('Olga reste immobile, les yeux fixes' (p. 12)) suggests that her reaction, whether to the information or to the rhetoric, cannot be one of sceptical indifference. Information apart, the interruption of the message ensures that the spectator–listener will, during the short pause which follows, be more conscious of the rhetoric than of the undeveloped import of the utterance, and will thus become doubly disengaged from the perlocutionary force of its persuasion: his interest is more directly engaged by its failure as a perlocutionary act vis-à-vis the stage-listener, or by its failure as a form of seductive 'action à distance'.

But the utterance as information creates its own problems. It is perhaps rare for the exposition of a play to open with such a baldly informative statement: exposition seems to be drawing attention in a parodic form to its own procedures. But it does so to deceive: at this stage the news item conceals more than it reveals. The most significant aspect of the statement is that it concerns events which, we discover later, should, according to Hoederer's prediction, have occurred a year earlier. However, this aspect of the information is suppressed, or, at least, its revelation is deferred until the fourth of the play's seven *tableaux*. That revelation is, however, crucial, for it allows us to evaluate the significance both of Hoederer as a historical agent and of his assassination by Hugo. For in 1943 (two years before the time of the opening scene) Hoederer's policy as outlined to the Prince and Karsky is dictated by his prediction that 'les Russes se rapprochent, avant un an ils seront chez nous' (IV, iv, p. 155). And the information which allows us to calculate the year's discrepancy (although not to assign a definitive significance to it) is itself deferred, is never emphasised, and must be reconstructed from a chronology which seems to serve a quite different expository function in establishing the two-year duration of Hugo's imprisonment in 1943, in alluding to the threat to his life shortly before his release, and in explaining his attempt to reconstruct his motive for killing Hoederer. Further, the value of exposition itself is called into question: when at the end of the first *tableau* exposition seems to be well under way with Olga's abrupt imperative: 'Commence par le commencement' (I, iv, p.

34), its validity is immediately questioned by Hugo: 'est-ce qu'il y en a un?' (p. 34). Hugo's attempt to tell his story suggests that narrative (and by extension historical) representations of experience are based upon arbitrary incisions in time:

Hugo. On peut commencer l'histoire en mars 43 quand Louis m'a convoqué. Ou bien un an plus tôt quand je suis entré au Parti. Ou peut-être plus tôt encore, à ma naissance. Enfin bon. Supposons que tout a commencé en mars 1943. (p. 34)

The signifying function of speech-acts is questioned: Olga's imperative 'Raconte' (p. 33) suggests a naive belief in an unproblematic relationship between narrative and meaning. But although her command is a successful perlocutionary act at one level – in that Hugo does begin his story – it may fail at another, for Hugo does not share her confidence: 'c'est une histoire que je connais par cœur [. . .]. Quant à dire ce qu'elle signifie, c'est une autre affaire' (p. 34). Here, the problem of ascribing meaning to actions and events serves only to underline the arbitrariness of linguistic constructs. But a nostalgia for confidence remains which motivates Hugo's abiding need to overcome the seeming heterogeneity of action and language. In the last words of the play – 'Non récupérable' – Hugo, in passing sentence of death upon himself, tries to ensure the coincidence of the speech-act's illocutionary force and perlocutionary effect. If he were to succeed, the *dénouement* of the play could be said to resolve, in a traditionally conclusive fashion, the metalinguistic (and therefore less traditional) problems posed in the exposition, and to resolve the problem of 'beginnings and ends' raised by the very convention of exposition and *dénouement*. For if the efficacy of both past and present action can be guaranteed only through the self-destructive utterance of the protagonist, what remains to be said or done?

An account in terms of such a resolution ignores, however, the initially suppressed secondary meanings of the apparently purely informative first two sentences of the play. For the apparent straightforwardness of the information results from a curious combination of a readily available external context for the spectator or reader – his own experience of receiving and evaluating such messages – and a temporary absence of textual or dramatic context, reinforced by the interruption of the message and by Olga's silence. But as the play proceeds, the familiarity of the external context will fade, while the textual context will become more and more complex, making the retrospective ascription of significance to those two opening sentences more uncertain. For in *Les Mains sales* two major levels of context can be distinguished. The chronology and context of Hugo's assassination of Hoederer are explicit and readily available; the reader, if he goes no further, may therefore readily infer that the 'message' of the play is located in this act and in the verbal events which accompany it. However, although accessible, the context is sufficiently manifold to allow for speculative suspense concerning the solution of the enigma conventionally seen as the traditional locus of plot interest: 'Why did Hugo kill Hoederer?' Or rather, 'Why is the fulfilment of Hugo's promise to kill Hoederer first deferred and then accomplished?' Furthermore, as we shall see, the complexity of this context at a detailed level allows for a number of local but ultimately significant indeterminacies.

The context of the fictive 'historical fact' of the year's delay in the successful advance of the Russian forces is, however, far more dispersed and implicit. It coincides with the fact of Hugo's assassination of Hoederer, and Hoederer's failure, in consequence, to meet Louis and convince him of the rightness of his policy, but the coincidence does not constitute an explanation. (The fact that it does not constitute an explanation is, however, part of the context of Hugo's subsequent actions.) The prediction by Hoederer (that the Russians will arrive within a year) which provides a retrospective context for the opening lines of the play is itself of ambiguous illocutionary force. Is it a rhetorical ploy exploited for the persuasion of the Prince and Karsky – an opportunistic threat masquerading as an assertion? Is it a forecast based on reasoned inference from readily available evidence or from 'inside knowledge' (although evidence within the immediate context is scant and communication with Russia, we later discover, has been cut)? Or is it indeed a prediction which, as such, would imply belief in a historicist theory of inexorable socio-political processes governed by rigid laws or impersonal forces – a view which Hoederer's slightly later explanation to Karsky might reinforce: 'vous avez perdu parce que vous deviez perdre' (IV, iv, p. 157) and which might be otherwise expressed as the view that 'the story of mankind has a plot'?[11] In short, is it pragmatic, empirical or Marxist? Further, is the fulfilment of the prediction deferred because of Hugo's interruption of Hoederer's complex illocution 'Hugo, veux-tu que je te donne ma parole que. . .' (VI, iii, p. 242) which demonstrates the fragility of word as bond? Or is it due, as Olga implies in the last scene (VII, p. 253), to the interruption of the

118

Party's lines of communication with the Soviet Union – a slight perturbation on the surface of an overall pattern? Is it due, in other words, to individual initiatives and interaction, with their apparently decisive beginnings and ends, or to a mere side-effect of war as part of the historical process?

Such questions of communication and of speech-acts and their status are closely related to the status of the assassination itself: is it a decisive moment, a random event, or one which, although intended, is irrelevant to the ultimate course of events? For Hugo 'le hasard a tiré trois coups de feu' (vii, p. 245); Hoederer regards his death as inevitable (iv, iii, pp. 139–140), the identity of his assassin becomes a convenient fiction (vii, p. 255), he himself is expendable. His life and death do not irretrievably affect the political situation, and Hugo, despite his last verbal gesture, is superfluous. Further, we are left to evaluate the significance of a year's delay within the larger perspectives of history, and to compare the effectiveness, in the short or long term, of physical action or verbal persuasion. Their interrelationship, associated with tension between urgency and indecision, itself generates a paradox: the assassination, deferred by Hugo, itself defers, when executed, the perlocutionary effects of Hoederer's argument with the Prince and Karsky. On the political level, the synthesis of speech-act and physical action occurs only within the impersonal, collective framework of re-established channels of communication (the 'party line') and of military advance. On the individual level, it occurs only with Hugo's final verbal act of self-destruction. In this episode of the 'plot of mankind's story', the two protagonists are mere *figurants*.

If, therefore, towards the end of the play we remember its opening sentences (and we are reminded of them by Olga's outline of the current political and military situation (vii, p. 253)), we are left wondering whether the action witnessed on the stage is not marginal to a supra-personal historical progression which is referred to but which cannot be represented. The context from which we might reconstruct such an interpretation is, however, dispersed and *lacunaire*, constituting one of the major ellipses of the play. It is in tension with the immediately represented action, which may rather reinforce the spectator's tendency to see historical change in terms of decisive events (assassination) or of 'great men' (Hoederer). At another level, the play suggests that the greatness of great men is less a question of what they do than of the way in which they are represented, whether naively or through a cynical exploitation of the cult of personality:

Hugo. Je suppose que vous avez réhabilité sa mémoire?
Olga. Il fallait bien.
Hugo. Il aura sa statue à la fin de la guerre, il aura des rues dans toutes nos
villes et son nom dans les livres d'histoire. (VII, p. 255)

The play both perpetuates and demystifies the 'myths' of decisive events and great men and, in so doing, it raises, but refuses to answer, the question of the locus of meaning in history. For the play also dramatises the problems involved in presenting such myths dramatically and thereby foregrounds the undecidability of history's meaning, since it suggests that meaning is more a function of variable modes of representation than of the stability of the content represented. For in its intertextual context *Les Mains sales* evokes other dramas which portray the equal futility of action and inaction, the failure to see that words themselves may be acts, and the self-cancelling permutations of choice, will and deliberation. Macbeth's 'tale told by an idiot [. . .] signifying nothing' is echoed in Hugo's 'Quant à dire ce qu'elle signifie, c'est une autre affaire. C'est une histoire idiote, comme toutes les histoires' (I, iv, p. 34), while Hamlet is more consciously recalled in his 'Etre ou ne pas être, hein? Vous voyez ce que je veux dire' (IV, vi, p. 169) and 'Pour écrire! Des mots! Toujours des mots!' (VI, ii, p. 234). The context of each allusion or quotation indicates that the problem posed is the question of the production of meaning or of the extent to which language can be said to connect with the world. The view that narrative can either represent experience or produce meaning is undermined; the problem of being is related, but purely interrogatively, to the problem of communicating meaning; the value of writing is questioned. So the failure to produce meaning is exemplified in the parodic repetition of existing texts. (Indeed, for Hugo the journalist, writing is itself a repetitive rather than a communicative activity, which simply reproduces already communicated 'news': by the time he writes, news has become history.) A nostalgia for a synthesis of meaning and action is also symbolised in Hugo's clandestine code-name, Raskolnikoff: Hugo's own name simply designates, while his adopted one also has a *sens*. Hugo aspires to a transference of its meaning to himself – to a coincidence of reference and meaning – through a form of magical, participatory 'action à distance', but it is an aspiration which ultimately condemns him to anonymity. Hoederer's apparently insignificant code-name is the only one we know for him, but it is he who, in the play's fictive future, will have 'son nom dans les livres d'histoire' (VII, p. 255).[12]

120

Sartre, then, specifically alludes to the 'already written' – to texts which themselves represent the problem of the ascription of meaning to historical and personal action. Other allusions, however, seem to satirise the protagonist's tendency to categorise experience in terms of more generic literary conventions, and thereby attempt to undermine the spectator's own tendency to 'read' his own theatrical experience in those terms. Hugo, for instance, represents himself in 'represented' speech as thinking in terms of a play in which he is at once author, actor and spectator, but to escape from the tyranny of representation he seeks to become both the agent of command and the executant of its per-locutionary effects:

Hugo, avec lassitude. Il y a beaucoup trop de pensées dans ma tête. [. . .]
   'Est-ce que je ne suis pas en train de me jouer la comédie?' Des trucs
   comme ça.
Hoederer, lentement. Oui. Des trucs comme ça. Alors, en ce moment, ta
   tête en est pleine?
Hugo, gêné. Non. . . Non, pas en ce moment. (*Un temps.*) Mais ça peut
   revenir. Il faut que je me défende. Que j'installe d'autres pensées
   dans ma tête. Des consignes: 'Fais ceci. Marche. Arrête-toi. Dis cela.'
   J'ai besoin d'obéir.   (III, iv, pp. 111–12)

But here Hugo's illocutionary acts of self-questioning and self-command are fictive (to the second degree) and have no direct effects. Such oblique force as they retain – for they also have the aim of informing Hoederer – miscarries ironically, for Hoederer mistakenly sees himself as the source of the commands which Hugo should obey:

Hoederer. Ça va. Si tu obéis, on pourra s'entendre.   (p. 112)

On its own terms, however, Hugo's obedience would bring with it not a greater 'entente', but Hoederer's death. The cliché of role-playing in 'jouer la comédie', thus emphasised and renewed, alerts the reader to the theatricality of the play itself, to the fragility of communication and to the problematic relationship of thought and language: Hugo professes *not* to be thinking the thoughts which he addresses to himself – a claim which invites speculation about the degree of deception or self-deception involved. Other allusions to dramatic genres serve in their very contradictions to underline the futility of such categories – and, by extension, of their application to *Les Mains sales* itself, as in Hugo's 'Je joue la comédie du désespoir' (IV, vi, p. 169), 'Je vivais depuis longtemps dans la tra-gédie. C'est pour sauver la tragédie que j'ai tiré' (VII, p. 244), 'Tout ce qu'il disait! C'est une farce' (VII, p. 256). Such over-definition, in itself contradictory, distances the reader from his own tendencies to over-define not only his own experience, but theatrical representation itself, in terms of genre. Moreover, it runs counter to a generic uncertainty at the heart of the play. At one level the 'present' of the play's action – the three hours which pass between Hugo's arrival in Olga's room and his final exit as 'non récupérable'[13] – coincides precisely with the duration of the performance, constituting the rigorous unity of time associated with classical tragedy. The consequence of the unity of time in which the spectator's time and represented time, or the time of performance and dramatic action, are superimposed is to isolate the immediate action from the historical and personal past of the characters. The relationship between the individual and history, and the source of the tragic action itself can only be evoked by and inferred from the characters' speech. The historical process which gave rise to the dramatic crisis (for instance, the Trojan war in *Andromaque*) is no longer at issue: its remaining force is symbolic and psychological. Consequently the unity of time is closely linked to the tragic sense of fatality. As Anne Ubersfeld puts it:

Le conflit historique est hors de l'histoire, c'est-à-dire hors de l'histoire en train de se faire. L'unité de temps inscrit l'histoire non comme *processus*, mais comme fatalité irréversible, inchangeable. La solution historique est nécessairement inscrite dès le départ dans le texte tragique [. . .]. L'ouverture tragique sur l'acte libre est toujours inscrite dans un *déjà-fait*, déjà vécu qui la détruit.[14]

Now it is clear that despite his efforts to interrogate his past, Hugo can neither revive nor revise it; his present experience is cut off from the lived time which should ensure the continuity of past and present. (His period of imprisonment, evoked but not represented, symbolises and reinforces this discontinuity.) Moreover, although he questions his past act in killing Hoederer, the political conflicts then involved are no longer at issue. And although Hugo's cry 'Non récupérable' may be a free act, it is tragically circumscribed by the *'déjà-fait*, déjà vécu'. Even the tension within Hugo's interpretation of his action between apparent contingency ('Ce n'est pas moi qui ai tué, c'est le hasard' (VII, p. 245)) and paradoxically willed inevitability ('Moi, je vivais depuis longtemps dans la tragédie. C'est pour sauver la tragédie que j'ai tiré' (VII, p. 244)) is dissolved in the broader inevitability of Hoederer's death and rehabilitation. The apparently inexorable historical outcome (socially 'positive' but deeply ironic from Hugo's point of view) which absorbs the initiatives of both Hugo and Hoederer is symbolised by Olga's reiteration of Hoederer's earlier words as his policy, once rejected, becomes Party policy. For Hugo, such an outcome mocks his attempt to define his own experience as tragedy. The echo of Hoederer's arguments as Olga tries to persuade Hugo to renounce his responsibility for the assassination reduces tragic inevitability to mechanical and derisory repetition: 'Tout ce qu'il disait! Tout ce qu'il disait! C'est une farce' (VII, p. 256). Hence the failure of Olga's persuasion, and hence Hugo's last futile desire to thwart the irreversibility of time itself: 'Je n'ai pas encore tué Hoederer, Olga. Pas encore. C'est à présent que je vais le tuer et moi avec' (VII, p. 259).

The framing of action and representation within a traditional unity of time is not, then, a reassuring source of generic stability. And there is, of course, a major disruption of that basically rigorous unity in that Hugo's narration of his past becomes enacted narration. The result is a clash of two views of time. One, arising from the three hours' duration of Hugo's meeting with Olga, implies the coincidence of the spectator's lived time, of the time of performance, and of represented time. The other, involving not only the longer, dispersed duration of the events 'narrated' by Hugo, but the lapse of two years between 'past' and 'present', creates a marked discontinuity between the time of the representation and represented time. Each view has different consequences for the extent to which the action of a play may be simply perceived, 'lived' or reconstructed by the spectator. The former view implies a more passive response:

L'unité de temps contraint le spectateur à la 'sidération' aristotélicienne (au sens brechtien du terme). L'histoire – que le spectateur n'a pas à reconstituer – apparaît du même coup spectacle étale, à jamais révolu dans son immutabilité, fait pour être vu, non pour être vécu: l'histoire est *spectacle fini*. [. . .] De même [. . .] la durée individuelle, le passé 'psychique' des protagonistes est vu dans la même lumière d'éternité.

(Ubersfeld, pp. 208–9)

And indeed at one level *Les Mains sales* follows the canons of classical representation, allowing for what Sartre would consider to be the effects of 'participation' theatre. The fact that despite the 'present' of performance the play's quasi-historical allusions refer (obliquely and fictively) to the spectator's prior experience, whether of similar actual events, of similar utterances or of other texts, is reinforced by the unity of time to create the sense of a *'spectacle fini'*. Further, in the context of personal 'destiny', it is clear that Hugo's death, threatened in the first *tableau*, is inevitable: like Ionesco's king, but less explicitly, 'il va mourir à la fin du spectacle'. At another level, however, the play exploits, or even flaunts, the distance between the time of representation and the time to which it refers, and between two modes of representing time. The spectator or reader, then, is obliged to reconstruct, through an active process of invention, reflection and revision, the events elided in the play's visual or textual discontinuities.

Now while in one sense the spectator or reader of *Les Mains sales* is given in the represented narration of the flashback the means of bridging the two-year interval between 'past' and 'present', in another sense, as we have seen, there is a discrepancy in the time-scheme of the play created by the deferred fulfilment of Hoederer's prediction, which leads the spectator to reflect upon that interval itself, but without producing a definitive explanation or significance. The indeterminacy of meaning is reinforced by a clash of conventions, by generic uncertainty. In *Les Mains sales* the clash is both radical and insidious, for the information which might account for the year's discrepancy is neither represented nor referred to, but can only be inferred. In Sartre's plays, such clashes, and such temporal discontinuities, are not explicitly emphasised, as they are for different purposes in, for instance, Claudel, Brecht or Ionesco. Their very implicitness creates, rather than a consistent distancing, to which the spectator can ultimately adjust, that sense of *malaise* which Sartre recommends in 'Théâtre épique et théâtre dramatique' and which, as we saw in the earlier discussion of *Huis clos*, undermines the over-simplifications of melodrama. Thus Sartre exploits our expectations of a certain genre by representing, in one time-scale, the critical moment of an individual destiny, only to subvert them, in another, by enacting the elusive contingencies of social relationships and the paradoxically inexorable unpredictability of an open-ended historical process.

As in *Huis clos*, the modes of representation displayed are closely associated with ideological assumptions. It is, of course, perfectly possible to account for Hugo's sardonically reflective or self-indulgently over-emphatic attempts at 'generic' self-representation in terms of his desire for unproblematic identity and action, and in terms of his need to see that action as the fulfilment of a personal destiny. But the text's emphasis on Hugo's literary allusions may also be seen to characterise the bourgeois intellectual for whom such allusion is part of a culturally determined linguistic code. And as we have seen, the implications of representation are also carried into the sphere of historical understanding: Hoederer's name, or rather his false (and, unlike Hugo's 'Raskolnikoff', initially unliterary) name will be perpetuated in order to absorb the contingencies of his death into the myth of the National Hero: an overtly ideological myth which in its ascription of meaning by *fiat* underlines the discrepancy between representation and the elusive significance of events.

The exploitation of ideologically weighted modes of representation is sometimes, thematically, less consciously pragmatic than the last example, but it has further metalinguistic implications. Hugo's speech, which refers so 'naturally' to the 'already written', is also traversed by the codes and assumptions which betray the bourgeois origins from which he wishes to free himself: assumptions which, for Sartre, become increasingly closely allied to the *lieux communs* and the stereotypes which characterise the inertia of language, and which themselves constitute modes of representation. Hugo's cliché-ridden tendency to assert his rights (for instance, the right to self-respect in III, ii) takes us at one level on to the 'terrain du droit' seen by Sartre as a thematically positive dramatic element in 'Le Style dramatique'. At another, however, it corresponds more closely to the views of *L'Etre et le Néant*, which not only associates the assertion of rights, as we saw earlier, with a false and univocal affirmation of pre-existing values, but also sees that assertion itself as inherently and negatively imbued with representational and theatrical qualities. For the 'sujet de droit' who affirms such rights is

précisément ce sujet que *j'ai à être* et que je ne suis point. Ce n'est pas que je ne veuille pas l'être ni qu'il soit un autre. Mais plutôt il n'y a pas de commune mesure entre son être et le mien. Il est une 'représentation' pour les autres et pour moi-même, cela signifie que je ne puis l'être qu'*en représentation*. Mais précisément si je me le représente, je ne le suis point, j'en suis séparé, comme l'objet du sujet, séparé *par rien*, mais ce rien m'isole de lui, je ne puis l'être, je ne puis que *jouer à l'être*, c'est-à-dire m'imaginer que je le suis. Et, par là-même, je l'affecte de néant. [. . .] Je ne puis l'être que sur le mode neutralisé, comme l'acteur est Hamlet, en faisant mécaniquement les *gestes typiques* de mon état.   (*EN*, p. 99)

While here, in the context of *mauvaise foi*, the relationship between rights and representation is discussed at the ontological rather than at the ideological or social level, the transition is foreshadowed later in *L'Etre et le Néant*. The problem of *de jure* identity and of the unrealisable possibility of self-coincidence is unexpectedly illustrated by a reference to property and conflict:

Il y possibilité lorsque, au lieu d'être purement et simplement ce que je suis, je suis comme le Droit d'être ce que je suis. Mais ce droit même me sépare de ce que j'ai le droit d'être. Le droit de propriété n'apparaît que lorsqu'on me conteste ma propriété, lorsque déjà, en fait, par quelque côté elle n'est plus à moi. La jouissance tranquille de ce que je possède est un pur et simple fait, non un droit. (p. 144)

In 1945, in his 'Présentation des *Temps Modernes*', Sartre more radically questions that apparently most fundamental and far-reaching assertion of rights – the Déclaration des Droits de l'Homme. He explicitly associates it with the would-be universalist but in fact class-bound 'esprit d'analyse' of the bourgeoisie, with its emphasis on the individual as a 'véhicule de la nature humaine' (*S* II, pp. 17–18). It is this bourgeois illusion which is implicit in Hugo's assumption – in contrast with the more down-to-earth concerns of those improbable proletarians, Georges and Slick – that the notion of rights is a universal value: 'Si je suis entré au Parti, c'est pour que tous les hommes [. . .] en aient un jour le droit' (i.e. 'de se respecter') (III, ii, p. 88–9). But such an attitude is infectious: Georges and Slick move from a cynical relativism ('T'a pas le droit de te respecter si t'es pas au moins secrétaire' (p. 88)) to an acceptance of the stereotype ('On ne lui veut pas de mal. On ne le blaire pas, c'est tout. On a tout de même le droit' (p. 99)). It is Hoederer, pragmatist rather than universalist, who undermines such claims by maintaining the value, however unstable, of action against the 'être en représentation' of the 'sujet de droit'. Such exchanges parody the conflict of rights which in 'Le Style dramatique' and 'Forger des mythes' is seen to be both dramatically and morally justifiable. *Les Mains sales* is not so much a drama of mutually contested rights as a contestation of the notion of rights, and the myth of universality is exposed as a form of ideology.

Hugo, then, is trapped in the codes of his class. They exemplify the pitfalls which lie between experience and expression. For Georges and Slick the pressure of hunger – envied by Hugo – resists formulation and communication. But the verbal fluency with which Hugo expresses his own childhood experience of surfeit and anorexia in an attempt to justify his apparently less urgent political commitment is a deceptive fluency. Creative expression, like the growth of the young child, is stunted by repetition and by a superficially ironic reworking of clichés: the stereotypes of stifling family concern, of hollow charity and of purely verbal solidarity with an equally stereotyped 'family of man':

Hugo. Mange, Hugo, mange. Une cuillerée pour le gardien qui est en chômage, une cuillerée pour la vieille qui ramasse les épluchures dans la poubelle. (III, ii, p. 98)

But the more basic irony is that Hugo is himself deceived in believing that his surfeited disgust led to positive action: 'une cuillerée pour la famille du charpentier qui s'est cassé la jambe. J'ai quitté la maison' (p. 98). As Jessica has already revealed, Hugo was in fact passive: 'ton père t'a chassé' (III, i, p. 69). Here the association of the inertia of the *lieu commun* with the theme of surfeit and passivity anticipates Sartre's analysis of a metaphysical 'anorexie' in *L'Idiot de la famille*[15] – an analysis which stresses a pathological failure to 'assimilate' the world into a process of growth and change. But Hugo (like the Flaubert of *L'Idiot*) also suffers in other ways from the pervasiveness of the cliché: the break, whether willed or passive, from his own milieu is frustrated by another set of stereotypes: 'Rien à faire! Je suis un gosse de riches, un intellectuel, un type qui ne travaille pas de ses mains' (III, ii, p. 100). The response of the reader to Hugo's plea for sympathy is not entirely against him. And such a response reflects, perhaps, a basic ambivalence of Sartre's which is more than that of the left-wing bourgeois intellectual. As we saw earlier, his view of the *lieu commun* in *L'Etre et le Néant* is relatively positive, and the much more sustained analysis of commonplaces in *L'Idiot de la famille* still allows for the possibility of *dépassement* within the dialectical movement between the apparent inertia of language and the 'activité synthétique [. . .] du parleur' (*IF*, pp. 621 *et seq.*). But as Sartre suggests in 1966 the individual's power of *dépassement* may be frustrated, and a retreat into the generality of the *lieu commun* may be interpreted either as a victory for conditioning or as a result of our complicity. In either case, it is an episode in the 'lutte de la répétition contre l'histoire':

Contre celle-ci nous nous défendons par celle-là. [. . .] La répétition, ce sont nos petits rites misérables et ce bavardage qui nous assourdit: les lieux communs. [. . .] Bien qu'ils soient appris et très proches de réflexes conditionnés, ils sont aussi maintenus en nous par notre complicité. Unique moyen, dans le monde actuel, de communication entre les hommes, ils sont aussi des agents d'absolue séparation.[16]

Such a view is anticipated in *Les Mains sales*. Hugo, tempted by historical action but condemned to 'repetition' by his activities as a journalist, is threatened by the linguistic conditioning and the *lieux communs* of his class, despite his resentful half-awareness of their spurious universality. But the shifting of allegiance to another class does not ensure escape from linguistic stereotypes. The Party has its own codes, designed to stigmatise its opponents or to conceal euphemistically the realities of action:

Olga. Nous ne pouvons pas nous permettre de liquider ce garçon sans même examiner s'il est récupérable.   (I, iii, p. 27).

Hugo is again half-aware of the ideological weight of such codes:

Jessica. J'irais trouver Hoederer et je lui dirais: voilà; on m'a envoyé ici pour vous tuer mais j'ai changé d'avis et je veux travailler avec vous. [. . .]
Hugo. C'est justement *ça qui s'appellerait* trahir.
(v, ii, p. 189) (my emphasis)[17]

Here the implied form of indirect speech suggests that Hugo is not unequivocally and unreservedly committed to the proposition that such acts are treacherous; it further suggests that although he refuses to accept Jessica's literal interpretation of the situation he cannot opt either for an attenuation of the distinction between facts and values or, on the other hand, for the commitment involved in recognising that values must be chosen precisely because they are *not* facts (i.e. the Sartrean position).

However, the fortunes of ideological codes and of their ultimate arbitrariness are perhaps best exemplified by the word which apparently guarantees a lack of arbitrariness: 'objectivement'. It is dramatically central, in that it sums up the ostensible and rationalised motivation of Hugo's 'intention' to kill Hoederer. It offers one of the most crucial semantic test-cases of the play, and Sartre also manipulates it in order to reveal the dangers of a fundamental confusion between facts and values. It is first used by the Party 'hard-liner', Louis, to emphasise the hollowness (in his view) of democratic mandate: despite the majority vote for Hoederer's policy of power-sharing, 'Objectivement, c'est un traître; ça me suffit' (I, iv, p. 51). When it is later preferred to Jessica by Hugo, in parrot-repetition of Louis, the word is associated again with the pseudo-scientific apparatus of Marxism, but in a context which itself wryly suggests both relativism and blind faith:

Hugo. Objectivement, il agit comme un social-traître.
Jessica, sans comprendre. Objectivement?
Hugo. Oui.

Jessica. Ah! (*Un temps.*) Et lui, s'il savait ce que tu prépares, est-ce qu'il penserait que tu es un social-traître?

Hugo. Je n'en sais rien. [. . .] Qu'est-ce que ça peut faire? Oui, probablement.

Jessica. Alors, qui a raison?

Hugo. Moi.

Jessica. Comment le sais-tu?

Hugo. La politique est une science. Tu peux démontrer que tu es dans le vrai et que les autres se trompent.

Jessica. Dans ce cas pourquoi hésites-tu? (v, ii, pp. 190–1)

The word 'objectivement' is parrotted again by Jessica in an attempt to save Hoederer's life by persuading him to listen to Hugo's arguments and to admit that he is in error – an attempt in which the illocutionary force of 'proving' objectivity would be crucial. In the event, what the word does has very little to do with what it 'means': its force depends not on its correspondence to an absolute state of affairs, but on its empty reiteration by someone who cannot understand its adequacy (or inadequacy). It succeeds neither in explaining nor in convincing, but it does succeed in warning Hoederer.

Jessica. Hugo, tu m'as promis! (*A Hoederer.*) Il dit que vous êtes un social-traître.

Hoederer. Un social-traître! Rien que ça!

Jessica. Objectivement. Il a dit: objectivement.

Hoederer, changeant de ton et de visage. Ça va. Eh bien, mon petit gars, dis-moi ce que tu as sur le cœur, puisqu'on ne peut pas l'empêcher.

(v, iii, p. 202)

For Hoederer, aware of the ideological status of such 'objectivity', sees that faith masquerading (in however opportunistic a fashion) as objective truth is more dangerous than mere opinion.[18] The illocutionary force intended by Jessica miscarries, then – although her intuitive sense of the status of 'objectivement' as part of the rhetoric of persuasion is more acute than Hugo's acceptance of its scientific pretentions. But its perlocutionary effect, although oblique, is unmistakable. Here, not everything 'meant' by the speaker is 'said', and what is understood both by the stage interlocutor and by the spectator is neither meant nor said. Ordinary language, ideological code and ellipsis combine in a dramatic effect which calls into question our ways of producing and receiving meaning, and of attempting to endorse the truth of our propositions.

In view of the obstacles which prevent the full engagement of word and world, word and action, or word and truth, it is unsurprising that Hugo and Jessica should take refuge in the apparent disengagement of language games or of 'fictive' utterances: the games of the revolutionary, of the jealous 'femme d'intérieur' or of the adventuress in the third *tableau* (scenes i and v), the game of the bored wife (IV, i), or the game of seriousness itself (III, i). A number of these exchanges are marked as 'fictive' (to the second degree) in relation to the remainder of the play: although, as we have seen, the problem of the representation of natural utterances is itself foregrounded, the fictive status of Hugo's and Jessica's 'play' is even further emphasised. Although couched largely in 'les mots de tout le monde' (*TS*, p. 33), their dialogue is clearly demarcated from everyday discourse by the linguistic 'frames' of play ('Pouce.' 'Pouce cassé.' (III, i. p. 68)). But more noteworthy still is the emphatic rhythm of their speech (a feature which, for Sartre, as we saw earlier, should exist in tension with ordinary language in dramatic style) – the rhythms of stichomythia and of sustained 'répliques sur le mot' which underline the self-referential and non-consequential nature of their exchanges.

The attractions of verbal play for those who find intolerable the commitments of the word as bond are obvious: an autonomous interplay of chance and rule, of resistance and control, of collusion and contest, an a-temporality involving pleasurable and willed rather than stereotyped and mechanical repetition, freedom of decision within strict limits, the apparent self-forgetfulness of absorption in disinterested activity, the experience of non-consequential tension and resolution, the irrelevance of truth-criteria. The distance of play from the concerns of the real world may take two forms: it may tend to isolate itself in secrecy; it may, on the other hand, constitute a representation or, as Huizinga suggests, 'a performance, a *stepping out* of common reality into a higher order'. The elements of collusion, contest and representation may be fused, in that 'the game "represents" a contest, or else becomes a contest for the best representation of something'.[19]

Apart from the demarcation from ordinary dialogue already noted, Jessica's and Hugo's playing illustrates – in perhaps unusual combinations – a number of the features mentioned above. Consciously melodramatic role-playing (so consciously melodramatic that it raises to a higher power the 'être en représentation' of the self in 'everyday life') or the mock hyperbole of pseudo-confession ('*Jessica*. Qu'est-ce qu'il y a dans cette valise? *Hugo*. Un secret honteux' (III, i, p. 67)) seem to place these exchanges firmly on the side of playful representation or of a ritual contest of concealment and discovery. At the same time, a sense of purely private play is clear, so that the spectator, normally at ease watching a naturalistic 'play', is transformed into an uneasy voyeur or eavesdropper. A further sense of *malaise* is provoked, moreover, by the repeatedly 'metacommunicative' tests (in Bateson's sense),[20] which the couple set each other. For in such questions as 'On joue ou on ne joue pas?' (III, i, p. 68) they seek to exchange 'messages that identify what sort of message a message is' in a fruitless attempt to define the verbal situation, thereby in fact underlining its instability and the precariousness of their own emotional commitments. The full illocutionary force of their exchanges, voluntarily suspended on the one hand by the controlled ritual fictions of play, is subverted on the other by the oblique and uncontrolled self-betrayal of their utterances. The attempt to disengage language from the word is as futile as any attempt to engage it fully.

But when the instrumental force of language as practical action is attenuated, can it be supplemented by its force as a magical 'action à distance'? In his final speech-act, the self-destructive 'Non récupérable' (VII, p. 260) which will lead to his death at the hands of the Party, Hugo seems to combine the two functions. His attempt to ascribe meaning by *fiat* to the earlier action of killing Hoederer, which has defied rational analysis, is properly an 'action à distance': it relies on the primitive logic of 'participation', with its elimination of space, time and the laws of contradiction, rather than on a rational logic of causal relations: 'C'est à présent que je vais le tuer' (p. 259). But the rider 'et moi avec' anticipates the direct perlocutionary effect of 'Non récupérable' (p. 260). Hugo tries to grasp the perpetually deferred realisation of full intelligibility in an absolute moment when the illusory coincidence of language, action, world and meaning might be possessed in a 'totalité instantanée' (*ETE*, p. 47).

In linguistic play, then, Hugo fruitlessly seeks a theoretically controlling but in practice fragile verbal 'frame' which will substitute the repetition of ritual for progressive action and maintain its own private conventions independently of an unstable world. But he also seeks the security of wider stabilised forms in would-be commitment to an ideological code and its linguistic stereotypes. When both fail, he finally attempts, in a single speech-act, to engage with the world by both exploiting and subverting that code in an ironic echo. But Hugo's irony is partial: subject to the logic of participation, it remains unaware of the contradiction

131

implicit in the cry 'Non récupérable', where the coincidence of self-assertion and self-destruction can only be expressed by the elision of the 'Je'.

At the end of *Les Mains sales* it is left to the reader or to the spectator to dismantle rationally the rhetoric of the condensed oxymoron, but he may also respond affectively to the futility of the self-inflicted verbal wound through which Hugo tries to redeem both himself and Hoederer. Does the spectator, then, experience that balance of participation and distance which may lead to a critical *prise de conscience* of the issues represented? Rather, Sartre seems to appeal in practice to two quite different levels of response in which the emotional and the rational may be strongly dissociated, and in which 'committed' consciousness may be inhibited rather than fostered. For the appeal to emotion involves at a thematic level, as we saw, an appeal to 'everyday' assumptions concerning the exercise of the will and the notion of rights which may run counter to Sartre's philosophical position. This may lead to facile identification and to an oversimplified view of political action and of political and moral polarities which could reinforce rather than question existing ideological commitments. (The reception of the play in 1948 and 1949 illustrates this danger.)[21] Rational 'distance', on the other hand, might lead to a dismissively non-committal view of such commitments. Further, at the linguistic level, Sartre's practice in *Les Mains sales* of his precept in 'Le Style dramatique' that the playwright should exploit 'les mots les plus banals, les plus usés' (*TS*, p. 35) may lead either to a falsely secure sense of the immediate accessibility of the theme and its ideological emphasis, or to a more detached but equally false sense of its triviality. In short, there is the threat of a possible imbalance between a superficial schema and an underlying complexity. It is, indeed, the latter which perhaps makes the former necessary – a necessity mirrored in Hugo's own tendency to schematise and melodramatise his own experience. Indeed, the tension between schema and complexity may correspond to the two levels at which *Les Mains sales* creates its effects – either as a slightly meretricious piece of 'good theatre' or as a more intellectually probing 'spectacle dans un fauteuil'. For as we have seen, the play offers, whether directly or obliquely, a commentary on its own psychological and linguistic procedures, in which the disjunction rather than the convergence of action, history, meaning and representation is dramatised in order to undermine the stabilising functions of representation, definition, stereotype or interpretation. It both expresses and questions a nostalgia for a smooth nexus of intention, action and identity, of sign and referent, illocutionary force and perlocutionary effect, of linguistic and cultural codes. And as one of the first examples of Sartre's own committed literature, it curiously questions, too, the communicative function of the writer's fictive speech-acts. Has the assertion of 'Le Style dramatique': 'le mot est un acte' (*TS*, p. 33) already been superseded, anticipating *L'Idiot de la famille*: 'Le discours théâtral n'offre pas de prise aux actes verbaux' (*IF* i, p. 168)? Rather, perhaps, 'Le Style dramatique', in its hint of the power of ellipsis, undermines its own thesis and senses the oblique and suggestive force of the unsaid: we must read between and beyond the noisy lines of Sartre's rhetoric, for 'le style c'est le silence du discours' (*IF* ii, p. 1618).

5

LES SÉQUESTRÉS D'ALTONA: IMAGINATION AND ILLUSION

Sartre's theory of imagination finds its most sustained and explicit critical application in *L'Idiot de la famille* (1971–2). It is strongly implicit in a number of his earlier essays, but in *L'Imaginaire* itself Sartre does not systematically relate his analysis of the imagining consciousness to its function in specific works of literature. This may explain why critics have in general been slow to follow up the connection between his theory and his own literary writing. I have already indicated the relevance of this theory to a reading of *La Nausée*; equally noteworthy, however, is the extent to which Sartre's psychology of the imagination is reflected, perhaps unwittingly, in the actual psychology of some of his dramatic characters, although they may appear in plays whose overt themes, in their socio-historical preoccupations, seem remote from his early phenomenological theory. This recurrent, if not always explicitly acknowledged, reflection reinforces the continuity which underlies the apparent changes of his position during his career – from phenomenology to Marxism, from disengaged philosopher to committed writer – until the synthesis of his study of Flaubert. One can see how Sartre's early theory can add to the richness of texture of quite a late play; it can add, too, to a certain moral ambiguity which safeguards his plays from the charge of propaganda or didacticism. For, as I suggested in Chapter 2, those characters who are morally negative from an existentialist point of view are often, perhaps, more interesting from a psychological or, more precisely, a phenomenological point of view. That is to say, although they may not be capable of responsible choice and of free commitment within a given situation, they may vividly enact Sartre's earlier theories of emotion and imagination. And this enactment implies a more delicate balance of sympathy and critical judgement within the plays than might otherwise have been achieved. For the purpose of illustrating this psychological and dramatic interest, and of demonstrating this particular continuity of preoccupation in Sartre's work,

I shall attempt to relate aspects of Sartre's theory, as set out in *L'Imaginaire*, published in 1940, to a play published in 1960, *Les Séquestrés d'Altona*.[1]

The play centres upon the figure of Frantz von Gerlach, a former Army officer, son of a wealthy and powerful German industrialist. When the play opens, Frantz has been living for the past thirteen years locked away in a room in his father's house, and refusing to see anyone other than his sister Leni. In the first act the ostensible reason for this withdrawal is made clear, although other, more complex motives emerge later. The 'official' explanation is this: Frantz, after returning from the war, had attacked an American soldier who, while billetted with the von Gerlach family, had attempted, under some provocation, to rape Leni. A condition of Frantz's pardon was that he should leave Germany: he is now supposed by the world outside his family to have died in Argentina a few years before. He had in fact taken refuge in his locked room, and already in the first act it becomes apparent that his withdrawal had been a voluntary one.

The action of the play begins when the father calls the family together – with the exception of Frantz, who still refuses to see his father – to break to them the news of his imminent death. His main purpose at this family council is to impose his determination that his younger son Werner, who will reluctantly inherit the industrial empire, should remain in the family house with his wife Johanna to protect Frantz. Werner is prepared to agree. He has always felt overshadowed by Frantz and accepts this imposition in order to earn his father's love. Johanna is more refractory, but her curiosity about Frantz wins the day. It leads her to accept another proposal of the father's: she is to try to see Frantz first in order to tell him about his father's fatal illness, later to persuade him to meet his father once more after their long separation. The father believes that the beauty of Johanna, who had previously been a successful film actress, will influence Frantz.

However, when we first meet Frantz in his room in the second act (he has previously only appeared in the complex flashbacks of Act I), it is not in the presence of Johanna, but of his sister Leni. She is the only person in the household who has seen him during those thirteen years, and she has developed an incestuous relationship with him. She is also an accomplice in what appears to be a form of madness on the part of Frantz – a madness which requires a particular setting. For the room in which Frantz has locked himself away contrasts sharply with the high bourgeois opulence of the 'salle des conseils' below. The room's peeling, cracked walls house broken furniture and ornaments; the bare bedstead has no mattress, and an incongruous portrait of Hitler is the frequent target of oyster shells hurled by Frantz. His officer's uniform, which he still wears with his medals, is in tatters. The function of this air of decay is to prolong Frantz's illusion that Germany had never recovered from the destruction which had overcome her at the end of the war. Somewhat at variance, however, with this general dilapidation is the presence of a tape-recorder and numerous spools of tape, on which Frantz records superficially incoherent 'speeches for the defence' before a mysterious tribunal of crabs which, in the thirtieth century, sits in judgement on the crimes of Frantz's own time. As the play progresses, it will reveal the true motives for Frantz's obsession with a judgement that will find him innocent, for his illusion about Germany and, by extension, for his withdrawal from the world. Revealed too will be the motives of those who connive at his illusions; Leni does so as a means of maintaining her power over him; we discover that Johanna, once she has gained access to his refuge, does so as a kind of bargain – as long as she can find confirmation of her own beauty in Frantz's eyes, she will confirm his belief that Germany still lies in ruins. But why is it necessary for Frantz to believe this? The overt motivation is the need to convince himself that he had failed Germany by not waging war sufficiently vigorously, by not, for instance, resorting to torture: 'j'ai tué l'Allemagne par sensiblerie' (IV, v, p. 179). A ruined Germany is the monument to this 'sensiblerie', for which he must feel constant guilt. But the true motives, which Frantz wishes to conceal, are quite other: they are revealed to the audience and to Johanna by Leni, in a brutal and successful attempt to destroy the growing collusion between Frantz and Johanna. It emerges that Frantz had himself been responsible for the torture of Russian partisans, earning thereby the name of 'le boucher de Smolensk' (v, i, p. 211). He *must* believe that total and irremediable disaster had overcome Germany in order to feel that such torture was justified, as it might remotely have been if the total destruction of his country had been threatened. Leni does not only, however, reveal the truth about Frantz's past actions; she reveals to him the feared and half-suspected truth about the present and about Germany's economic recovery, thus robbing him of his precarious self-justification. A final interview with his father, who had three years earlier discovered but suppressed the truth about Frantz's actions, confirms his sense of impotence. His only alternative to assuming full responsibility for the unjustifiable is suicide. In the last scene he and his father drive together to their death, but Frantz leaves behind him one of his tape-recorded speeches to his tribunal of crabs. The curtain falls on an empty stage as his recorded voice intones a final plea to future generations for the comprehension of his time and of himself as an individual.

Even this very schematic account – one that omits, for instance, to describe the intense relationship of power, resentment, vulnerability and love which Sartre establishes between Frantz and his father – suggests that this highly complex play can be interpreted on a number of different levels. These levels can be separated, however, only with some contrivance, for the play's personal, interpersonal, socio-political and historical implications are closely interwoven. On the personal and interpersonal levels, the play leads us back to some of Sartre's earliest existentialist themes. Frantz is a person who cannot face the truth or assume responsibility for what he has done or for what he is: he is the embodiment of inauthenticity. The interpersonal relationships presented in the play either involve a struggle between power and would-be self-assertion, like that of Frantz and his father, or they suggest that any kind of co-operation between human beings must be based on a mutual self-deception which is ultimately vulnerable to exposure, like that of Frantz and Johanna. In its socio-political emphasis the play reflects later developments in Sartre's thinking: critics have analysed the way in which it allegorically expresses Sartre's views on the evils of modern capitalism, its relevance to the problem of torture in the Algerian war, and to the justifiability or otherwise of Stalinist crimes in relation to the development of Soviet communism. The theory of conflict in personal relationships is also seen to pervade by implication the socio-political field, which reflects, moreover, the ambiguous view of history set out in the *Critique de la raison dialectique* – a view which, according to different critics, may be either a pessimistic or an optimistic one.[2]

There is, however, one level of experience and meaning within the play which has not hitherto been analysed: that is, the quality of the imaginary world which Frantz creates for himself. On close inspection, it becomes increasingly clear that his experience provides us with a concrete enactment of aspects of Sartre's theory of imagination, and that the quality of that enactment has much to do with the complexity of the audience's final response to the play. But before going on to look at the relationship between theory and enactment, it would be well to isolate, for the sake of clarity, certain elements within the theory – those which are basic to any understanding of it and those which are particularly relevant to the play in question. Some of Sartre's premises have, in any case, to be taken as axiomatic for the present purpose: his contention, for instance, that imagining and perceiving consciousness are distinct and mutually exclusive; and also, the phenomenological principle that the image is not a *content* of consciousness, but a spontaneous *act* of consciousness which intends (i.e. is 'directed towards') a transcendent object, although the object of that act of consciousness is either absent or non-existent. In the act of imagining, we are not aware of the image itself, but we become aware of objects by means of images – or, as Sartre says, we become aware of an object-in-image, otherwise defined as an unreal or imaginary object.

These two premises – that of the distinction between imagining and perceiving consciousness and that of the absence or non-existence of the imaginary object – need further clarifying. For Sartre, imagining consciousness is distinguished from perceiving consciousness not only by the 'unreality' of the object-in-image, but by the phenomenon of quasi-observation. In perception we can add to our knowledge of a given object through our observation of it; we can learn more about it. I can, for instance, count the columns of the Panthéon as I walk around it. Also, in perception, I can observe and learn more about the relationship of the object with other objects, or about the relationship of parts within the object. In imagination, on the other hand, the object is given once and for all in the act of intending it; it is entirely determined or created by the concepts I use in evoking it; since it *is* only what I put into it, I cannot learn more about it. It has an arbitrary, once-and-for-all quality – an arbitrariness shared by relationships between imaginary objects and by the relationships between their parts. I cannot count the columns of the Panthéon-in-image. If I imagine one side of the Panthéon and then the other, two quite separate and discontinuous acts of consciousness are involved. I have not learned more about the Panthéon-in-image; I have had two separate images of the Panthéon and there is no relationship between them.

Quasi-observation, then, is a characteristic of the imagining consciousness; non-existence or absence are primary characteristics of the imaginary object, for 'la conscience imageante pose son objet comme un néant' (*Im.*, p. 23). It can do so, according to Sartre, in any one of four ways. First, the imaginary object can be posited as being non-existent in the manner, for instance, of a centaur. Or, secondly, the object can be posited as absent, in the sense that one can produce an image of an absent friend. Third, it can be posited as existing elsewhere, as in the case of a friend seen in another specific imaginatively defined context. Or, fourth, the 'acte positionnel [. . .] peut aussi se "neutraliser", c'est-à-dire ne pas poser son objet comme existant' (p. 24). With the exception of the last, all these 'actes positionnels' involve, whether explicitly or implicitly, a negation of 'l'existence présente et actuelle de l'objet' (p. 24).

In Sartre's description of the image, however, the terms 'néant', 'absence', 'inexistant' and 'irréel' have a somewhat paradoxical character. For Sartre also maintains that the 'objet irréel' (i.e. the 'objet-en-image') does have its own mode of existence: 'il existe comme irréel, comme inagissant, sans doute; mais son existence est indéniable' (p. 180). Similarly, when I 'see' the Panthéon in my imagination 'd'une certaine manière, le Panthéon visé est présent: il se donne dans sa réalité affective. [. . .] Mais le Panthéon existe *ailleurs* et il se donne précisément comme existant ailleurs: ce qui est présent, en quelque sorte, c'est son absence' (pp. 115–16). For Sartre, this present absence and this unreal existence constitute the magical, irrational and contradictory character of the image.

It is not surprising, then, that the relationship which Sartre postulates between the imaginary object and the world of reality should be a complex one:

Poser une image c'est constituer un objet en marge de la totalité du réel, c'est donc tenir le réel à distance, s'en affranchir, en un mot le nier. Ou, si l'on préfère, nier d'un objet qu'il appartienne au réel, c'est nier le réel en tant qu'on pose l'objet; les deux négations sont complémentaires et celle-ci est condition de celle-là. Nous savons, par ailleurs, que la totalité du réel, en tant qu'elle est saisie par la conscience comme une *situation* synthétique pour cette conscience, c'est le monde. La condition pour qu'une conscience puisse imaginer est donc double: il faut à la fois qu'elle puisse poser le monde dans sa totalité synthétique et, à la fois, qu'elle puisse poser l'objet imaginé comme hors d'atteinte par rapport à cet ensemble synthétique, c'est-à-dire poser le monde comme un néant par rapport à l'image.

(p. 233)

The imaginary and the 'réel comme monde' exist at the expense, so to speak, of each other, and yet they are interdependent. To imagine is to be able to withdraw from the world and to transcend the real, 'mais, réciproquement, la possibilité de constituer un ensemble est donnée comme la structure première de l'acte du recul. [. . .] Pour pouvoir imaginer, il suffit que la conscience puisse dépasser le réel en le constituant comme monde, puisque la néantisation du réel est toujours impliquée par sa constitution en monde' (p. 234). From the ability of imagining consciousness to detach itself from the world and 'nihilate' it, Sartre infers the freedom of consciousness itself, but in addition to that freedom, imagining consciousness possesses a greater spontaneity than perceiving consciousness, to which objects are literally present, and in which, therefore, 'l'élément purement représentatif correspond à une passivité de la conscience' (p. 27). To 'nihilate' the world and the real in the act of imagining, then, is to reveal both the freedom of consciousness and the spontaneity of imagining consciousness – a point which has interesting implications for the case of Frantz von Gerlach.

Apart from the freedom and spontaneity of imagining consciousness, its 'nihilating' character has other consequences for the nature of the imaginary object. For Sartre, the unreality of the imaginary object has three aspects. It is first characterised by a spatial unreality, and, second, by a temporal unreality; third, although the ability of consciousness to 'poser le monde [i.e. the real world] dans sa réalité synthétique' (p. 233) is a necessary condition for it to, be able to imagine, the imaginary world is not, itself, 'un tout lié' (p. 170): it is characterised by what Sartre calls the unreality of intra-world relationships.

Spatial relationships within the imaginary world are absolute. They are not grasped as an organised series of external relationships. In my image of Pierre, I do not see him five yards away from me; the image simply presents him to me with the size and appearance that he would have if I had perceived him at a distance of five yards in reality. Distance and size have become intrinsic qualities of the imaginary object and do not depend, as they do in the real world, upon comparative relationships between objects. For Sartre, imagined space has a much more qualitative character than that of perceived space. This not only affects the size and the distance away from me of the imaginary object; it also affects the imaginary space surrounding the imaginary object – for instance, the imaginary room in which one intends the friend-in-image. Such a room is not *situated* in relation to real space, otherwise the perspective would be modified in relation to one's position at the moment of the act of intending. In fact, this room is posited as being related *only* to the friend-in-image. One could not go so far as to say that the room is an intrinsic quality of the friend, yet the relationship between them is not one of pure exteriority and contiguity, as it would be in the real world; it is rather 'un rapport interne d'appartenance' (p. 167).

Sartre's view of the unreality of the temporal dimension of the imaginary world involves an apparent paradox: he sees the duration of the imaginary object as not being commensurate with the duration of the imagining consciousness. The imaginary object may appear to consciousness as being 'sans aucune détermination temporelle' (p. 167): Sartre affirms, perhaps dubiously, that the imagined centaur is timeless. Or the imagined object may be a synthesis of different past durations within a present immobility, Pierre's present imagined smile being a synthesis of past remembered ones. Or the time of the imagined object may be more rapid, or far slower, than the time of the imagining consciousness. Also, unlike real time, it is not irreversible. The time of the imaginary object is intrinsic to it, and absolute.

The third characteristic of the imaginary world is, as we saw, the unreality of intra-world relationships. Indeed, the term 'imaginary world', Sartre suggests, is an inappropriate one:

Lorsque nous parlons du *monde* des objets irréels, nous employons pour plus de commodité une expression inexacte. Un monde est un tout lié, dans lequel chaque objet a sa place déterminée et entretient des rapports avec les autres objets. L'idée même de monde implique pour ses objets la double condition suivante: il faut qu'ils soient rigoureusement individués: il faut qu'ils soient en équilibre avec un milieu. C'est pourquoi il n'y a pas de monde irréel parce qu'aucun objet irréel ne remplit cette double condition. (p. 170)

The imaginary world, then, lacks two characteristics of the real world: its objects lack both the degree of individuation and the relational stability of real objects. Whereas in perception the different parts or qualities of an object are related to one another in a coherent way, such relationships do not hold good in the imaginary object. If I attempt to modify a part or quality of an imaginary object, then the relationship between its parts or qualities will disintegrate. For instance, if I imagine Pierre and then wish to imagine Pierre wearing a moustache, I shall in fact create two quite distinct and discontinuous imaginary objects, and in the second, several characteristics of the first will be lost. The imaginary world, Sartre maintains, is the world of all or nothing (p. 172). Hence, for Sartre, the discontinuous, jerky quality of the imaginary object and the imaginary world, in which every object is isolated from every other, acting upon nothing, being acted upon by nothing. As Sartre says, the image is *without consequence* in the proper sense of the term (p. 174).

And yet, it has one particular and radical consequence for the imagining consciousness: my 'participation' in the unreal world of the image with its 'ombre de temps, [. . .] ombre d'objet, avec son ombre d'espace' (p. 170) can occur only at the cost of my own 'irréalisation':

L'objet en image est un irréel. Sans doute il est présent mais, en même temps, il est hors d'atteinte. Je ne puis le toucher, le changer de place: ou plutôt je le peux bien, mais à la condition de le faire irréellement, de renoncer à me servir de mes propres mains, pour recourir à des mains fantômes qui distribueront à ce visage des coups irréels: pour agir sur ces objets irréels, il faut que moi-même je me dédouble, que *je m'irréalise*. Mais d'ailleurs aucun de ces objets ne réclame de moi une action, une conduite. Ils ne sont ni lourds, ni pressants, ni astreignants: ils sont pure passivité, ils attendent. La faible vie que nous leur insufflons vient de nous, de notre spontanéité. Si nous nous détournons d'eux, ils s'anéantissent; [. . .] ils sont totalement *inagissants*: termes ultimes, ils ne sont jamais termes d'origine. Même entre eux, ils ne sont pas cause ni effet.   (p. 162)

Although in this context Sartre is not referring to that special kind of image, the aesthetic object, such a view is, as we shall see, relevant to the nature of 'participation' theatre and to the role of the spectator. This has, in turn, a crucial bearing on the dramatic effects of *Les Séquestrés d'Altona*.

The lack of individuation of imaginary objects accounts for their ambiguous, rather amorphous quality. Further, this lack involves the fact that none of their characteristics can be the object of prolonged and constantly developing observation: lack of individuation is closely related to the quasi-observational characteristic of the imagining consciousness. Whereas the perception or observation of a real object can be continued indefinitely and still reveal new facets, the imaginary object can only reveal what I have already put there. Moreover, the imaginary object lacks 'cette infinité de rapports – en même temps que l'infinité des rapports que ses éléments soutiennent entre eux – [. . .] qui constitue l'essence même d'une chose' (p. 20). From these characteristics Sartre somewhat dubiously infers the 'pauvreté essentielle' of the imaginary world in comparison with the richly overflowing world of things (pp. 20 and 171). However, since critics have tended to isolate and take exception to this negative aspect of Sartre's theory, it is worth emphasising one crucial qualification. Despite its poverty, the imaginary world can be rich in *meaning*, and this perhaps paradoxically arises from the fact that the imaginary object is nothing more than what I have put into it:

L'objet en image est donc contemporain de la conscience que je prends de lui et il est exactement déterminé par cette conscience: il ne comprend en lui rien de plus que ce dont j'ai conscience; mais, inversement, tout ce qui constitue ma conscience trouve son corrélatif dans l'objet. Mon savoir n'est autre qu'un savoir *de* l'objet, un savoir *touchant* l'objet. Dans l'acte de conscience, l'élément représentatif et l'élément de savoir sont liés en un acte synthétique. L'objet corrélatif de cet acte se constitue donc à la fois comme objet concret, sensible, et comme objet de savoir. Il en résulte cette conséquence paradoxale que l'objet nous est présent du dehors et du dedans à la fois. Du dehors, car nous l'observons; du dedans, car c'est *en lui* que nous percevons ce qu'il est. Voilà pourquoi des images extrêmement pauvres et tronquées, réduites à quelques déterminations de l'espace, peuvent avoir pour moi un sens riche et profond. Et ce sens est là, immédiat, *dans* ces lignes, il se donne sans qu'on ait besoin de le déchiffrer.

(p. 22)

This distinction between the poverty of the image and the richness of its *sens* will have fundamental consequences for Sartre's discussion of that special kind of *objet-en-image*, the aesthetic object. It will enable him to affirm that the 'world' of the poem or the painting, although distanced from the real world, creates magically and irrationally a *sens* which seems to have the immanent density, opacity and richness of the world of things.

The imaginary world, then, is a world of triple unreality. But beyond this, two other major characteristics of the image must also be considered: its spontaneity, and its status as an affective–cognitive synthesis (p. 98). In perception, as we saw, consciousness may seem to be passive in relation to the object it perceives: my situation motivates my perception. When I imagine, however, the object of my intention cannot motivate or determine my consciousness because the object of the imagining consciousness is non-existent. The image owes nothing to its object because the object is created in the act of imagining.

For Sartre, there are, however, variations in the degree of spontaneity implicit in the act of imagining. From this point of view, Sartre distinguishes between the purely mental image, which possesses the highest degree of spontaneity, and images in which the imaginary object is related to what he calls an 'analogon' (p. 31), which may be more or less material in nature. In the case of a portrait, for instance, it is the perceived patterns of pigment on the canvas which refer us to the imaginary object, the absent person-in-image. Sartre classifies images according to the extent to which they are related to a more or less physical analogon: from the portrait, where the spontaneous creative act of consciousness is most highly 'motivated' by a material analogon, to mimed gesture and schematic drawings, through to hypnagogic imagery, in which the relationship between analogon and image approximates most closely to the purely mental image. The details of Sartre's classification need not concern us here: it is sufficient to note that the general theory of the relationship between image and analogon is particularly relevant to the world of Frantz von Gerlach, as it raises the question of the degree of spontaneity of his imagining consciousness.

Equally relevant, however, is the synthesis of affectivity and knowledge in the imagining consciousness – a characteristic which is in turn related to the familiar Sartrean theme of self-deception. For Sartre, the act of imagining is 'un acte magique' (p. 161) which attempts to possess in its totality an object which would yield itself only gradually and partially to perception, and then only rarely in accordance with the desire of the perceiver. In perception, the world of objects presents resistance to our desires. Or, in other words (which echo those of *Esquisse d'une théorie des émotions*), the act of imagination is an 'incantation destinée à faire apparaître l'objet auquel on pense, la chose qu'on désire, de façon qu'on puisse en prendre possession' (p. 161). Hence the affective charge of the image; hence, too, the fact that, for Sartre, the image is associated with self-deception. The coincidence of the image with the apparent fulfilment of desire leads to the illusion that the act of imagining is 'really' efficacious. However, the 'unreal' nature of the fulfilment leads, in turn, only to an exacerbation of desire.

But despite the fact that the intended effect of the image is illusory, it is through the image that affective consciousness, according to Sartre, aspires to a form of knowledge:

l'image est une sorte d'idéal pour le sentiment, elle représente pour la conscience affective un état limite, l'état dans lequel le désir serait en même temps connaissance. L'image, si elle se donne comme la limite inférieure vers laquelle tend le savoir lorsqu'il se dégrade, se présente aussi comme la limite supérieure vers laquelle tend l'affectivité lorsqu'elle cherche à se connaître. (p. 97)

Here, the hierarchy established between knowledge, image and affectivity is clear. It is further reinforced by the fact that the element of knowledge within the affective–cognitive synthesis of the image is subject to a form of entropic 'dégradation'. It is a 'savoir dégradé' in two senses (p. 82). Whereas in perception we learn more about the object, in imagination we find in the object nothing more than what we have already put there. In addition, there is the possibility of reacting to the image as though it were perceived: the *objet-en-image* is regarded as an object which can be 'known' although it is non-existent and contains nothing which consciousness has not put into it. The 'degradation' of knowledge thus involved again constitutes – in a characteristic Sartrean slide from the psychological to the moral – a form of self-deception:

Si vive, si touchante, si forte que soit une image, elle donne son objet comme n'étant pas. Cela n'empêche pas que nous puissions réagir ensuite à cette image comme si son objet était présent, était en face de nous: nous verrons qu'il peut arriver que nous tentions, avec tout notre être, de réagir à une image comme si elle était une perception. Mais l'état ambigu et faux auquel nous arrivons ainsi ne fait que mieux mettre en relief ce qui vient d'être dit: en vain cherchons-nous par notre *conduite* envers l'objet à faire naître en nous la croyance qu'il existe réellement; nous pouvons masquer une seconde, mais non détruire la conscience immédiate de son néant.

(p. 26)

One last point needs to be made. Although Sartre distinguishes between those feelings and emotions which are instrumental in evoking the image, and those which constitute our reaction to it, creation and reaction are clearly very closely linked: 'produire une image plus ou moins vive c'est réagir plus ou moins vivement à l'acte producteur et, du même coup, attribuer à l'objet imagé le pouvoir de faire naître ces réactions' (p. 178). Furthermore, the emotion or the affective element involved in the generation of the image becomes a self-sustaining and self-reinforcing 'response'. Sartre takes as his example the affective complex of 'répugnance' and 'dégoût':

elle peut bien s'enfler jusqu'à la nausée, rien n'empêchera que ce soit *d'elle-même* qu'elle s'enfle. Il lui manque cette part de passivité qui fait la richesse des sentiments qui constituent le réel. Elle se soutient elle-même par une sorte d'autocréation continuée, par une sorte de tension sans repos: elle ne saurait se laisser aller sans s'évanouir avec son objet, elle s'épuise à s'affirmer et en même temps à se gonfler, à réagir à elle-même. De là une dépense nerveuse considérable. (pp. 180–1)

The impression we may have of being passive vis-à-vis the intensity of the affective 'response' is an illusion: it is, rather, a 'spontanéité qui échappe à notre contrôle' (p. 181). Sartre also postulates, however, a more deliberate form of reaction or 'conduite' vis-à-vis the image, which may, indeed, be contrived in order to provoke a desired response – the revival, for instance, of a specific feeling of tenderness. This should be distinguished from the self-reinforcing 'sentiment imageant' described above. In the case of the 'deliberate' reaction

le savoir réflexif précède le sentiment même et le sentiment est visé sous sa forme réflexive. L'objet en outre est reproduit précisément pour qu'il provoque le sentiment. En un mot nous connaissons déjà sa liaison avec cet état affectif et nous faisons apparaître l'objet en tant qu'il contient comme une de ses qualités le pouvoir de faire naître cet élan de tendresse.

(p. 183)

But an *objet-en-image* itself has no causal efficacy: the affirmation that it can produce the tenderness that I feel must come from myself: 'je vais affirmer que l'objet irréel agit sur moi, tout en ayant immédiatement conscience qu'il n'y a pas, qu'il ne saurait y avoir d'action réelle et que je me crispe pour mimer cette action' (pp. 183–4). In consequence the feeling itself becomes 'degraded' and schematised, deprived of the richness and unpredictability of my experience of the real object, and expressed in increasingly rigid forms. Further, imaginary feelings, and the 'moi imaginaire' which they help to constitute, may well be put to flight by renewed contact with the real object – a tendency which has crucial consequences for Frantz von Gerlach. But the attraction of the act of imagining is that the imaginary situation can be controlled and limited, because it *is* only what consciousness has put into it. Imaginary actions have only the results which I wish to give them, whereas the real situation can contain the possibility of unexpected developments which are beyond the control of consciousness.

Such, then, are the chief characteristics of the imagining consciousness and of the imaginary object for Sartre: the image is an act of consciousness intending the transcendent object, not a content of consciousness; the attitude of the imagining consciousness is one of quasi-observation; the imagining consciousness posits its object as absent or non-existent, and the act of imagining is an act of negation in that the image negates the world; the act of imagining is spontaneous, but the degree of spontaneity of the image depends upon the nature of the analogon; finally, the image is an affective–cognitive synthesis.

To what extent are these characteristics reflected in *Les Séquestrés d'Altona*? Their chief relevance is undoubtedly to the behaviour of Frantz von Gerlach, the central figure. It is he who creates the imaginary world described earlier – a world in which the imaginary object is a ruined, desolate, doomed Germany, and in which the physical analogon is the locked room in which Frantz lives, insulated from the demands and the unpredictabilities of the 'real' world – an impoverished, comfortless wreck of a room, with its doubly symbolic portrait of Hitler. Even Frantz's uniform is part of the material analogon, with its tatters and its row of make-believe medals. It is through this analogon, created by himself but endowed by him with its own autonomy, that he 'intends' the imaginary object of a still fallen Germany. This specific rela-tionship, in Frantz's case, of physical analogon and imaginary object is linked in a number of ways to Sartre's general theory of the image. First, it raises the question of the degree of spontaneity involved in the creation of the imaginary world, and in the second place, it reveals a complex interplay between imagination and emotion, both in the genesis of the image and in the sustaining of the emotion. Further, the fact that the material analogon consists of everyday objects which have their 'real' associations in 'real' life creates its own series of problems. These in turn are linked first with Sartre's view that the characteristic attitude of the imagining consciousness is one of quasi-observation; secondly with the negating force of the image; and thirdly with the theory of triple unreality.

If we first examine the degree of spontaneity in the creation of Frantz's imaginary world, we find that it is extremely closely re-lated to his emotional experience. There is a high degree of spon-taneity in the genesis (if not in the evolution) of his obsessive image, and it is motivated by the emotional response of guilt. Frantz sees that the justification for his acts of torture could only have been an extreme situation in which Germany faced inevitable ruin. He needs, therefore, to believe in a ruined Germany in order to feel that his act was justified. His attitude towards the act of torture – an attitude of guilt – was freely chosen, and involved a free choice of the justifying image. In genesis, then, his act of imagining is spontaneous and free. (It is also motivated, as Sartre's theory would suggest, by the desire for a world other than the world of reality.) However, the response of guilt, although chosen, is intolerable (if anything, it is intolerable *because* it is chosen). Therefore, in order to obviate his guilt as far as possible, Frantz must believe that the image he has freely created in fact limits and constrains his freedom, and in so doing he must also, incidentally, deny the irreversibility of time. Now Sartre argues, as we saw, that an imaginary situation cannot be considered to determine a response: the imaginary situation is nothing more than what we choose to put into it. But Sartre also maintains that in emotional behaviour we *believe in* the world that our emotion has created for us, and he also maintains that our bodies are the vehicles of this belief. As we saw in Chapter 2 our belief in a world to be feared, for instance, is expressed in our trembling, in our flight, or in our fainting – in 'magical' physical behaviour designed to change the world by other than rational means. Frantz's creation of a material analogon – his room and his clothes – which refers to the imaginary object of a ruined Germany, is partly a denial of the fact that an imaginary situation is not a determining one; partly, therefore, a denial of freedom and spontaneity; and partly a physical manifestation of belief designed to change the world by irrational means. Hence the necessity for Frantz to create a three-dimensional analogon in which he may literally live, sustaining the bodily phenomenon of belief in a transformed world – a world to which he can commit himself. He is tempted by the imaginary world, since it is the only one with which he thinks he can deal effectively, but he wishes it to have the opacity of reality. This is an indication of the need to *possess* the world, which, Sartre maintains, can only be done in the imaginary mode. It is a symptom, too, of the necessity to respond to the image as though it were an actual perception – an example of the 'degraded' knowledge which is part of the affective–cognitive synthesis created in the image. Other aspects of Frantz's behaviour also suggest the need for belief in the real existence of the imaginary world: as Sartre says, we seek 'par notre *conduite* envers l'objet à faire naître en nous la croyance qu'il existe réellement' (p. 26). Thus, for thirteen years, Frantz has only admitted his colluding sister Leni to his seclusion, and has literally blocked his window to the outside world. He has sought to preserve the integrity and autonomy of his own world by cutting himself off entirely from any possibility of the puncturing of the illusion.

Indeed, Frantz's determination to respond to an image as though it were perception, to the extent of creating a three-dimensional 'living' space, can eclipse the spontaneity which initially created the image. The original 'développement du sentiment imageant' is transformed into the more deliberate reaction to the image which we noted earlier. The image is maintained in order to preserve the reaction and Frantz's original emotion is reflexively sustained. It is characterised by that 'crispation' and that intensifying self-mimicry described in *L'Imaginaire* (p. 184). Gestures, like the repeated play with the oyster-shells, are mechanical but convulsive; verbal formulae, like the invocations to the tribunal of crabs, are ritualised but still nervously exhausting in their willed futility: 'le

sentiment va se schématiser et se figer dans des formes rigides'
(p. 186). For Leni, the spectator–accomplice within the play, such
forms have become banal. But they are none the less vulnerable,
and new, spontaneous modes of imaginary rationalisation become
a matter for comment. Such fluctuations occur when a new threat
to Frantz's imaginary world generates a new image which dispels
the old. Leni attempts to persuade Frantz that if his family
discovers the signal which will gain admittance to his room, he will
lose the precious tape-recordings addressed to History – the
tribunal of crabs sitting in the thirtieth century. That image 'spon-
taneously' gives way after a struggle to maintain its 'rigidity' to one
in which the physical analogon of the spools of tape has no place:

Leni. Ils prendront les bobines. [. . .] (*Frantz éclate de rire.*) Frantz, je t'en
supplie, changeons le signal. (*Frantz cesse de rire. Il la regarde d'un air
sournois et traqué.*) Eh bien?
Frantz. Non. (*Il invente à mesure ses raisons de refuser.*) Tout se tient.
L'Histoire est une parole sacrée; si tu changes une virgule, il ne reste
plus rien.
Leni. Parfait. Ne touchons pas à l'Histoire. Tu leur feras cadeau des
bobines. Et du magnétophone, par-dessus le marché.
Frantz va vers les bobines et les regarde d'un air traqué.
Frantz, d'abord hésitant et déchiré. Les bobines. . . Les bobines. . . (*Un
temps. Il réfléchit, puis d'un geste brusque du bras gauche, il les balaye
et les fait tomber sur le plancher.*) Voilà ce que j'en fais! (*Il parle avec
une sorte d'exaltation, comme s'il confiait à Leni un secret d'importance. En fait, il invente sur l'instant ce qu'il dit.*) Ce n'était qu'une
précaution, figure-toi. Pour le cas où le trentième n'aurait pas dé-
couvert la vitre.
Leni. Une vitre? Voilà du neuf. Tu ne m'en a jamais parlé.
Frantz. Je ne dis pas tout, sœurette. (*Il se frotte les mains d'un air réjoui,
comme le Père au premier tableau.*) Imagine une vitre noire. Plus fine
que l'éther. Ultrasensible. Un souffle s'y inscrit. Le *moindre* souffle.
Toute l'Histoire y est gravée, depuis le commencement des temps
jusqu'à ce claquement de doigts. (II, i, pp. 83–4)

New images can, then, be generated to sustain the overall autonomy of the imaginary world. And for the theatre audience, even
more than for the conniving Leni, Frantz's behaviour, fluctuating
disconcertingly as it moves from the spontaneous to the reflectively
rigid to the 'normally' self-aware, has the essential qualities of
Sartre's 'vie imaginaire': it is spasmodic, jerky, literally inconsequential, and, above all, ambiguous:

Frantz. (*Avec une inquiétude dont on ne sait pas si elle est sincère ou jouée.*)
Et si nous y étions déjà? [. . .] Au trentième siècle. Es-tu sûre que

cette comédie se donne pour la première fois? Sommes-nous vifs ou reconstitués? (*Il rit.*)   (pp. 85–6)

For Sartre, the inconsequentiality of imaginary changes stands in marked contrast to the unpredictable but consequential changes of reality. In this connection, it is interesting to see Frantz's response to the first intrusion of the 'real' world into his own, when Johanna breaks into his seclusion. Sartre maintains that our feelings vis-à-vis 'unreal' objects may be banished by the appearance of 'real' objects. Frantz's reaction to Johanna is, however, perhaps more complex. He is at the same time wary and fascinated: wary because the controllable world of imagination is threatened, fascinated because of the infinitely rich, if refractory, possibilities which she offers as a real person – a richness in marked contrast to what Sartre calls the impoverishment of the imaginary world. The change of intention which can occur when the imagining consciousness is again motivated to become aware of the real world is illustrated by a curious incident, comically *grinçant* in its deflatory effect, when Frantz suddenly removes one of the medals decorating his chest and eats it, because it is in fact made of chocolate. He later suggests to Johanna: 'Non, prenez plutôt les croix: c'est du chocolat suisse' (II, v, p. 108). Here at least, Sartre seems to suggest, is a moment of action within Frantz's otherwise static world – a moment which, although bathetically trivial, nevertheless demonstrates that Frantz is actually free to change his way of intending the world.

The temptation of the real, then, is introduced by Johanna. Frantz's other response to it is, predictably, to attempt to draw Johanna into his own world. Another specific gesture underlines its effect. At a given moment Frantz hurls oyster shells at the portrait of Hitler; this gesture – a ritual for Frantz – is repeated twice by Johanna with her shoes and her wine-glass, first when she appears to humour Frantz's desire to share his seclusion with her, and again when she is genuinely fascinated by this possibility. In this instance it is not that the imagining consciousness has suddenly switched to a 'realising' attitude, as in the episode of the chocolate medal; it is rather that an actual gesture is used to reinforce the illusory idea that the imaginary world has its own autonomous consistency, which is refractory to the ineffectively destructive gesture. And even when this reinforcement begins to give way before encroaching reality the portrait of Hitler – doubly 'imaginary', symbolic both of Germany's past power and downfall and of Frantz's present refusal to recognise her renewal – is the last surviving accessory of Frantz's illusions. In the fourth act Frantz, awaiting another visit from Johanna, still invokes his tribunal of crabs, but the details of the décor have changed: '*La chambre de Frantz. Même décor qu'au II. Mais toutes les pancartes ont disparu. Plus de coquilles d'huîtres sur le plancher. Sur la table une lampe de bureau. Seul, le portrait de Hitler demeure*' (p. 151).

Reality, once admitted, is inexorable:

> *Frantz.* Vous me détruirez lentement, sûrement, par votre seule présence. Déjà ma folie se délabre; Johanna, c'était mon refuge; que deviendrai-je quand je verrai le jour? (IV, ii, p. 165)[3]

But these intimations are only the prelude to the eventually disastrous collision of the imaginary and the real. In the face of Johanna's *real* horror at the *reality* of his past actions as a torturer, Frantz's imaginary world disintegrates; but his dependence upon it has become so total that suicide is the only recourse. It is not simply the imaginary world that is illusory: in the final outcome Sartre demonstrates that our belief in that world is also ultimately illusory: 'en vain cherchons-nous par notre *conduite* envers l'objet à faire naître en nous la croyance qu'il existe réellement; nous pouvons masquer une seconde, mais non détruire la conscience immédiate de son néant' (*Im.*, p. 26). Eventually, it is the awareness of the 'néant' of his imaginary world, as well as the correlative recognition of his guilt and impotence in the real world, which destroys Frantz.

Frantz's creation, then, of a material analogon for his *objet-en-image* has several consequences. It demonstrates that he wishes to deny the possible spontaneity of the imagining consciousness in order to believe (or to persuade himself to believe) that the imaginary world determines his conduct. It further demonstrates the emotional force which constitutes the imaginary world, and which constitutes a reaction to that world: the image, for Frantz, is undoubtedly an affective–cognitive synthesis involving what Sartre calls a 'savoir dégradé'. Further, the creation of the material analogon enables Sartre to enact the possible changes of intention from the imagining to the realising, together with the psychological and moral significance of such changes. This enactment is, of course, all the more striking because the analogon consists of three-dimensional objects which might normally be seen to have specific, practical functions in the world of reality. Furthermore, this fact adds considerably to the ambiguity and richness of the world portrayed by Sartre, despite his theoretical views on the 'pauvreté essentielle' of the image. It may appear paradoxical, for instance, that Frantz's creation of a concrete, tangible milieu in fact underlines the essential negativity and non-existence of the imaginary world as Sartre defines it. As we saw, to imagine is to attempt to keep the world at a distance, to attempt to free oneself from it, to deny it. Frantz, in effect, attempts to negate reality as completely as he can by giving the imaginary world as concrete a *presence* as possible. The intensity of his desire to do so is demonstrated by the fact that when the created world eventually fails him, Frantz finds that he must deny the real world through the ultimate negation of total withdrawal, of suicide.

Frantz, then, attempts to confer upon his *objet-en-image* an observable reality. But is it observable or 'quasi-observable'? To observe an object in perception is, for Sartre, as we saw, to be able to learn more about the object; we cannot learn more about the imaginary object. It is in fact essential for Frantz's illusion that the objects surrounding him should remain quasi-observable: they must be preserved at all costs with the meaning originally attributed to them, and they must be kept insulated from the world of change. One could, of course, envisage one sense in which they could be observed to change; a crack might develop in a chair, the damp on the wall might spread. But this would be observation rather of the kind that one might bestow on the pigment of a picture which one would normally see through, as it were, in order to intend the imaginary object. The *objet-en-image* for which Frantz's room is the analogon does not have the hidden but potentially discoverable 'profiles' of a perceived object. Until the intervention of Johanna, Frantz's world is cut off from the richness and unpredictability of developing relationships in the real world. It is also impervious to action, unless the intending consciousness flickers between the imagining and realising modes, as we saw in the curious case of the chocolate medal, or switches more radically from one to the other, as it finally does when Leni betrays Frantz to Johanna. The very possibility of such a change in intention adds to the ambiguity and dramatic interest of Frantz's world, but on the whole it shares what Sartre considers to be the impoverishment of the imaginary world vis-à-vis the richness of the real. This quality is reflected in the wilful psychological impoverishment of seclusion but, as we saw earlier, it is not incompatible with a wealth of *sens*. The imaginary status of Frantz's world is also confirmed by the fact that those who witness it for the first time, like Johanna, see it not as an extension of the real world, but as a kind of spectacle – a spectacle in which one can participate only if one denies the real world, a spectacle with the eeriness of the non-instrumental and the static.

This sense of stasis leads one to ask whether Frantz's created world shares the triple unreality attributed by Sartre to the imaginary – unreality of space, of time, and of intra-world relationships. There is no doubt, in the first place, that Frantz's attempt to create real space, as it were, from a series of symbolic objects is ambiguous in a way very similar to the ambiguity which Sartre notes in imaginary objects. The qualities of imaginary objects – such as the size or distance away from me of my friend Pierre in the image I have of him – are absolute in the sense that they are simply given. They are not evaluated in terms of their relation to other objects or to the qualities of other objects existing in reality. Yet, Sartre maintains, neither are they completely divested of their relativity: each of these absolute qualities took its origin in a perceptible appearance of the object, hence from a relative quality. (Sartre argues that the contradiction thus involved is not an obtrusive one because of the 'caractère brouillé de l'objet irréel' (*Im.*, p. 165).) It is certainly true that the material arrangements, as it were, of Frantz's world participate in the relativity of everyday objects; but also that he has tried to confer upon them as absolute a quality as possible. The symbol of this attempt is the wall which he has had built outside his window to sever, precisely, the relationship between the space of his world and the real space of the world outside. A further point concerns not so much the qualitative nature of Frantz's spatial world for himself, as the relationship of the spectator to Frantz in his room. Sartre maintains that if we *see* a friend in his room and *imagine* a friend in his room, the relationship between room and friend is different in the two cases. In perception we see the relationship as an external one of contiguity; in the imagination, as an inner one of 'appartenance'. Although the room-in-image is not seen as a *quality* of the friend, it is, unlike the perceived room, seen as *part* of him. This is precisely the impression conveyed by the relationship between Frantz and the space in which he lives: they go *together* in a more intensely qualitative way than would be probable in the world of everyday perception. (The question of whether rooms and persons are never *perceived* in a 'rapport interne d'appartenance' (p. 167) is perhaps more doubtful.)

We discover, similarly, that Frantz's world does not share the time of the real world: 'Jamais d'heure ici: l'Eternité' (ii, viii, p. 117). The notice which he puts up when he wishes to communicate with his crabs is quite arbitrary: 'Absent jusqu'à demain midi' (ii, i, p. 89). It is only when Johanna's intrusion disrupts his world that the reality of time breaks in – a change underlined, perhaps rather heavily, by Frantz's half-reluctant, half-eager play with the wrist-watch and his imitation of the speaking clock (iv, i and ii). But a heightened awareness of clock-time is simply the transition to a duration charged with the emotional urgency of waiting for a real person and to a sense of the temporality, both dynamic and destructive, of the outside world.

When we come to consider the unreality of intra-world relationships, it is the ambiguity of Frantz's world which strikes us most forcefully. At one level, the fact that the material analogon consists of real objects means that in theory certain changes in their relationships could be brought about without the collapse of the whole. But their individual autonomy as objects is limited: we as spectators of the play cannot learn more about them, and Frantz refuses to do so. Moreover, the relationships between them are preserved without change; they remain static until Johanna's arrival. Frantz's capricious decision to regard his tape-recordings as irrelevant is, as Sartre puts it in L'Imaginaire, 'sans conséquence' (p. 174). But later we see that Frantz's world lacks precisely the equilibrium of the real world. Johanna's presence – the element of change – does not simply modify Frantz's world; it undermines it. Frantz struggles for a while to maintain its precarious integrity and stasis, but it eventually falls apart in the face of change. It corresponds essentially to Sartre's definition of the imaginary as the world of all or nothing.

These, then, are some of the ways in which Frantz's created world seems to correspond to Sartre's theory of imagination: in its spontaneity, its negativity, its character as an affective–cognitive synthesis, the element of quasi-observation, the triple unreality of time, space and intra-world relationships. Yet these correspondences are drawn only from those aspects of the play which involve the creation of an imaginary world through the medium of a physical analogon. The play exemplifies other forms of imaginative activity: Frantz's evocation of images drawn from memory, for instance, or the impassioned speeches addressed to his tribunal of crabs. More significant still, however, are those aspects which take us beyond the psychological import of Sartre's theory of imagination towards its aesthetic implications, and, thence, to its ultimate effect upon the audience. What is the consequence of the fact that Frantz's imaginary world is presented to us within the *objet-en-image* of Sartre's play and through the medium of *its* physical analogon? What is the effect of the clash within the play between Frantz's contrived décor and the 'realist' décor of the bourgeois 'salle des conseils' in which the dying patriarch meets his family? Is the realism of the latter setting the criterion against which we measure the illusions of the former, or do the rituals and drama-tised gestures of the family within the 'realist' room clash, in turn, with its apparent solidity and suggest that 'reality' itself is nothing more than a tissue of theatrical gesture, ritual and illusion?

Each of these two hypotheses might, if confirmed, have different consequences for a thematic interpretation of the play, but neither need imply anything other than a consistent level of stylisation and, hence, the likelihood of a relatively consistent and unam-biguous response on the part of the spectator. In practice, however, such a likelihood is remote: of all Sartre's plays, *Les Séquestrés d'Altona* generates the greatest sense of enigmatic *malaise*, and it does so when the most intricate demands are made upon the spectator's own imagining consciousness.

It could be argued that this response of disquiet is at its most complex and tense in the last scene of the play when Frantz and his father have driven to their deaths at the Teufelsbrücke, when Leni, Johanna and Werner have withdrawn, and when Frantz's recorded voice is heard speaking for the last time to his 'tribunal de la nuit': the only sign of 'life' on an empty stage. It could also be argued that this tension and its almost intolerable lack of resolution is due to the hesitation of the aesthetic *objet-en-image* between presence and absence. This in turn creates an unstable interplay of percep-tion and imagination; 'participation' and alienation; reluctant identification, complex revulsion and critical judgement; frus-trated but colluding impotence and the desire for action. For Sartre, the paradox of simultaneous presence and absence is characteristic of all images: 'On se rappelle *la caractéristique essen-tielle de l'image mentale: c'est une certaine façon qu'a l'objet d'être absent au sein même de sa présence*' (*Im.*, p. 98). But this quality is particularly striking in the case of a complex 'embodied' art-object such as a play, and it has equally striking consequences for our belief in the *objet-en-image*. We saw that Frantz seeks to give his own imaginary world as concrete a 'presence' as possible: it is this presence which traditional theatre tends to exploit, while never-theless ensuring that the synthesis of presence and absence remains 'hors d'atteinte'. Such a presence clearly raises the question of the role of perceiving consciousness itself – a question acknowledged by Sartre in ways which threaten to attenuate his fundamental distinction between imagining and perceiving intentional acts, and which are particularly exemplified in the theatre arts. Sartre considers, for instance, the music-hall artist impersonating Maurice Chevalier:

seule une volonté formelle peut empêcher la conscience de glisser du plan de l'image à celui de la perception. Dans la plupart des cas ce glissement se fait tout de même, de temps à autre. Il arrive même souvent que la synthèse ne se fasse pas entièrement: le visage et le corps de la fantaisiste ne perdent pas toute leur individualité; et cependant, sur ce visage, sur ce corps de femme, la nature expressive 'Maurice Chevalier' vient d'apparaître. Il s'ensuit un état hybride, ni tout à fait perception ni tout à fait image [. . .]. Ces états sans équilibre et qui ne durent pas sont évidemment, pour le spectateur, ce qu'il y a de plus plaisant dans l'imitation.   (p. 45)

Similarly, the spectator who watches the curtain rise at the theatre discovers a world which, although it is neither the world of perception nor that of the purely mental image, has affinities with the former. Its 'existence irréelle' is the correlative of a particular kind of mental operation: 'ces synthèses même, je les opère à la façon de synthèses perceptives et non de synthèses signifiantes' (p. 88). It is as though, to use a favourite word of Sartre's when he describes the activity of the imagination, the absent *objet-en-image* comes to 'haunt' perceived presence.[4]

For the spectator of *Les Séquestrés d'Altona* the tension between perceived and imaginary space and time is at its most acute at the point of Frantz's suicide and of the recorded speech which eerily bridges life and death. As Leni counts out the minutes of his last drive to the Teufelsbrücke 'stage' time parallels with a mocking urgency the duration of perceived time. But this accelerating convergence of the imaginary and the real is then abruptly set against the evocation of the end of history in the paradoxically timeless 'future-in-the-past' of Frantz's recorded speech, as he pleads with his sub-human tribunal for judgement and acquittal *in absentia*. Now, as the past utterance, through the uncannily present voice of the absent speaker, invokes a future of silent judgement, the 'participation' of the spectator is at once most acutely engaged and most fundamentally called into question. For as Frantz speaks and as Leni, Werner and Johanna leave, the image of the unresponding crabs and their symbolic dehumanising of history itself fades: 'Le trentième ne répond plus. [. . .] Tout sera mort: les yeux, les juges, le temps. Nuit' (v, iii, pp. 222–3). The audience itself becomes the sole listener and judge, the only witness to Frantz's now futile affirmation of his destroyed humanity: 'O tribunal de la nuit, toi qui fus, qui seras, qui es, j'ai été! J'ai été!' (p. 223). But with this affirmation each member of the audience has been reminded, not of collective solidarity, but of his isolation – the 'seriality' chillingly evoked by Frantz and analysed by Sartre in *Critique de la raison dialectique*: 'Un et un font un, voilà notre mystère' (p. 222). The function of sole witness is, then, that of each spectator alone, and it is a complex one. With what should he identify? With the apostrophised 'siècles' of a dehumanised history, with the deformed present – the accused – or with a denial of any future? With the silent judgement of the 'toi' invoked by Frantz? With a futile affirmation of humanity, or with an affirmation of humanity against the odds? Or with the echo of an absent consciousness which had, in life, sought to escape the 'real' world through its own self-dramatising fantasies but which now claims total responsibility? 'Moi, Frantz, von Gerlach, ici, dans cette chambre, j'ai pris le siècle sur mes épaules et j'ai dit: j'en répondrai' (p. 223).

The situation of the audience is not so much ambiguous as undecidable. The only certainty is its awareness, whether explicit or inexplicit, of its own inability to act within or upon the imaginary world of the play: it has simply a choice of roles 'sans conséquence' (*Im.*, p. 174). Yet this perhaps reassuring certainty is questioned as Sartre forces yet another decision. The 'volonté formelle' which prevents 'la conscience de glisser du plan de l'image à celui de la perception' (p. 45) is itself ultimately undermined by the sheer physical presence of the empty stage, and notably so after the voice of Frantz eventually falls silent. Then, the overwhelming presence of the analogon eclipses the absent image.

In *L'Imaginaire*, Sartre seeks to explain the difficulty we experience in passing from the world of imagination to the world of reality, in terms of the relationship between analogon and image:

Celle-ci [la Septième Symphonie] ne peut se manifester que par des analoga qui sont datés et qui se déroulent dans notre temps. Mais pour la saisir *sur ces* analoga il faut opérer la réduction imageante c'est-à-dire appréhender précisément les sons réels comme analoga. Elle se donne donc comme un perpétuel ailleurs, une perpétuelle absence. [. . .] Elle n'est pas simplement – comme les essences, par exemple – hors du temps et de l'espace: elle est hors du *réel*, hors de l'existence. Je ne l'entends point réellement, je l'écoute dans l'imaginaire. C'est ce qui explique la difficulté considérable que nous éprouvons toujours à passer du 'monde' au théâtre ou de la musique à celui de nos préoccupations journalières. A vrai dire il n'y a pas passage d'un monde à l'autre, il y a passage de l'attitude imageante à l'attitude réalisante. La contemplation esthétique est un rêve provoqué et le passage au réel est un authentique réveil. On a souvent parlé de la 'déception' qui accompagnait le retour à la réalité. Mais cela n'expliquerait pas que ce malaise existe, par exemple, après l'audition d'une pièce réaliste et cruelle, en ce cas, en effet, la réalité devrait être saisie comme rassurante. En fait ce malaise est tout simplement celui du dormeur qui s'éveille: une conscience fascinée, bloquée dans l'imaginaire est soudain libérée par l'arrêt brusque de la pièce, de la symphonie et reprend soudain contact avec l'existence. Il n'en faut pas plus pour provoquer l'écœurement nauséeux qui caractérise la conscience réalisante. (pp. 244–5)

In connection with *Les Mouches* we noted Sartre's inference, from this description of the unreality of the imaginary world, that the aesthetic and the moral should not be confused. The later Sartre, however, takes a more complex view of their relationship, with crucial consequences for his dramatic practice. In *Les Séquestrés d'Altona* the awakening of the spectator from the 'dream' of 'l'attitude imageante' occurs *before* the curtain falls. The will to submit to illusion, to 'look through' the analogon at an imaginary, absent world in which nothing is of consequence and in which we lose our real selves, gives way to the alienating possibility of seeing the stage simply as a stage and the play simply as a play. Such a possibility would encourage the 'évanouissement du mirage théâtral' (*TS*, p. 302) which Sartre, speaking in 1960 to the Brechtian critic Bernard Dort, sees as essential to the spectator's *prise de conscience*.[5] His practical method of achieving it towards the end of *Les Séquestrés d'Altona* is perhaps more radical, however, than his insistence, in the same interview, on 'le déplacement dans le temps ou dans l'espace' as the instrument of such a 'distanciation'. But, as in *Huis clos*, distance stops short of total alienation: 'la distanciation ne doit pas détruire l'*Einfühlung*' (p. 305). The 'évanouissement du mirage théâtral' displaces, rather than destroys, the focus of empathy or identification. We do not identify ourselves with the protagonist. Instead, we identify the protagonist with ourselves, and with our own dilemmas and shortcomings: 'Je voudrais [. . .] que, petit à petit, ce spectateur soit gagné par un malaise, pour finalement reconnaître que ces Allemands, c'est nous, c'est lui-même. Disons que le mirage théâtral devrait s'effacer pour laisser la place à la vérité qui est derrière ce mirage' (p. 301). The flicker of consciousness between imagination and perception reminds Frantz von Gerlach and ultimately reminds us that our actions, whether we like it or not, can and do have consequences in the real world.

6

COMMITMENT AND WRITING

Sketch for a theory of commitment

In 1960, Sartre said of Mallarmé: 'son engagement me paraît aussi total que possible: social autant que poétique'.[1] In the perspective of *Qu'est-ce que la littérature?* such a claim may seem startling: for the Sartre of 1947 poetry could not rank as committed writing. Is he, then, playing on two senses of the word 'engagement', making the banal point that, on the one hand, Mallarmé is committed *to* poetry while, on the other, he is implicated *in* society by virtue of his *être-dans-le-monde*? We recall that also in 1960, in the 'Question de méthode' which introduces his *Critique de la raison dialectique*, Sartre attempts to devise and in part apply a theory which would account for the insertion of the individual into society and history: a theory presenting the family as the crucial mediation through which an individual internalises, from his childhood, the pressures of his social context, whether of class, group structures, economic conditions or ideology. In 'Question de méthode', anticipating his monumental study, *L'Idiot de la famille*, Sartre takes the example of another writer, Flaubert, and indicates how his *dépassement* of his immediate family situation leads to his 'engagement littéraire' (*CRD*, p. 72).[2]

Such an emphasis might indeed reinforce the view that Mallarmé, too, exemplifies two parallel but independent forms of *engagement*: an inevitable involvement in society (even if the reaction to that involvement takes the form of a superficial detachment), and a more positive commitment to literature (which might indeed result from such a detachment). The word 'total' in Sartre's comment on Mallarmé suggests, however, a potential interrelationship. For in 'Question de méthode' Sartre proposes in addition to his theory of mediation, with its synthesis of Marxist and psychoanalytic approaches, a 'progressive–regressive' and 'totalising' method of investigating the interpenetration of individual and society. This aims to reveal the dialectical relationship of social conditioning and the individual project (for instance, the project of writing) through which that conditioning is at once 'dépassé' and 'conservé' (p. 68). The regressive phase would analyse the formative historical and socio-political circumstances internalised by the individual in the opacity of childhood and would thus reveal both his 'singularité historique' (p. 89) and 'la profondeur du vécu' (p. 92). It would investigate three levels of significance: that of the abstract 'significations universelles' of a given period (for instance, capitalism); of a specific social group within that period (for instance, the *petit-bourgeois* family); and of the individual member of such a family (for instance, Flaubert) in his unique and subjective attitudes and behaviour, revealing 'la réalité concrète comme totalisation vécue' (p. 88). The regressive stage would also involve a study of the processes whereby one level of significance is 'differentiated' (pp. 88 and 92) at a higher level; how, for instance, capitalism is variously 'lived' and objectified by different families of the intellectual *petite-bourgeoisie* in the mid-nineteenth century. Within this stage there is therefore a constant 'va-et-vient', as Sartre calls it, between interpretations of the period's 'universal' social structure, the immediate social context of the individual, and the 'singularity' of his experience lived at the subjective level. The analysis of each level of significance reciprocally enriches the interpretation of others, but at the regressive stage each level is none the less irreducible to any other. It is then the task of the progressive phase of the method to reveal synthetic – rather than reductive – relationships between these levels: it would show how the individual, through his project, transcends and yet preserves his social conditioning in order to create his own *être-dans-le-monde* as an objective but not definitive totality. It would show, too, how the individual's project, in its relation of tension and contradiction with the pressure of conditioning, may become modified or distorted, leading to an alienated form of self-objectification in which 'l'objectification terminale ne correspond peut-être pas exactement au choix originel' (p. 93). The interpretation of such distortions – which may be, in turn, transcended – would again involve recourse to a regressive phase which would refine the significance of the biographical and historical context. The *va-et-vient* of the method would therefore match the movement of the project itself: 'une vie se déroule en spirales; elle repasse toujours par les mêmes points mais à des niveaux différents d'intégration et de complexité' (p. 71). The method can be said to be a 'totalising' one in that it sees the object of its study – the integration of individual, society and history – as a never fully accomplished process of unification which is constantly permeated and 'detotalised' by the forces of negation and temporality. Further, complete (as distinct from 'totalising') knowledge of the process of totalisation from an external point of view is impossible: the knower is implicated in the known and is part of the very movement of totalisation. As a mode of explanation, Sartre's method, while recognising the validity of Marx's own thought, seeks to avoid what he sees as the mechanistic emphasis of contemporary versions of Marxism, its view that the movement of history can be defined in terms of a single predetermined meaning, and its reliance upon a 'reflection' theory of knowledge in which ideas are the direct consequences of social structures.

The project of writing, then, implicates the social and psychological situation of the writer, and also interacts with it. But does such an interaction imply a positive *engagement* of the kind which the word 'commitment' might suggest? The evolution of Sartre's thought in the 1960s suggests that an 'engagement poétique' might imply such a positive 'engagement social': his reappraisal of Mallarmé in 1960 anticipates the revaluation of committed writing set out in *Plaidoyer pour les intellectuels* (1965).[3] In 1947 Sartre had argued that the function of committed writer can provisionally be characterised as that of revealing to the reader both his situation and his freedom to change it, in order that he might effect the critical *prise de conscience* necessary for a transcending of that situation. The medium of such a revelation would be prose – in Sartre's view (at that time) an essentially instrumental or practical use of language. In *Plaidoyer*, however, which owes much to the reflections of 'Question de méthode', Sartre offers a more complex view of situation, 'dévoilement', and the writer's mode of expression. In *Qu'est-ce que la littérature?* (1947) the action of writing 'dévoile pour changer' (*S* ii, p. 73); in 1965 'praxis' is more fully dialectical: it is 'le moment du savoir pratique qui révèle, dépasse, conserve et déjà modifie la réalité' (*S* viii, p. 379). The intellectual and writer, although he is not a 'spécialiste du savoir pratique' in that his work is neither technical nor unproblematically conceptual, is nevertheless engaged in a crucial form of praxis. His contesting of the dominant ideology is more complex than the action of the *technicien* upon reality in that it involves particularly refractory internal contradictions: it does not reveal the world in the mode of explicit knowledge but bears witness to it as 'vécu' rather than 'connu' (p. 453). Further, the poet has been promoted to the rank of 'écrivain': poetry and prose are seen as complementary rather than mutually exclusive modes of writing. In the process, it is the definition of prose which undergoes the most radical transformation: the 'transparence' of the prose sign (essential, earlier, to its 'committed' function but reserved, later, for purely technical language) is reconciled with the 'materiality' of the word (hitherto the hallmark of poetic language). The reconciliation creates an ambiguity which is now seen to be characteristic of all literary expression, and which pre-eminently exemplifies the tension between transcendence and alienation implicit in all human experience: 'les mots sont à double face comme l'*être-dans-le-monde*. D'une part ce sont des objets sacrifiés: on les dépasse vers leurs significations, lesquelles deviennent, une fois comprises, des schémas verbaux polyvalents [. . .]. D'autre part, ce sont des réalités matérielles: en ce sens, ils ont des structures objectives qui s'imposent et peuvent toujours s'affirmer aux dépens des significations' (p. 446). This ambiguity in turn expresses that of the writer's situation, an expression essential to the *dépassement* of that situation in commitment:

le but de l'écrivain n'est aucunement de supprimer cette situation paradoxale mais de l'exploiter au maximum et de faire de son *être-dans-le-langage* l'expression de son *être-dans-le-monde*. Il utilise les phrases comme agents d'ambiguïté, comme présentification du tout structuré qu'est la langue, il joue sur la pluralité des sens, il se sert de l'histoire des vocables et de la syntaxe pour créer des sursignifications aberrantes.

(p. 448)

And as the languages of poetry and prose converge, they hold in tension 'l'unité et la contradiction explosive du singulier et de l'universel' (p. 450): 'elle [l'œuvre littéraire] doit se faire elle-même le dévoilement à soi du monde par la médiation d'une partie singulière qu'il a produite, en sorte qu'on présente l'universel partout comme le générateur de la singularité et réciproquement qu'on saisisse la singularité comme courbure et limite invisible de l'universel' (p. 451). The literary work, then, makes manifest the 'universel singulier': a synthesis of the subjective and the objective, the individual and the socio-historical – a totalising synthesis which constitutes the *engagement* of the writer, represents his creative freedom (p. 445) and sustains his communication with the reader.

Both the brief allusion to Mallarmé and the more sustained analyses in *Plaidoyer* challenge, then, the position adopted in *Qu'est-ce que la littérature?*, which, despite its own inner contradictions, is still considered to be one of the classical statements of the function and characteristics of committed writing. Moreover, as I have already suggested, 'Question de méthode' can also be seen to propose a more complex view of the nature and intelligibility of the individual's socio-historical situation – an intelligibility which, as we shall see, is essential to any theory of committed writing or, indeed, of committed action in general.

My present purpose is not, however, to give an exhaustive account of Sartre's theory of committed action and committed writing, or of his own practice of either (whether overtly political, journalistic or literary). It is rather to suggest that the challenge to *Qu'est-ce que la littérature?* occurs earlier in Sartre's development than has hitherto been supposed, both at the theoretical level and in the investigation of the practice of writing. For two recently published and substantial fragments of texts dating from the late 1940s and early 1950s anticipate the growing problems and complexities of *engagement*. Such problems, involving the question of the intelligibility of a social situation and its historical development, and the interpretation of the basis and goals of individual action within that situation and that development, are usually associated with *Critique de la raison dialectique*, with the essays of the sixties, and with *L'Idiot de la famille*. Both the early texts, however, suggest that this more complex view is in its elaboration contemporary with or, at all events, only slightly later than, the relative simplifications of *Qu'est-ce que la littérature?*.

The first text is a series of fragmentary *pensées* salvaged from the two thousand unpublished pages of notes for the treatise on ethics promised at the end of *L'Etre et le Néant* and never completed. The extracts which concern us were published by Michel Sicard in the review *Obliques* in 1979 under the title '*La Grande Morale*, extraits d'un *Cahier de Notes*'.[4] The first notebook was drafted in 1947 and, according to Sicard's introduction, the project was abandoned in, probably, 1949. In the treatise, Sartre had intended to develop the ethical implications of *L'Etre et le Néant* through phenomenological descriptions and analyses of individual behaviour and action. However, the published fragment – forty-eight pages of the original manuscript – discusses the ambiguity of historical action, the problematic nature of historical knowledge, and the difficulties inherent in a totalising theory of history, as well as the question of the limits and necessity of a moral framework for action.

The second early text is a much more substantial and sustained fragment of an originally lengthy study of Mallarmé, and I shall correspondingly discuss it in greater detail. It would, indeed, be hazardous to claim for Mallarmé a decisive role in the development of Sartre's thinking if the only evidence were Sartre's familiar essay, first published in 1953.[5] But the recently published additional section makes it easier to assess Mallarmé's relevance to Sartre's theory of committed literature and, by extension, to his practice of existential biography. Drafted between approximately 1948 and 1952 and appearing in *Obliques*, again in 1979, as *L'Engagement de Mallarmé*, the published section consists of a hundred or more of the original five hundred manuscript pages, of which the remainder were apparently lost in the bomb attack on Sartre's flat in 1962.[6] The state of the surviving text reflects the unsystematic character which Sartre was later to ascribe to the whole project.[7] While the long first section seems to be a finished draft, later there are breaks in continuity: relatively sustained passages are interrupted by missing pages or fragmentary notes. The later section appears to have served as a rough copy for the even more highly compressed 1953 essay. The chronology of the analysis is not clear, although one of the interesting features of the essay is its occasional deliberate departure from orthodox chronology by way of an incipient 'progressive–regressive' method. Apart from its fragmentary character the unprepared manuscript does however in other respects resemble Sartre's 'completed' works. His style is elliptical, allusive, assertive and hyperbolic. His method, as in *Saint Genet* and *L'Idiot de la famille*, involves an attempt to reconstruct the subject's experience through the process of empathy and hypothesis which in *Critique de la raison dialectique* Sartre defines as 'compréhension' in conscious accord with the German tradition of 'das Verstehen' (see above, p. 88).

A third early text which I shall also discuss – 'Orphée noir' – was in fact published in 1948,[8] but its relevance to the theses of *Qu'est-ce que la littérature?* has not, perhaps, been discussed as fully as it deserves. For, like *L'Engagement de Mallarmé*, it asserts the possibility, although in a very different social context, of committed poetry: in the work of francophone Black African poets 'le plus authentique projet révolutionnaire et la poésie la plus pure sortent de la même source' (*S* III, p. 285) – a project which, far from

164

assuming the transparency of language, experiences, exploits and transcends its alienating power.

But what are the presuppositions, assertions and arguments of *Qu'est-ce que la littérature?* which these other texts may be seen to modify? Its arguments presuppose that consciousness is free but situated, that consciousness is negation, and that consciousness is capable of imagining what is not the case. Consciousness is responsible for conferring meaning upon, or creating a human world within, an impassive, undifferentiated, impersonal ground of being. It therefore changes what is by revealing it and endowing it with meaning – or, as Sartre more specifically affirms in *Qu'est-ce que la littérature?*, by naming it: 'toute chose qu'on nomme n'est déjà plus tout à fait la même' (*S* II, p. 72). Hence, for Sartre, the privileged role of the writer as a committed agent: 'L'écrivain "engagé" sait que la parole est action: il sait que dévoiler c'est changer, et qu'on ne peut dévoiler qu'en projetant de changer' (p. 73). The writer invites the reader to effect a critical judgement, to realise freely his responsibility for bringing about change. This threefold activity has freedom both as its source and as its end: it translates metaphysical freedom into personal and political freedom: 'nous devons dans nos écrits militer en faveur de la liberté de la personne *et* de la révolution socialiste' (p. 298). And for its medium this activity requires the transparency of prose, in which for Sartre (at this stage) words are referential and directly transitive bearers of unitary meanings. Poetry cannot serve the committed writer: for poets, words have the opacity of objects rather than the transparency of signs. By functioning as the image or the symbol of an affective atmosphere – 'une angoisse faite chose' (p. 61) – they embody a *sens* rather than reveal a *signification*. Poets deny the instrumentality of language which is necessary to our action within and upon the world. There are moments, it is true, when the starkness of this opposition between prose and poetry is undermined within *Qu'est-ce que la littérature?* itself, but Sartre nevertheless maintains that for the committed writer simplicity of designation is imperative: 'la fonction d'un écrivain est d'appeler un chat un chat' (p. 304).

The formulation of Sartre's arguments raises a number of problems, some of which will be more clearly and fully acknowledged in *La Grande Morale,* in *L'Engagement de Mallarmé* and in later works. For instance, since, in *Qu'est-ce que la littérature?*, the distinction between metaphysical and socio-political freedom is not rigorously defined or sustained, the relationship between them cannot be fully clarified. In later works a more consciously complex view of their interrelationship and of the social aspects of the alienation of freedom will be possible. The earlier lack of definition means that in *Qu'est-ce que la littérature?* there are times when committed action seems to presuppose a degree of the very freedom which it is its function to promote. Further, in relation to the writer, Sartre fails to envisage fully the problem of how the freedom of judgement rather inexplicably available to an enlightened intellectual élite might be universalised. This problem is not convincingly solved by his attempt to demonstrate how a 'virtual' public may be transformed into a 'real' public, and his argument results in both a somewhat facile appreciation of the potential of the mass media and a paternalistic attitude towards the working-class public whom it is the writer's duty to enlighten: 'Ainsi le guidera-t-on par la main jusqu'à lui faire voir que ce qu'il veut en effet c'est abolir l'exploitation de l'homme par l'homme et que la cité des fins qu'il a posée d'un coup dans l'intuition esthétique n'est qu'un idéal dont nous ne nous rapprocherons qu'au terme d'une longue évolution historique' (p. 297). Yes, despite the enlightenment of the writer, it sometimes appears that 'littérature engagée' in its fullest sense – both 'committed to' change and 'fully involved in' its social context – would seem possible only in the Kantian extra-historical utopia which is also its goal: a 'cité des fins' which, notwithstanding Trotskyist overtones, presupposes an idealist notion both of the perfect society and of the essence of literature: 'la littérature est, par essence, la subjectivité d'une société en révolution permanente' (p. 196). It is therefore not clear whether Sartre is concerned to describe what committed literature is, or to consider what it might ideally be. At one point it seems as though the writing of the eighteenth century provides Sartre with a historical exemplification of the ideal and allows him to combine description and prescription. However, despite its promising reconciliation of writer and public, it still falls short of the synthesis of negation and project which he requires of committed literature: its critique of immediate social injustices implicates 'la Négativité, comme pouvoir d'arrachement au donné' (p. 196), but in its concern with abstract and universal rights it fails to specify a concrete and positive social order for the future.

Sartre's essay poses, then, a number of problems of definition. And it might, indeed, be more fruitful to define *engagement* not in terms of some quiddity, but differentially and cumulatively in relation to other terms which intersect with it. From this point of view *engagement* can be most usefully related to three concepts which Sartre alludes to unsystematically: 'embarquement', 'témoignage' and 'embrigadement'.[9] The first and last are related to the problem of the socio-historical context of writing as a mode of committed action and to the agent's freedom of reflection and judgement, while the second is concerned with the modes of action and expression available to the committed agent or writer.

Embrigadement is least relevant to my present concerns, although the problems associated with commitment to a party line or with action in a party-political context are far from peripheral in Sartre's own career. Indeed, they are so important that they deserve, and have received, full-scale study.[10] But from the point of view of *embrigadement* the essays and fragments at present under review are relatively straightforward. Although in *Qu'est-ce que la littérature?* Sartre's own commitment to the 'révolution socialiste' (p. 298) might seem to imply the espousal of a party-political line, he makes it clear that enrolment in the simultaneously conservative and opportunist Communist Party (p. 285) is inimical to the activity of the enlightened bourgeois intellectuals from whose ranks, Sartre seems to think, committed writers are chiefly drawn. Party membership appears to have equally negative effects for the proletarian, by setting him beyond the reach of effective communication: 'la classe opprimée, engoncée dans un parti, guindée dans une idéologie rigoureuse, devient une société fermée; on ne peut plus communiquer avec elle sans intermédiaire' (p. 271). Sartre also seems to reject the CP's claim to a monopoly of historical wisdom and, with it, the theoretical framework of orthodox Marxism. This point is made again in *La Grande Morale*: 'aucun parti ne peut se présenter comme l'interprète de l'histoire' (*GM*, p. 249).

The problem of the intelligibility of the historical situation is one which is crucial, of course, both to the nature of *embarquement* and to the efficacy of *témoignage*: it is posed, with different emphases, in *La Grande Morale* and in *L'Engagement de Mallarmé*. It is already clear in *Qu'est-ce que la littérature?* that the notion of *embarquement* goes beyond that of banal involvement, but it none the less falls far short of the individual's implication in history as specified by the theory of the 'universel singulier' in *Critique de la raison dialectique*. The intermediate essays may, however, provide a bridge.

For Sartre, being *engagé* always entails being *embarqué*, but it cannot be restricted to the fact of being so. In *Qu'est-ce que la littérature?*, in order to stress the distinction between the two terms, he takes up a criticism of his 'Présentation des *Temps Modernes*' made by Etiemble. First, Etiemble's quotation from Sartre's earlier essay is given, followed by his comment: '"L'écrivain [. . .] est dans le coup quoi qu'il fasse, marqué, compromis jusque dans sa plus lointaine retraite."[11] [. . .] Je reconnaissais à peu près le mot de Blaise Pascal: "Nous sommes embarqués." Mais du coup je voyais l'engagement perdre toute valeur, réduit soudain au fait le plus banal, au fait du prince et de l'esclave, à la condition humaine' (*S* II, p. 123). In his reply to Etiemble, Sartre then attempts a more precise definition: 'Je dirai qu'un écrivain est engagé lorsqu'il tâche à prendre la conscience la plus lucide et la plus entière d'être embarqué, c'est-à-dire lorsqu'il fait passer pour lui et pour les autres l'engagement de la spontanéité immédiate au réfléchi' (p. 124). And reflection involves choice; as Sartre succinctly puts it in 'Présentation des *Temps Modernes*' 'il [the individual] est engagé, il faut parier, l'abstention est un choix' (p. 28).

Reflection, then, is a necessary element of *engagement*, taking it further than an inevitable *embarquement*. It is, by implication, the committed writer's own capacity for reflection upon the situation which may lead him to induce a reflective *prise de conscience* in his public, and which should, in theory, allow him to construct a framework of interpretation from which the practical imperatives of action might emerge. And one might also infer that such reflection and such interpretation should generate in the writer a greater sense of the complexity of the situation in which he is *embarqué* – whether in the short-term perspective of immediate events or in the context of longer-term historical developments. It is indeed Sartre's own awareness of the complexities of the recent past and the present which motivates his description of the 'Situation de l'écrivain en 1947' in *Qu'est-ce que la littérature?*. However, here reflection seems to lead to an *impasse* in which the opacity of the situation is recognised on the one hand, and its intelligibility is asserted, against all the odds, on the other:

La vision lucide de la situation la plus sombre est déjà, par elle-même, un acte d'optimisme: Elle implique en effet que cette situation est *pensable*, c'est-à-dire que nous n'y sommes pas égarés comme dans une forêt obscure et que nous pouvons au contraire nous en arracher au moins par l'esprit, la tenir sous notre regard, donc la dépasser déjà et prendre nos résolutions en face d'elle, même si ces résolutions sont désespérées.   (*S* II, p. 289)

I shall return to the notion of the 'situation pensable'; in the meantime it is worth noting that no framework for 'thinking about' the situation, for defining one's 'résolutions' or for passing from decision to effective action is offered. And although it is at this point that 'notre engagement doit commencer' (p. 289), Sartre's practical imperatives are, as far as the committed writer is concerned, correspondingly vague. He should, Sartre suggests, 'recenser nos lecteurs *virtuels*' (p. 290), harness the potential of the mass media (pp. 290–2), be both negative and constructive (p. 300), and effect both a 'nettoyage analytique' and an 'élargissement synthétique' of language (p. 305). However, after Sartre's apocalyptic description of the situation itself, such exhortations have an air of anticlimax.

When the role of the reader is considered, the definition of action is more problematic still. Early in his essay Sartre is fruitfully concerned to define the reader's function in the creation of the literary work, but the question of a transition to practical action leads only to a dilution of the concept: 'si la perception même est action, si, pour nous, montrer le monde c'est toujours le dévoiler dans les perspectives d'un changement possible, alors, dans cette époque de fatalisme nous avons à révéler au lecteur, en chaque cas concret, sa puissance de faire et de défaire, bref, d'agir' (p. 311). If perception itself and, as we discover elsewhere, the very process of articulation,[12] are themselves forms of action, at what point does that action become *engagé*, and what are the specific modes of that *engagement*? Sartre's relative evasiveness concerning these modes may, at least in relation to literature, be due to his horror of propagandist writing, but there seems to be a more basic uncertainty. There are times when he envisages that the function of committed literature is to convey a direct denunciation of the current situation, or to act immediately upon the sensibility of the reader: 'La force d'un écrivain réside dans son action directe sur le public, dans les colères, les enthousiasmes, les méditations qu'il provoque par ses écrits' (p. 223). Elsewhere, however, he suggests a more indirect form of effect, in that the *subject* of committed literature should be action – none other than the enterprise of making history: 'La *praxis* comme action dans l'histoire et sur l'histoire, c'est-à-dire comme synthèse de la relativité historique et de l'absolu moral et métaphysique, avec ce monde hostile et amical, terrible et dérisoire qu'elle nous révèle, voilà notre sujet' (p. 265). But yet again, in that ideal society in which, we had thought, literature, for Sartre, would be most fully *engagée*, its active role is attenuated further, and with the emphasis on its purely reflexive function, Sartre's argument seems to have come full circle:

En un mot, la littérature est, par essence, la subjectivité d'une société en révolution permanente. Dans une pareille société elle dépasserait l'antinomie de la parole et de l'action.[13] En aucun cas, certes, elle ne sera assimilable à un acte: il est faux que l'auteur *agisse* sur ses lecteurs, il fait seulement appel à leurs libertés et, pour que ses ouvrages aient quelque effet, il est nécessaire que le public les reprenne à son compte par une décision inconditionnée. Mais dans une collectivité qui se reprend sans cesse et se juge et se métamorphose, l'œuvre écrite peut être une condition essentielle de l'action, c'est-à-dire le moment de la conscience réflexive.   (pp. 196–7)

In view of these inconsistencies it may not be surprising that this fragment of *La Grande Morale* ends, by way of a resolution, with a nostalgic evocation of what appears to be the Hegelian theory of action: 'Ainsi s'entrevoit, par-delà l'antinomie de la morale et de l'histoire, une morale concrète qui est comme *la logique de l'action effective*' (*GM*, p. 262).[14]

The relationship between situation, reflection and action is, then, far from straightforward. Still more complex problems are posed by the relationship between individual action and longer-term historical perspectives. Sartre's early definition of *praxis*, quoted above, suggests that he sees the relevance of these perspectives. But he has difficulty in reconciling a number of different views of time: his definition of individual consciousness as an absolute which creates its own temporality (the view proposed in *L'Etre et le Néant*), the vision of the extra-historical utopian society postulated in *Qu'est-ce que la littérature?* as the ideal context of committed literature, the 'moment' of reflective consciousness, and the relativising force of History. The need for such a reconciliation and its consequences, for instance, for the familiar problem of means and ends, are recognised. But the means whereby individuals of 'bonne volonté, intemporelles, *s'historialisent* en conservant leur pureté et [. . .] transforment leurs exigences formelles en revendications matérielles et datées' (*S* II, p. 293) – the means whereby the individual is inserted into history – is assumed but not theoretically grounded or explained. The difficulty of such a grounding seems to be repressed or shelved in *Qu'est-ce que la littérature?*, but its intractability is explicitly recognised and explored in *La Grande Morale*: 'Peut-être l'histoire est un problème insoluble mais de mieux en mieux posé' (*GM*, p. 252).

The 'position' of the problem, albeit fragmentary, is undertaken in *La Grande Morale* both in relation to the short-term context of events as they are immediately experienced, and to longer-term developments. And while its provisional conclusions may appear, in their relative negativity, to undermine the superficially optimistic assertions of *Qu'est-ce que la littérature?*, they prepare the way for the interim practical example of Mallarmé's historical role, the much more fully elaborated and positive theory of *Critique de la raison dialectique*, and, eventually, the *summa* of *L'Idiot de la famille*.

For instance, in *Qu'est-ce que la littérature?* the 'pluridimensionnalité' of the event or the 'fait historique' is seen to justify the novelistic technique of multiple point of view, but Sartre does not explore the difficulties posed by the complexity of the event for the process of reflection, interpretation and involvement – whether for the writer, or for the historical agent in general. These are set out more systematically in *La Grande Morale*. First, the event is seen to synthesise (or, as Sartre prefers to say, syncretise) the familiar Sartrean antinomy of nature and consciousness. 'En tant qu'il est nature' the event is vulnerable to a form of disintegration: it is governed by a series of external causal relationships which are themselves subject to entropy and destruction, and to the intervention of chance. On the other hand, the event may be seen as a comprehensible unity by an individual consciousness which '[le] saisit selon ses propres principes' (*GM*, p. 255) and therefore internalises it. However, the very multiplicity of separate consciousnesses and of 'interprétations vécues' means that each event remains refractory to a full 'internalisation' by any given consciousness: indeed, the interpretations themselves come not only to be seen as external to each other but to be externalised as an objective aspect of the event (p. 255). The event is therefore subject to an unstable relationship of interiority and exteriority. Further, while an event may appear to be comprehensible to the agent, for the multiplicity of observers it may appear as chance, reinforced by the contingency of 'l'être-dans-le-monde de l'homme' (p. 255), and by the synthesis of freedom and inertia, activity and passivity which human consciousness now exemplifies for Sartre. And again, set within an institutionalised framework, the event becomes a purely statistical unit: an abstract and, by extension, a dehumanised and dehumanising concept: '"Les cheminots se sont mis en grève." A noter que "les cheminots" sont des fonctions à ce moment là' (p. 255). Further, the 'singularité' of the event (associated positively by Sartre with the free activity of individual consciousness) is always threatened by the inert 'généralité' which negatively represents the universality of matter (pp. 256–7). This tension within the event or within the 'historical fact' is in turn reflected in the ambiguity of human work. On the one hand 'le travail en abrutissant généralise, ce qui fait aussi le respect ou la faim'; on the other, 'le travail, Hegel l'a montré, fournit à la conscience une image de soi en lui reflétant son action sur les objets' (p. 257). These different possible emphases mean that the event, in its exteriorising of 'interprétations vécues' (p. 255) is essentially unstable and elusive: 'inattendu-attendu, extériorité-intériorité, contingent-nécessaire, inventé-subi, matériel-spirituel, perpétuellement unifié-émietté par cette unification même, objet-sujet, perdu et retrouvé' (p. 255).[15] And the very act of ascribing meaning to events emphasises that instability: 'précisément parce que cette signification agissante est pluridimensionnelle, l'événement est déséquilibre, c'est une prolifération décentrée' (p. 255).

For the Sartre of *La Grande Morale*, then, the event is the locus of fundamental and dialectically unresolved contradictions. Later, in 'Question de méthode', the notion of the group as agent – scarcely touched upon in *La Grande Morale* – will allow Sartre to define the historical event in its concrete reality as an 'unité organisée d'une pluralité d'oppositions qui se dépassent réciproquement' (*CRD*, p. 83). And while the event may react upon the agents involved in it and while its results may seldom be clear-cut, its very ambiguity, Sartre now thinks (taking as his example the events of 10 August 1789) may confer upon it precisely its concrete historical efficacy (p. 84).

Moreover, in *Plaidoyer pour les intellectuels*, the status of the event as the concrete expression of a particular ideology enables the committed intellectual, in his specific response to it, to escape the charge of being 'un être abstrait qui vit de l'universel pur' (*S* VIII, p. 405). For the event no longer exemplifies an unresolved tension between the singular and the general – whether the 'general' or 'universal' be defined as the abstract, as in *Plaidoyer*, or as the material, as in *La Grande Morale*. It now synthesises action, thought and history: the role of the intellectual is to

travailler *au niveau de l'événement* à produire des événements concrets qui combattent le pogrom ou le jugement raciste du Tribunal en montrant la violence des privilégiés dans sa nudité. J'appelle *événement*, ici, un fait porteur d'une idée, c'est-à-dire un universel singulier car il limite l'idée portée, dans son universalité, par sa singularité de fait *daté* et *localisé* qui *a lieu* à un certain moment d'une histoire nationale et qui résume et la totalise dans la mesure où il en est le produit totalisé. (*S* VIII, p. 407)

If, then, we trace the development of Sartre's analysis of the event back from *Plaidoyer*, we find that there the synthesis of 'fait' and 'idée' is effected by the interaction of individual and event, which are both seen to exemplify the 'universel singulier'. In 'Question de méthode' the idea of the group-agent supersedes the view of the subject offered in *La Grande Morale*, where the agent is 'decentred' in relation to the event. Here, in turn, Sartre seems concerned to explore problems which are repressed in *Qu'est-ce que la littérature?*, where the 'embarked' individual is still the centred subject of reflection and action. At this early stage, despite an acknowledgement of the opacity of events, Sartre seems, as we noted, optimistically determined to affirm that the situation is 'thought about'. Clearly, the notion of individual reflection upon the situation might be supposed to imply the possibility, or perhaps even the necessity, of the individual's representing his historical situation to himself – or, at least, of having it represented to him: 'C'est notre tâche d'écrivain que de représenter le monde et d'en témoigner' (*S* ii, p. 307). But in *Qu'est-ce que la littérature?* a theoretical framework which might inform the intelligibility of the situation or the practical imperatives of committed action is not developed.[16] In *La Grande Morale*, however, Sartre does address himself – although, again, not conclusively – to problems of theory and representation from the point of view of both historical interpretation and historical action, and with consequences for *engagement* and *embrigadement*. In his fragment on *Ambivalence de l'Histoire: Ambiguïté du fait historique* Sartre, apart from contending that 'aucun parti ne peut se présenter comme l'interprète de l'histoire' (*GM*, p. 249), maintains (not altogether originally, but with fruitful consequences for his later views) that the representation of history is itself a historical factor:

Du coup l'histoire n'est déjà plus ce qu'ils [historical agents] en pensent: elle est *cela* plus l'action de la représentation qu'ils en ont. Mais cette action elle-même est d'un type particulier: elle est par proposition. Même si les consciences jouent l'inertie elles ne sont pas inertes, on n'agit pas sur elles par causalité. Elles doivent *reprendre* le thème proposé; du coup il sert à d'autres fins. Ainsi l'action de la théorie de l'histoire considérée ne peut avoir lieu que dans et par la déformation de la théorie. (p. 249)

Here, clearly, Sartre sees a positive sense, foreshadowing the links between theory and *praxis* developed in *Critique de la raison dialectique*, in which theories and modes of the representation of history can be taken to be instruments of historical change. (In *La Grande Morale*, however, such an historical process can be said to be dialectical only in a weak sense, in that historical action and, furthermore, reflection and judgement change, but are also changed by what they purport to act upon or explain.) But the negative corollary is that the subject's act is alienated by the very factor of representation, that theory is distorted by its very application, and that the attempt to confer meaning upon a situation distorts that situation. In short, from the point of view of the agent, the situation in the short term, or 'history' in the longer term, never *is* what one thinks it is. Indeed, Sartre maintains, it could only be otherwise for that ultimate 'totaliser', the Hegelian Spirit: 'l'histoire a un sens si l'Esprit est un' (p. 249). But this is a hypothesis which, as we know from *L'Etre et le Néant*, Sartre refuses to accept, and to which, despite the Hegelian overtones of *La Grande Morale* and *L'Engagement de Mallarmé*, he remains resistant.[17] Rather, he has to settle for a plurality of unstable meanings and for a series of provisional totalisations – of 'totalités' which are constantly 'détotalisées'. And again, precisely because of the intervention of representation, these cannot be implicated in a fully dialectical progression: 'toute dialectique une fois représentée (réflexion) agit par représentation de la dialectique donc non dialectiquement' (*GM*, p. 256).[18] Their relationship is one of unresolved paradox:

l'histoire a un sens si l'Esprit est un. Dans la mesure où l'Esprit est totalité ce sens existe, donc il y a *direction donc progrès*; dans la mesure où il est aliéné à lui-même par le néant qui le transit (détotalisation) il n'y a ni direction ni progrès: piétinement. La situation c'est donc une Histoire qui n'est pas histoire, un progrès piétinant, une explication *totale* par le nécessaire et *totale* par le contingent. (p. 249)

These changing Sartrean perspectives on the nature of the situation and of the historical event, and on the representation of history, offer a far more complex and problematic context for committed action – whether in terms of motivation or effect – than did *Qu'est-ce que la littérature?*. There, Sartre maintains that the situation of the agent is *pensable* and recoverable through reflection. In *La Grande Morale* it has become increasingly *impensable*. But in *La Grande Morale* a yet more radical questioning is to come. History seems to make reflection itself impossible for the subject, and to reinforce his inaccessibility, *qua* subject, for others. For while 'le fait historique' is 'un événement de la subjectivité humaine' it is also

objet devant ma conscience et du même coup j'entre dans une subjectivité qui n'est pensée par personne, une subjectivité ignorante-ignorée, un au-delà du savoir qui *est* encore et surtout l'histoire. Une subjectivité qui n'est plus subjectivité parce qu'elle ne peut pas s'atteindre elle-même par la réflexivité. Et c'est précisément ce non-savoir cette subjectivité aliénée qui se refermera sur elle-même pour devenir objet pour la génération postérieure (ou encore pour *un autre* qui me saisira à ce moment).

(p. 257)[19]

Here the reflection and understanding postulated as necessary pre-conditions for commitment in *Qu'est-ce que la littérature?* are called into question at two levels: first at that of the subject's understanding of his own self, situation and action; secondly, at that of their availability for interpretation by others. The committed act would seem, now, to have become a blind and incomprehensible wager. But those who are familiar with the Sartrean wager will know that 'qui perd gagne' and, indeed, 'le non-savoir' is later enlightened by another form of understanding more sensitive, both for subject and interpreter, to the opacities of living. For the subject, this understanding will involve a preconceptual and primarily affective grasp of his personal and social situation; for the interpreter, it will involve an imaginative recreation, through empathy, of the subject's situation and response. For Sartre, the recourse to 'compréhension' is a crucial method of resolving the subject/object dichotomy in knowledge.[20]

La Grande Morale, then, openly confronts the problem which is evaded in *Qu'est-ce que la littérature?*, but it is left to 'Orphée noir', *L'Engagement de Mallarmé* and *Saint Genet* to anticipate the solution offered by the relationship between 'compréhension' and the 'vécu' set out in *Critique de la raison dialectique*. Moreover, the first two, more concisely but perhaps more explicitly than *Saint Genet*, look forward to its application specifically to the situation of the committed writer in *Plaidoyer pour les intellectuels*. There, the function of the intellectual is to effect – apparently as in *Qu'est-ce que la littérature?* – the 'prise de conscience réflexive' (*S* VIII, p. 427) which society itself, suffering its own contradictions at the level of the 'lived', cannot achieve. But at first, as in *La Grande Morale*, the scope of this reflection is severely attenuated by the intellectual's 'ignorance historique': he represents simply 'l'*ignorance minima* [Sartre's italics] qui structure sa société' (p. 428). None the less, although the intellectual as committed writer may internalise his situation in an affective and pre-conceptual rather than fully cognitive mode, his representation of it – unlike the distorting representation analysed in *La Grande Morale* – will effect a genuine 'totalisation' of the individual and of the society by which he is conditioned. The literary work of art will '[livrer] un homme au point qu'on sent presque son souffle mais *sans le donner à connaître*' (p. 449), and will '[rendre compte] du *tout* sur le mode du non-savoir, du vécu. Le tout, c'est-à-dire le passé social et la conjoncture historique en tant qu'ils sont *vécus* sans être *connus*' (pp. 452-3).[21] The 'work' (used in the strong sense – for Sartre, as we shall see in the Mallarmé study, the literary work is also a form of 'labour') will constitute an 'universel singulier' in which the existing world is constantly called into question (p. 443). The transparency of consciousness and reflection is no longer the basis for contestation and change. Their locus is, rather, the relatively opaque affectivity of the *vécu*, which transcends its initial passivity in a dynamic, progressive 'totalising' of objective structures and of an 'enracinement particulier' which leads to an 'effort d'universalisation qui naît de la singularité et la conserve en la niant' (p. 453). This dialectical process transcends conventional distinctions between personal and social existence, and the interpreter will therefore seek to comprehend it through a synthesis of psychoanalytic and Marxist methods. This synthetic approach was to be most exhaustively applied in *L'Idiot de la famille* (1971-2). It was conceptualised, as we saw, in *Critique de la raison dialectique*, was less in evidence in the more metaphysical *Saint Genet*, but was already fundamental to Sartre's approach in *L'Engagement de Mallarmé*.

Embarquement, then, evolves into a more complex form of *engagement* through a synthesis of activity and passivity, conditioning and autonomy, which qualifies Sartre's earlier more rationalistic approach and rehabilitates affectivity as a mode of being-in-the-world. We shall see later how Sartre attempts to integrate this understanding of the *vécu* into his study of that apparently most reflective of poets, Mallarmé. But in 'Orphée noir' (1948), the situation of Black African poets, alienated by the fact of colonial oppression, alienated by the very language which they speak, is already mediated by affectivity rather than by reflection. It is true that Sartre introduces the theme of reflection early in his essay: 'ainsi le noir qui revendique sa négritude dans un mouvement révolutionnaire se place d'emblée sur le terrain de la Réflexion, soit qu'il veuille retrouver en lui certains traits objectivement constatés dans les civilisations africaines, soit qu'il espère découvrir l'Essence noire dans le puits de son cœur' (*S* III, p. 239). But his reference is less straightforward than it might at first seem: the notion of reflection is developed not in terms of conceptualised thought, but of a mirror-image in which a presence-to-self is implicit, and in which the poet's *négritude* is felt rather than known – all-pervasively but none the less elusively, for the distortion of his self-image through the refracting medium of white culture destroys the possibility either of direct apprehension or of total self-coincidence, and condemns the poet to a sense of exile. Unlike the concept of class, the experience of race, which is concrete and individual, is accessible, therefore, to 'ce que Jaspers nomme compréhension' rather than to 'l'intellection' (p. 280). Subsequently, Sartre will acknowledge that class-consciousness, too, claims its share of 'compréhension'; for the time being, the situation of Black African poets – opaque, pervasive, elusive and yet manifest – inspires an increasingly typical Sartrean oxymoron: it is lived in 'la nuit lumineuse du non-savoir' (p. 285).

But if it is to be demonstrated that poetry is a form of action, an appropriate medium for literary commitment, it must also be shown that the apprehension of *négritude* transcends the passivity which Sartre so often associates with affective responses and, through affectivity, with poetry itself. Moreover, poetry must bridge, although it can never fully eliminate, the alienating rift between the subjective and the collective – a rift deepened, in Sartre's view, by the conflict between native race and colonial culture internalised by Black African poets. Poetry must become implicated in the movement of history. Finally, since Sartrean commitment must overcome both ontological and socio-political alienation, poetry, if it is to be committed, must both make manifest and heal the rift between man and world.

For Sartre, poets like Aimé Césaire confront and surmount this dichotomy at its most fundamental: the antinomy between nature and consciousness still postulated in *La Grande Morale* is resolved, for the white's technical, utilitarian and instrumental attitude to nature – the attitude usually associated with practical action – is supplanted by a 'compréhension par sympathie' of the natural world. This involves its own modes of intuitive and yet dynamic creativity, an incarnation of 'l'Eros naturel' (*S* III, p. 269), which is androgynous in its union of patience and power:

Le rapport technique avec la Nature la dévoile comme quantité pure, inertie, extériorité: elle meurt. Par son refus hautain d'être *homo-faber*, le nègre lui rend la vie. Comme si, dans le couple 'homme-nature', la passivité d'un des termes entraînait nécessairement l'activité de l'autre. A vrai dire, la négritude n'est pas une passivité, puisqu'elle 'troue la chair du ciel et de la terre': c'est une 'patience', et la patience apparaît comme une imitation active de la passivité. L'action du nègre est d'abord action sur soi. Le noir se dresse et s'immobilise comme un charmeur d'oiseaux et les choses viennent se percher sur les branches de cet arbre faux. Il s'agit bien d'une captation du monde, mais magique, par le silence et le repos: en agissant d'abord sur soi, le nègre prétend gagner la Nature en se gagnant.

(p. 264)

The writing of the black refuses, then, 'une prose d'ingénieurs' (p. 265), and transcends the Narcissism previously associated with the poet.[22] The emotional and the magical are no longer, as they were in Sartre's *Esquisse d'une théorie des émotions*, an evasion of practical action, nor is the magical any longer a symptom of 'l'esprit traînant parmi les choses'. Both are now seen to be the mode of a participation in Being, or a form of cosmic energy more profound than any technical appropriation of the world: 'Le secret du noir c'est que les sources de son existence et les racines de l'Etre sont identiques' (p. 265).

For Sartre, the black poets' return to the original simplicity of existence (p. 252) which precedes the exile of socio-cultural alienation is effected perhaps rather obviously but none the less powerfully through a rediscovery of ancient desires and energies, of ancestral rhythms and incantations – a spiritual exercise (p. 253) or an 'objective method' (p. 260) which converges with the subjectivity of the poet's Orphic descent into his own soul. And at first, Sartre, acknowledging also the debt of Césaire and Senghor to Surrealism, sees the fruit of this double enterprise as a 'poésie objective' (p. 254) designed to evoke by incantation 'la négritude-objet' (p. 260).[23] As such, it seems initially to correspond to the art-object of *Qu'est-ce que la littérature?*, in which the medium – whether poetic language, music or pigment – does not designate an object, as would the language of prose, but constitutes it:

Et finalement ce qui s'arrache de Césaire comme un cri de douleur, d'amour et de haine, c'est la négritude-objet. Ici encore il poursuit la tradition surréaliste qui veut que le poème objective. Les mots de Césaire ne décrivent pas la négritude, ne la désignent pas, ne la copient pas du dehors comme un peintre fait d'un modèle: ils la font; ils la composent sous nos yeux: désormais c'est une chose qu'on peut observer, apprendre.

(p. 260)

But the last words indicate a fundamental distinction between the *couleur-objet* or the *phrase-objet* of *Qu'est-ce que la littérature?* and the object constituted by the work of the black poet. His creation transcends the limitations of the *objet imaginaire* or the aesthetic object which cannot, as we saw earlier, be observed in the same way as a perceived object, and about which nothing can be learned. In other words, poetry can now communicate in ways which were denied it in *Qu'est-ce que la littérature?*.

Sartre does not explicitly explain or justify this change of attitude on his part, but we may infer that his admiration for the 'revendication haute de la non-technicité' which accompanies the revolutionary aspirations expressed in the poetry, for instance, of Césaire, has helped to attenuate his own earlier emphasis on prose as the technical instrument of action through writing. But this attenuation may be explained, too, by Sartre's revised view of the relationship between poetry and failure. In *Qu'est-ce que la littérature?* poetry is seen to be a 'valorisation absolue de l'échec' (*S* II, p. 87), of a failure to overcome by practical means the 'obscure finalité' or the 'coefficient d'adversité' (p. 86) of the universe, and, by extension, of a failure to use language as an instrument: 'S'il est vrai que la parole soit une trahison et que la communication soit impossible, alors chaque mot, par lui-même, recouvre son individualité, devient instrument de notre défaite et receleur de l'incommunicable' (p. 86). In 'Orphée noir', however, this metaphysical defeat has a specifically socio-political and cultural basis. Speaking and writing in an alien language, the black poet is constantly exposed to a 'décalage léger et constant qui sépare ce qu'il dit de ce qu'il voudrait dire, dès qu'il parle de lui' (*S* III, p. 245). Prose fails him, and all language is therefore poeticised: 'les vocables gisent en face de lui, insolites, à moitié signes et choses à demi' (p. 245). But the black poet transforms this metaphysical defeat into the instrument of a specific subversion:

A la ruse du colon ils répondent par une ruse inverse et semblable: puisque l'oppresseur est présent jusque dans la langue qu'ils parlent, ils parleront cette langue pour la détruire. Le poète européen d'aujourd'hui tente de déshumaniser les mots pour les rendre à la nature; le héraut noir, lui, va les défranciser; il les concassera, rompra leurs associations coutumières, les accouplera par la violence. [. . .] C'est seulement lorsqu'ils ont dégorgé leur blancheur qu'il les adopte, faisant de cette langue en ruine un super-langage solennel et sacré, la Poésie. Par la seule Poésie les noirs de Tananarive et de Cayenne, les noirs de Port-au-Prince et de Saint-Louis peuvent communiquer entre eux sans témoins.   (pp. 247–8)

The black poet's complex *engagement* in his oppressive colonial situation has, then, generated a new form of subversive expression, and poetry has become a means of committed communication. As so often in Sartre, 'qui perd gagne' – a reversal which, indeed, is already seen in *Qu'est-ce que la littérature?* to be the essence of poetry itself: there, it is the poet's sensitivity to the failure of prose as a medium of communication which animates his power to suggest the incommunicable. And by a further reversal, it is the 'loser wins' mechanism which establishes the poet's function of *témoignage* – a function which, I suggested earlier, is closely associated with the theme of *engagement*. Whether it should generally be so associated is, however, a matter of some controversy. *Témoignage*, in its strong sense, has its source in the notion of 'bearing witness' through martyrdom, an imitation of Christ's Passion, sacrifice and suffering. Sartre's terminology is constantly reminiscent, if in a secularised way, of this origin. But *témoignage* so defined may perhaps be only uneasily reconciled, if at all, with socio-political efficacy. It may remain an end in itself. Conversely, the *embrigadement* associated with the cult of efficacy may precisely deny those spiritual or moral values which *témoignage* may bring to commitment.

Engagement proper, then, may have to occupy an uneasy middle ground between the two peripheral concepts of *témoignage* and *embrigadement*. Sartre, however, seems much more ready to accept the relevance of the former.[24] In *Qu'est-ce que la littérature?* it is the duty of all committed writers to 'représenter le monde et d'en témoigner' (*S* II, p. 307), and that *témoignage* is all the more intense, extreme and essential *because* it is secularised: in the experience of the war-time torture risked by the resistance writer 'l'angoisse commence pour un homme et le délaissement et les sueurs de sang, quand il ne peut plus avoir d'autre témoin que lui-même; c'est alors qu'il boit le calice jusqu'à la lie' (p. 250). In such a context it may seem strange that poetry, too, is already seen as a form of committed *témoignage*, albeit metaphysical and negative:

La poésie, c'est qui perd gagne. Et le poète authentique choisit de perdre jusqu'à mourir pour gagner. [. . .] Si donc l'on veut absolument parler de l'engagement du poète, disons que c'est l'homme qui s'engage à perdre. [. . .] Il est certain de l'échec total de l'entreprise humaine et s'arrange pour échouer dans sa propre vie, afin de témoigner, par sa défaite singulière, de la défaite humaine en général. (p. 87)

Here Sartre's hyperboles underline his tendency to see *engagement*, however negative, in terms of extremism – but a form of extremism which inverts the expected association of action with efficacy. *La Grande Morale*, even in a context more concerned,

ostensibly, with historical than metaphysical *engagement*, simultaneously reinforces this attitude, reveals the paradox of *embrigadement*,
and expresses Sartre's nostalgia for a unified but impossible totality:

> Plus l'agent historique choisit pour moyen la violence, le mensonge et le
> machaviélisme [*sic*], plus il est efficace. Mais plus il contribue à la division,
> plus il met l'accent sur la détotalisation; plus il est lui-même objet en his-
> toire et plus il défait l'histoire (dont l'existence idéale serait par totali-
> sation). Le véritable agent historique est moins efficace mais en traitant les
> hommes comme lui-même, il tâche à faire exister l'esprit comme unité donc
> l'histoire. C'est par lui qu'une histoire est possible (par l'écrivain, le phi-
> losophe, le saint, le prophète, le savant). (*GM*, p. 250)

It is therefore not surprising that *La Grande Morale* develops, too,
the theme of failure, although the emphasis has slightly but significantly changed from *Qu'est-ce que la littérature?*. The authenticity of
the poet's peculiar form of negative *engagement* has now become a
more general human authenticity:

> La poursuite de l'Etre c'est l'enfer. L'échec peut conduire à la conversion. Il
> peut aussi être nié de mauvaise foi. S'il est aimé et reconnu à la fois, sans
> conversion ou en dehors de la conversion, c'est la Poésie. L'homme authent-
> ique ne peut pas par la conversion supprimer la poursuite de l'Etre car il n'y
> aurait plus rien. Mais il peut aussi aimer se perdre, alors il est poète.
> Malédiction issue de poésie, c'est-à-dire de l'amour de l'échec. Amour de
> l'impossible. L'homme authentique ne peut pas faire qu'il ne soit par quel-
> que côté poétique. (p. 256)[25]

It is left, however, to 'Orphée noir' to reconcile the more positive
aspects of socio-political as well as metaphysical *engagement* with
both *témoignage* and poetry. For the patience of the black poet, both
the source and the consequence of his empathy with nature, is also
taken in its strict etymological sense and is transformed into a de-
christianised re-enactment of the Passion, *révolté* rather than
resigned:

> A l'absurde agitation utilitaire du blanc, le noir oppose l'authenticité re-
> cueillie de sa souffrance; parce qu'elle a eu l'horrible privilège de toucher le
> fond du malheur, la race noire est une race élue. Et, bien que ces poèmes
> soient de bout en bout antichrétiens, on pourrait, de ce point de vue,
> nommer la négritude une Passion: le noir conscient de soi se représente à ses
> propres yeux comme l'homme qui a pris sur soi toute la douleur humaine et
> qui souffre pour tous, même pour le blanc. [. . .] Si l'on voulait systéma-
> tiser, on dirait que le noir se fond à la Nature entière en tant qu'il est sym-
> pathie sexuelle pour la Vie et qu'il se revendique comme l'Homme en tant
> qu'il est Passion de douleur révoltée. (*S* III, pp. 270–1)

But the universal and timeless implications of this redemption of the natural and the human become specifically historical, through the experience of slavery and of colonial oppression, and through the double *témoignage* of suffering, and of bearing witness through writing. The fundamental experience of suffering 'est à la fois la saisie intuitive de la condition humaine et à la fois la mémoire encore fraîche d'un passé historique' (p. 274). Further, the refusal of complicity with suffering ensures a future goal: 'la souffrance comporte en elle-même son propre refus; elle est par essence refus de souffrir, elle est la face d'ombre de la négativité, elle s'ouvre sur la révolte et sur la liberté. Du coup il s'historialise dans la mesure où l'intuition de la souffrance lui confère un passé collectif et lui assigne un but dans l'avenir' (p. 276). The poetry of *négritude* is thus open to a dialectical 'becoming' in which negation 'vise à préparer la synthèse ou réalisation de l'humain dans une société sans races. Ainsi la Négritude est pour se détruire, elle est passage et non aboutissement, moyen et non fin dernière' (p. 280).

Yet poetry itself, Sartre finally affirms, not only encapsulates but outlasts and indeed neutralises the relativising movement of history, and thus becomes not simply the possible but the necessary medium of the experience he has tried to evoke. As such, it subverts even the conceptual framework of his own prose, which becomes increasingly the vehicle of empathy – rhetorical, fervent, powerful, perhaps wishful:

Parce qu'elle est cette tension entre un Passé nostalgique où le noir n'entre plus tout à fait et un Avenir où elle cédera la place à des valeurs nouvelles, la Négritude se pare d'une beauté tragique qui ne trouve d'expression que dans la poésie. Parce qu'elle est l'unité vivante et dialectique de tant de contraires, parce qu'elle est un Complexe rebelle à l'analyse, c'est seulement l'unité multiple d'un chant qui la peut manifester et cette beauté fulgurante du Poème, que Breton nomme 'explosante-fixe'. Parce que tout essai pour en conceptualiser les différents aspects aboutirait nécessairement à en montrer la relativité, alors qu'elle est vécue dans l'absolu par des consciences royales, et parce que le poème est un absolu, c'est la poésie seule qui permettra de fixer l'aspect inconditionnel de cette attitude. Parce qu'elle est une subjectivité qui s'inscrit dans l'objectif, la Négritude doit prendre corps dans un poème, c'est-à-dire dans une subjectivité-objet [. . .]. La Négritude c'est le contenu du poème, c'est le poème comme chose du monde, mystérieuse et ouverte, indéchiffrable et suggestive: c'est le poète lui-même. Il faut aller plus loin encore; la Négritude, triomphe du Narcissisme et suicide de Narcisse, tension de l'âme au delà de la culture, des mots et de tous les faits psychiques, nuit lumineuse du non-savoir, choix délibéré de l'impossible et de ce que Bataille nomme le

182

'supplice', acceptation intuitive du monde et refus du monde au nom de la 'loi du cœur', double postulation contradictoire, rétraction revendicante, expansion de générosité, est, *en son essence, Poésie*.   (pp. 284–5)[26]

Much of the climax of Sartre's argument in 'Orphée noir' recalls in its vocabulary and emphasis his answer in the second part of *Qu'est-ce que la littérature?* to the question 'Pourquoi écrire?' (*S* II, pp. 89–115). There, aesthetic value has its origin in 'la constatation d'une harmonie rigoureuse entre la subjectivité et l'objectivité' (p. 108). There, too, the artist is closest to absolute creation when 'c'est dans la passivité même de la matière que nous rencontrons l'insondable liberté de l'homme' (p. 106), and when aesthetic response transcends practical life and its utilitarian confusion concerning means and ends, in a positive appeal to freedom and generosity (pp. 115 and 107). In this section of *Qu'est-ce que la littérature?* the literary object is still defined in terms of prose forms – the writer is 'essayiste, pamphlétaire, satiriste ou romancier' (p. 112) but not yet, it would seem, poet. And yet, as I suggested in my first chapter, Sartre is already undermining – apparently unknowingly – the distinction between transparent *signification* and opaque *sens*, between prose and poetry, established in the earlier part of his argument: 'Ainsi, dès le départ, le sens n'est plus contenu dans les mots puisque c'est lui, au contraire, qui permet de comprendre la signification de chacun d'eux; et l'objet littéraire, quoiqu'il se réalise *à travers* le langage, n'est jamais donné *dans* le langage; il est, au contraire, par nature, silence et contestation de la parole' (p. 94). In 'Orphée noir', too, 'il faut faire du silence avec le langage' (*S* III, p. 247).

But 'Orphée noir' goes further. In *Qu'est-ce que la littérature?* the eternal and absolute qualities inherent in Sartre's definition of the literary object are uneasily related to a specific situation and a specific public by a not altogether convincing transition from metaphysical to socio-political freedom. In 'Orphée noir', however, the qualities of poetry as absolute creation arise from a specific political, cultural, linguistic situation and enact its evolution. Does this mean, then, that the creation of committed poetry is unique to that situation – that, for instance, the black poets' subversive recourse to indirect language is a purely contingent result of their subjection to an alien tongue? Sartre seems to recognise this uniqueness and this reductive contingency: 'Pour une fois au moins, le plus authentique projet révolutionnaire et la poésie la plus pure sortent de la même source' (*S* III, p. 285). If the capacity for commitment is inherent in poetry itself, it must be shown to be so in that most indirect and absolute of poets, writing in the '"langue neutre par excellence"' (*S* III, p. 244) of his native tongue: Mallarmé.

A practical example: *L'Engagement de Mallarmé*

'L'acte, par moi choisi, a été d'écrire.'[27] 'Choisir', 'écrire', 'agir': Mallarmé's affirmation in *Sur L'Idéal à vingt ans* lacks only 'changer' to complete a Sartrean programme of commitment. And indeed, in Sartre's evolving definition of the committed function of literature his reading of Mallarmé plays a crucial role. For while 'Orphée noir', as we have seen, is a major acknowledgement of the possibility of committed poetry, and while in *Saint Genet* the aesthete is transformed into the 'écrivain', *L'Engagement de Mallarmé* (contemporary in genesis with the former, contemporary in elaboration with the latter)[28] may be considered as the complement and supplement of both. Mallarmé, indeed, offers a more extreme test-case. Since in his work the transformation of existing social values is not thematically dominant, the poetic act itself must be seen to be constructively critical if poetry and commitment are to be reconciled. Further, insofar as the theme of subversion is, in Senghor, Césaire or Genet, inseparable from specific linguistic practices, it is Mallarmé, more than the surrealists, who is the *éminence grise* of Sartre's analyses: 'puisque le français manque de termes et de concepts pour définir la négritude, puisque la négritude est silence, ils useront pour l'évoquer de "mots allusifs, jamais directs, se réduisant à du silence égal"'.[29] And insofar as poetic creation enacts an ontological and metaphysical drama, Mallarmé, or his 'emblématique Hamlet' is again the touchstone:

Genet changera par la puissance des mots sa vie de paria en une 'aventure originelle'. On ne saurait se défendre de songer à Mallarmé: Mallarmé aussi veut *alléger* l'être. [. . .] Lui aussi, il veut s'arracher aux anecdotes, aux 'incarnations contemporaines' pour devenir 'un imaginaire héros à demi mêlé à de l'abstraction', personnage unique d'un drame originel [. . .] et qui est le drame de l'homme 'seigneur latent qui ne peut devenir' et de 'l'antagonisme du rêve [sic] avec les fatalités à son existence départies par le malheur.'[30]

It is in the context of existential biography that the manuscript of *L'Engagement de Mallarmé* must first be situated – as an attempt to 'affronter dans le concret l'interprétation de la psychanalyse et celle du marxisme' (*EM*, p. 184): an 'affrontement' which is eventually partially reconciled in a Hegelian analysis.[31] (Sartre, however, recognises the impossibility of a fully Hegelian synthesis.) For in placing the experience of the writer in an elaborated socio-political context, *L'Engagement de Mallarmé* goes further than *Saint Genet*, anticipating the still more sustained attempts at synthesis of 'Question de méthode' (1957) and *L'Idiot de la famille* (1971–2), and demonstrating that Sartre increasingly emphasises the reconciliation in the writer of 'l'universel' and 'le singulier' – a prerequisite for commitment.

Mallarmé's commitment is partly demonstrated by negative implication, for Sartre contends that Mallarmé's immediate predecessors and contemporaries – the poetic 'génération de 1850' – failed to effect this reconciliation. In a peremptory, sweepingly polemical and superficially Marxist account of the 'superstructure' of Second Empire society and its aftermath, Sartre maintains that institutional changes (the fall of the monarchy), ideologies (in philosophy, the growth of materialism and of a 'nominalisme désespéré'; in religion the 'death' of God), culture (the marginal situation of the artist), and class attitudes (the professed but hollow egalitarianism of the bourgeoisie; the *ressentiment* of the *petite-bourgeoisie*; the 'false consciousness' of both) are all interrelated. In turn they are themselves related to a complex of poetic attitudes, themes and functions: the sterility of the poet (as theme or as actual experience); the sense that poetry, no longer a mode of knowledge, has lost its religious and social vocation; an emphasis on technique and artifice at the expense of inspiration and spontaneity; an ascetic 'refus du bonheur'; misanthropy and élitism; and a negativism which conveniently anticipates cosmic catastrophe ('il paraissait plus commode et moins dangereux de refroidir le Soleil en pensée que de toucher à l'ordre social' (*EM*, p. 178)). Nor does Sartre neglect the 'economic base': competition and the free market interact with an 'atomisme social' which cultivates the solitary and the incommunicable. The poverty of the *petit-bourgeois* poet may reinforce asceticism. Metaphysical alienation and economic alienation coincide: 'Et quand il [the poet] s'aliène à l'Absolu, affectant de considérer l'Idéal comme essentiel et son Ego comme inessentiel, il ressemble encore à ses parents qui se sont aliénés pour toujours à l'invisible Capital' (p. 174).

However, despite the allusion to economic alienation, Sartre's analysis is of course *marxisant* rather than Marxist in the 'orthodox' sense of, at least, the Parti Communiste Français. Sartre rejects a causally determining relationship between 'economic base' and 'superstructure', or between social milieu and individual response:

he maintains that those writers who seem to illustrate the orthodox 'reflection' theory of Marxism do so through their own collusion, their own choice of passivity and escapism rather than of *dépassement*: 'Aucun d'eux n'est capable de résumer en une tension suprême, les aspects multiples et contradictoires d'une situation et d'un choix. [. . .] A cause de cela, ils deviennent des "populaires", représentations collectives qui tirent leur expérience de la seule conjoncture historique, bref des superstructures qui ne sont guère plus que des reflets du social' (p. 179).[32] The Marxist category of 'false consciousness' seems inadequate to explain their lack of commitment. Likewise, dialectical materialism offers no solution. If we may anticipate the Hegelian terminology which later becomes dominant in Sartre's argument, we may say that to rescue poetry in an active *Aufhebung* from this 'objectivité passive', Sartre (or History?) needs the mediation of a voluntarist and an extremist. He finds him in Mallarmé. It is Mallarmé who eclipses Marx: 'si l'idée poétique devient en quelqu'un une maladie mortelle et volontaire, si une conscience vaste et lucide en fait tenir ensemble toutes les nuances, dans l'unité d'un même acte, elle échappera aux interprétations marxistes et au conditionnement social' (p. 179). The limits of a Marxist explanation of the 'universel' have been reached: can psychoanalysis offer a supplementary method which will reconcile the 'singulier', the 'destinée personnelle' of the subject, with the 'moment de l'histoire sociale'? Sartre seeks to go beyond the scepticism of *La Grande Morale* and to establish their 'action réciproque'. Such a reciprocity assumes that both the personal and the social must be actively, rather than passively, 'lived'.

Sartre's 'thèmes collectifs' are powerfully energised by Mallarmé. Readers of Mallarmé will be able to furnish their own examples of his intense experience and conscious *dépassement*, particularly since the publication of the *Correspondance*. Sartre explicitly regrets its absence at the time of his own reading (p. 189), and most of his representative instances (culled largely from Henri Mondor's life of Mallarmé and quoted, apparently, from memory) will by now be familiar ones. Thus, the metaphysical 'ideology' of the 'death' of God is lived as an individual and physical drama: '"Une lutte terrible avec ce vieux et méchant plumage, terrassé heureusement, Dieu! Son aile osseuse par une agonie plus vigoureuse que je ne l'eusse soupçonné chez lui m'avait emporté dans des Ténèbres. Je tombais, victorieux"' (p. 192).[33] The philosophical struggle of materialism and idealism is enacted (but the free paraphrase introduces purely Sartrean overtones – the emphases are mine): 'Bref seule existe la Matière, dans son absurde et perpétuel présent. Nous en sommes de "vaines formes". Certes "bien sublimes"; pour avoir inventé l'Ame et Dieu. "Mais bien *absurdes* aussi, car la Matière, en nous et par nous s'élance forcément vers *l'Idéal* [for Rêve] qu'elle sait n'être pas"' (pp. 192–3; *C* I, p. 207). The poetic theme of sterility intensifies the experience of creative impotence: '"*Hérodiade*, œuvre solitaire, m'avait stérilisé"'; 'un sujet effrayant,' Sartre might have added, 'dont les sensations, quand elles sont vives, sont amenées jusqu'à l'atrocité' (*EM*, p. 191; *C* I, pp. 166 and 161). The economic plight of the *poète-fonctionnaire* becomes a physical sensation: 'la vraie et bonne misère, [. . .] en me promenant par la nuque à travers tout ce qui n'est pas ma vocation, m'a fait [. . .] épuiser les vilenies et les mécomptes des choses extérieures' (*C* I, p. 342). The social attitude of *petit-bourgeois ressentiment* is expressed but transcended by the 'Elu' of *La Cour*: '"le seul, au nom de qui des changements sociaux, la révolution, s'accomplirent pour que surgi il se présentât librement, sans encombre, vît et sût"' (*EM*, p. 192; *O.c.*, p. 414).

The active 'assuming' of the historical situation does not in itself, however, ensure the reciprocity of the personal and the social. To establish their interrelationship, Sartre implicitly anticipates the theory of mediation outlined in 'Question de méthode' and elaborated in *L'Idiot de la famille*: a theory in which the institution of the family is central, in which the role of affectivity and of the *vécu* is recognised, and which involves the development of a psychoanalytic method: 'la famille, en effet, est constituée dans et par le mouvement général de l'Histoire et vécue d'autre part comme un absolu dans la profondeur et l'opacité de l'enfance' and, in turn: 'La psychanalyse, à l'intérieur d'une totalisation dialectique, renvoie d'un côté aux structures objectives, aux conditions matérielles, et, de l'autre, à l'action de notre indépassable enfance sur notre vie d'adulte' (*CRD*, pp. 47 and 48). The psychoanalytic method which Sartre has in mind in the Mallarmé manuscript is, however, like his Marxism, again far from orthodox: although he refers to Freudian concepts (the 'work of mourning', the Oedipus complex, identification, regression), he often does so in order to expose their inadequacy or their irrelevance. But his criticisms, in arguments which will be familiar from *L'Etre et le Néant*,[34] go beyond points of specific interpretation. He objects more fundamentally to what he sees as the Freudian notion of the subject as a biologically conditioned, passive and atomistic aggregate of supposedly irreducible elements which are linked by mechanical and contingent 'relations de contiguïté' rather than by 'la totalité des relations synthétiques d'intériorité' (*EM*, p. 184).[35] (This notion, Sartre believes, is itself part of a positivist and empiricist 'superstructure'.) At the 'applied' level, although he acknowledges the links between manifest and latent content (p. 183), he takes to task those critics who attempt a 'dream analysis' of texts by deciphering a 'coded' series of universal symbolic relationships. (We can perhaps infer that Freudians, for Sartre, fail to account for the uniqueness of the 'singulier'.) He finds Charles Mauron's interpretation of *Un Coup de dés* particularly suspect ('On veut que le *Coup de Dés* soit un poème "œdipien" parce que "la mer est un des symboles les plus fréquents de la mère"' (p. 183))[36] for what might at first seem to be a curiously tangential reason: because it fails to take into account the derivative character in Mallarmé's *early* poetry of the sea imagery inspired by Baudelaire. His objection is in fact an oddly circuitous way of contending, not altogether originally, that poetic themes may become absorbed into the 'superstructure' (i.e. the 'universel') but that they may be subsequently revivified and lucidly transformed. Such is Mallarmé's case: 'Si le poète a marqué [les motifs poétiques], c'est *par son travail*, par trente ans d'une réflexion qui peu à peu leur a conféré des significations nouvelles' (p. 183). Hence, the imagery of sea and shipwreck in *Brise marine*, far from reflecting fixed and reiterated obsessions, finds new 'fonctions symboliques' in later poems (*Salut, Au seul souci de voyager, A la nue accablante tu, Un Coup de dés*). For in the meantime, apart from the '"complexité marine et stellaire"' (p. 184; *O.c.*, p. 435) of *Igitur*, and given the pervasiveness of the '"rêverie aquatique"' (*EM*, p. 184; *C* I, p. 191), 'l'eau semble tout entière engagée dans sa fonction de miroir. Elle est eau dormante, fleuve calme ou lac ou bassin; elle se congèle ou se liquéfie selon les besoins' (*EM*, p. 184). However, symbolic dynamism interacts with psychological evolution and thematic change: 'lorsque le narcissisme du jeune poète a cédé la place à la conception tragique du héros, le pur *milieu* du reflet s'est changé en puissance inhumaine de l'extériorité', 'l'obsession chaque jour croissante du Naufrage [. . .] figurera, dans les toutes dernières années, l'infini désordre de la matière et le règne du Hasard' (p. 184). This 'esquisse d'une critique thématique', although directed against a reductive approach, fails nevertheless to recognise the complexity and polyvalence of Mallarmé's 'rêverie aquatique'.[37] Sartre's own interpretation, apart from expressing his dualistic tendencies, has clearly been dominated by the need to find a transition in Mallarmé from narcissism to a self-transcending concern with cosmic and metaphysical drama. (Of the poems mentioned by Sartre, *Salut* and *Au seul souci* are particularly difficult to account for in terms of his schema.) But even if we accept Sartre's over-simplification, is the transition from narcissism to a broader metaphysical vision, or the modification of a 'thème collectif' 'par son travail' enough, we may ask, to qualify Mallarmé as a committed poet? It does at least appear that the transformation is conscious and active, that it is effected 'sous l'influence de préoccupations d'*adulte*, et que la transformation ait été consciente d'elle-même' (p. 184).

None the less, it seems implicit in Sartre's argument that the consciousness attributed to Mallarmé is no longer the consciousness of *L'Etre et le Néant*. Given that Sartre now recognises (as he failed to do in his earlier work) the opacity of childhood, his earlier uncompromising rejection of the unconscious,[38] whether infantile or adult, becomes increasingly problematic, if not self-contradictory. On the one hand 'il y a en effet un inconscient au cœur même de la conscience' (p. 183), on the other 'il ne s'agit pas de quelque puissance ténébreuse et nous savons que la conscience est conscience de part en part' (p. 183). Sartre still believes that such consciousness is accessible to a 'compréhension préontologique' (*EN*, p. 658; *EM*, p. 184), if not to explicit knowledge and conceptualisation,[39] but the modes of reflection and activity available to consciousness have radically changed. Whereas in *L'Etre et le Néant* 'tout est là, lumineux, la réflexion jouit de tout, saisit tout' (*EN*, p. 658), now the 'inconscient' which is nevertheless 'conscience' is defined as a 'finitude intériorisée' (*EM*, p. 183), and its activity is sharply attenuated by 'le non-savoir': 'Mallarmé est affecté et flétri jusqu'au cœur de son intimité par ce que nous savons *aujourd'hui* et qu'il n'a pas su' (p. 183). He is the 'subjectivité ignorante', if not the 'subjectivité ignorée' of *La Grande Morale* (*GM*, p. 257). Sartre has clearly modified the relationship of consciousness and situation postulated in *L'Etre et le Néant* and basic to the argument of *Qu'est-ce que la littérature?*: 'puisqu'il [le pour-soi] est aussi celui qui *se fait être*, quelle que soit donc la situation où il se trouve, le pour-soi doit assumer entièrement cette situation [. . .] avec la conscience orgueilleuse d'en être l'auteur, car les pires inconvénients ou les pires menaces qui risquent d'atteindre ma personne n'ont de sens que par mon projet' (*EN*, p. 639).

Such a modification should not, however, be taken to suggest that Mallarmé reprehensibly fails to meet the strenuous specifications of the earlier Sartre – those expressed in his savage insistence on the free choice and the total responsibility of the seven-year-old Baudelaire. Rather, Sartre is already beginning to think in terms of the *vécu*, that more complex and humane definition of 'la réalité humaine' which characterises the experience of the committed writer of *Plaidoyer* and the Flaubert of *L'Idiot de la famille*: 'L'introduction de la notion de vécu représente un effort pour conserver cette "présence à soi" qui me paraît indispensable à l'existence de tout fait psychique, présence en même temps si opaque, si aveugle à elle-même qu'elle est aussi "absence de soi"'.[40] The *vécu* no longer involves a unilateral 'assumption' or choice, nor even a simply reciprocal relationship: it is, as we saw earlier, a dialectical 'totalising' of objective structures and of an 'enracinement particulier', an 'effort d'universalisation qui naît de la singularité et la conserve en la niant'.[41] It is a synthesis of activity and passivity, conditioning and autonomy. And already, Mallarmé, passively 'affecté et flétri', modifies and creates the 'objective structures' of poetry 'par son travail' (*EM*, p. 183). Moreover, despite its relative opacity, the *vécu* is still accessible to 'compréhension' but not to the subject's explicit knowledge nor to direct denotation: 'la plus haute forme de compréhension du vécu peut engendrer son propre langage – qui sera toujours inadéquat mais qui aura souvent la structure métaphorique du rêve'.[42]

But Sartre would still reject, as he does in the Mallarmé manuscript, the deciphering of such metaphoric structures in terms of instinctual or biological drives. The alternative categories which he originally postulated are familiar ones. At the ontological level, the irreducible 'drive' is the desire to be God, to fill the 'lack' of the *pour-soi* – a desire which grounds our efforts to possess, to create and to know, and of which all empirical desires are symbolic. At the factual level of the 'given', the fundamental project is a free 'assumption' of the subject's alienated being-for-others. But while the 'relation [. . .] de l'existant à l'être' (p. 184) remains basic to the psychoanalysis of Mallarmé, a number of its more fundamental specifications have been implicitly transformed. Sartre no longer stresses the originally basic negating function of consciousness, but its more positively relational activities; the rationalistic abstraction of free choice becomes a 'sensibilité vivante et créatrice' (p. 185); relationships with others are now grounded in *Mitsein* (p. 185) – a co-operative being-with-others which was explicitly rejected in *L'Etre et le Néant* in favour of an antagonistic *être-pour-autrui*,[43] and which clearly offers a more propitious basis for commitment.

These changes are crucially implicit in Sartre's hypothetical reconstruction of Mallarmé's early years – a reconstruction which, moving from ostensible description to the imaginative recreation of an individual experience, becomes a universalising myth in its imagery of the primitive and the sacred, but which also purports to offer a normative account of infancy and childhood. Now consciousness is no longer 'nihilating' nor negating, as it irremediably was in *L'Etre et le Néant*; there is no fissure in its presence to the world; the mediation of the mother – embodiment of a gentle Nature – is paradoxically felt as warm immediacy, as a bulwark against the alienation of alterity. The Sartrean psychoanalytic category of appropriation and assimilation ('la mère mange le monde, et l'enfant la mange à son tour' (p. 185))[44] does not result from the frustration of ontological desire, but from its fulfilment; the potential rivalry of the Oedipal triangle is forestalled in unproblematic identification; *le regard*, far from being a sinister threat, is a refuge; vision, far from implying an imperceptible distance between self and world, is the medium of secure and luminous affinity (p. 185).[45]

Sartre finds the quality of the mother's vision ('éblouissant miroitement à la surface de l'être' (p. 185)) and the child's response to the world transmuted by her vision, in the lines of *Toast funèbre* and of *Le Nénuphar blanc*:

A chaque pas il retrouve, épars dans les jardins de cet astre

> '. . . Pluie et diamant, le regard diaphane
> Resté là sur ces fleurs dont nulle ne se fane.'

Pour lui 'la buée d'argent glaçant des saules n'est que la limpidité du regard (maternel) habitué à chaque feuille'.

(p. 185; O.c., pp. 55 and 284)

Though deciphering a 'latent content', Sartre still follows his characteristic and deliberate method of illuminating his subject's 'past' by reference to his 'future', rather than by the reverse, perhaps more typically Freudian, procedure. Further, it would appear that the most negatively charged of Sartrean categories – *le regard* – can only be given positive value by invoking the most fundamental human relationship of all: one which Sartre claims he had himself experienced as the love of a mother 'non seulement dévouée mais aussi totalement pleine de tendresse'.[46]

Consciousness, then, is no longer a flicker of negation, nor being a sickening superfluity. The terms of Sartrean dualism, we discover, are not after all ontological but rather genetic categories: 'les enfants heureux découvrent la plénitude comme une donnée immédiate; la négation, l'absence et toutes les formes du Néant leur apparaissent ensuite sous l'aspect d'insuffisances locales, de lacunes provisoires, de contradictions volatiles; bref, le Néant est postérieur à l'Etre' (*EM*, p. 186). The 'douce confusion natale' (p. 185) is the *préhistoire* of negating consciousness which will itself be subsumed, in Sartre's later thought, within the *vécu*. Sartre has moved away, too, from his earlier assertion of radical responsibility ('je *choisis* d'être né' (*EN*, p. 641), 'en naissant [. . .] je suis responsable de la place que je prends' (p. 576)). Will this attenuation of responsibility also attenuate commitment?

Mallarmé's 'history' begins with his mother's death. Sartre takes issue again with Mauron, who sees the death of Mallarmé's sister as the decisive event of his life.[47] For Sartre the death of a parent is the most crucial experience in its radical consequences for our existential relation to the world – a relation which, it may be noted, while 'conscious' in the Sartrean sense, is expressed here entirely in terms of a 'lived' rather than an explicitly reflective or empirically affective response:

elle [the death of a parent] révèle une fois pour toutes notre possibilité de n'être-plus-au-monde comme un des caractères de l'être-dans-le-monde; ce dévoilement de la condition humaine comme *paradoxe* [. . .] peut agir sur notre *distance aux objets*, sur notre intuition de l'être, sur le goût même que nous avons pour nous-mêmes; il peut relâcher le lien au monde, l'invertir, accroître ou diminuer notre obliquité par rapport à l'expérience. (*EM*, p. 185)

For the young Mallarmé, the death of his mother brutally inverts the priority of *l'être* over *le néant*: an inversion which Sartre, alluding to Merleau-Ponty's discovery of 'des maladies du Cogito' (p. 185),[48] characterises as pathological. Mallarmé consequently experiences not a 'désir d'être' but a 'liaison [. . .] du désir au Néant', reducing the world to an undifferentiated neutral background ('"l'évidence de tout l'être pareil"' (p. 186; *O.c.*, p. 648)) which is impervious to the perpetual evanescence of the mother – a reduction and an evanescence relived with empathy, it would seem, by Sartre, as Mallarmé's words become his own ('voltiger', 'palpiter', 'trembler', 'éparpiller', 'volatile', 'vertigineux', 'miroitement', 'ombre') in a décor abandoned by 'l'absente de

toute maison' which recalls the 'meubles vacants' and the 'glace hor-
riblement nulle' of *Igitur* (*O.c.*, p. 440).

In his sixth year, then, Mallarmé 'conçoit l'être-dans-le-monde
comme un exil' (*EM*, p. 186): a formulation which neatly evades
the issue of 'responsible' choice while conveying the 'sense-giving'
rather than purely passive nature of the child's response. The
symptoms, too, of this 'maladie du Cogito' sustain a precarious
balance between activity and passivity: a preference for indirect
modes of knowledge rather than intuition; a vain attempt to re-
capture the mother's unifying vision of the world in a series of
'fausses synthèses évanescentes' (p. 186); an alienation of the self
not to the other but to the death of another; a static sense of the
déjà vécu (p. 186).

The symptoms persist, for the healing 'work of mourning' is
frustrated by familial and social 'mediations' which accentuate the
lack of dynamism of the child's affectivity. The father and grand-
father reflect back to him the apparently ineluctable future of the
Administrator: 'carrière à laquelle on me destina dès les langes'
(*O.c.*, p. 661). But the possibly revivifying response of revolt is
inhibited, following his mother's death, by a wordless sense of the
'creuse inanité de tout': a sense unconceptualised (or repressed?)
and therefore indirectly expressed in, for instance, the symbolism
of *Igitur* (victim, through his family, of '"une accablante sensation
de fini"' (*EM*, p. 187; *O.c.*, p. 440), forbidden by his mother to go
down the 'corridors oubliés depuis l'enfance' (*O.c.*, p. 450)). Only
rarely does intensity find expression, and then still obliquely: for
instance in the highly over-determined, condensed yet consciously
reworked evocation of family relationships disclosed in the successive versions of *Réminiscence* or in the menacingly ambivalent
compassion for the future assassin of *Pauvre enfant pâle*[49] (*EM*, pp.
189 and 187).

But that intensity, whether latent, oblique or icy, is the precon-
dition for a fragile salvation and an unforeseen commitment. So,
paradoxically, is the initial experience of sterility and of an 'âme
purement passive' (*O.c.*, p. 261), as Sartre seeks to show in a dialectical argument which centres on the years of crisis and 'conversion' at Tournon but which spirals outwards to encompass
Mallarmé's earlier and later writing. For sterility and passivity
move, first, into an antithetical sense of the imperative to create a
'moi pur' through poetry. Sartre develops critically the Kantian
comparisons made by others (alluding, presumably, to Valéry),[50]
by assimilating the moral and poetic imperative to the Mallarmean

Ideal, whose exigencies elicit the despair and aspiration which motivate the early poetry. However, since, for Sartre, Mallarmé's 'Idéal', as the 'Rien pur' (*EM*, p. 191), lacks even the theoretical content of Kant's formalism, it cannot establish the autonomy of the poet's will, but simply reflects back to him his impotence and negativity. Although for Mallarmé the imperative persists, the even more extreme attempt to resituate consciousness through the total recreation of self and world (the '"devoir de tout recréer [. . . pour avérer qu'on est bien là où l'on doit être"]' (p. 191; *O.c.*, p. 481)) must also fail. 'Une pensée, quand bien même elle viserait l'universel ou découvrirait une éternelle vérité, est un événement de l'âme, historique et singulier, dont le motif doit être cherché dans notre être-là contingent' (*EM*, p. 191). But despite this insistence, Sartre's ambivalence is clear in his response to the more arduous anguish of Mallarmé's struggle, not with humble contingency, but with 'le Hasard', and to the heroic metaphysical suicide of *Igitur* – a mythical and exemplary rather than a historical drama.

How, then, can Mallarmé reconcile his desired universality, his impersonal mediation of 'l'Univers spirituel' (*C* I, p. 242) with historical action? By moving, Sartre implies, from pure negativity to a critical reflection which is in turn the source of change – a movement expressed in the 'Hegelian' letters to Cazalis and Lefébure of 14 and 16 May 1867 (*C* I, pp. 240–50). It originates in the discovery of 'la Poésie critique' and culminates in the dialectic of classical, renaissance and modern art – of Phidias:

la Beauté complète et inconsciente, unique et immuable,

of Leonardo:

la Beauté ayant été mordue au cœur depuis le christianisme par la Chimère, et douloureusement renaissant avec un sourire rempli de mystère, mais de mystère forcé et qu'elle *sent* être la condition de son être,

and of Mallarmé:

la Beauté, enfin, ayant par la science de l'homme, retrouvé dans l'Univers entier ses *phases corrélatives*, ayant eu le suprême mot d'elle, s'étant rappelé l'horreur secrète qui la forçait à sourire – du temps du Vinci, et à sourire mystérieusement – souriant mystérieusement maintenant, mais de bonheur et avec la quiétude éternelle de la *Vénus de Milo* retrouvée ayant su l'idée du mystère dont *La Joconde* ne savait que la sensation fatale.

(*C* I, p. 246)

For Sartre, this dialectic is essentially Hegelian: 'quiétude dans l'immédiat, passage au médiat et inquiétude, réconciliation en soi et pour soi dans l'Absolu-sujet. Une seule différence mais capitale: l'Absolu-sujet, ici, c'est Mallarmé' (*EM*, p. 193).[51]

This is the moment of Mallarmé's 'conversion', and is also the turning point of Sartre's own 'dialectic': a movement from the earlier quasi-Marxist and psychoanalytic analyses to a modified Hegelianism. Through Mallarmé's negation of the pure negativity generated in him by his family, he becomes the critical consciousness which transforms art and history. Yet this grandiose role must be played out at a human level: for all Sartre's hyperbole he asserts that Mallarmé, like himself, eventually rejects the abstractions of the final Hegelian synthesis. Metaphysical impersonality becomes a humanity shared with humility, critical appraisal and pride: '"l'Elu, [c'est] quiconque veut. Toi ou moi. . ."' (p. 192; *O.c.*, p. 414).[52]

But in Sartre's theory of commitment, critical consciousness must also be free consciousness. Hegel, again, helps to demonstrate Mallarmé's active freedom: the freedom of the sceptic rather than of the stoic. For Hegel, stoic 'formalism' is purely the empty concept of freedom, which does not penetrate into the variety and plenitude of concrete being; it is a form of abstract negation. Scepticism, however – 'antithèse du Stoïcisme vide et symbole de la Conversion mallarméenne' (*EM*, p. 194) – is

'la réalisation de ce dont le stoïcisme est seulement le concept; il est l'expérience effectivement réelle de ce qu'est la liberté de la pensée; cette liberté est *en soi* le négatif. [. . .] La pensée devient la pensée parfaite anéantissant l'être du monde dans *la multiple variété de ses déterminations*, et la négativité de la conscience de soi libre, au sein de cette configuration multiforme de la vie, devient négativité réelle'. (p. 194)[53]

Sartre seems to claim, then (although this is the most elliptical part of his argument) that Mallarmé's critical negation is no longer abstract: it takes place within time and in relation to a specific content: his 'négation pure [. . .] doit nécessairement redescendre dans les choses et s'y manifester sous forme d'un travail négatif' (p. 194). As a mode of 'work' and of action, rather than of representation, his writing ultimately negates the nihilism which Sartre sweepingly attributes to his early work:

Le premier mouvement de Mallarmé a été le recul du dégoût et la condamnation universelle de toutes les formes de la vie. Mais, en relisant 'Hérodiade', il s'aperçoit tout à coup que la négation universelle équivaut à l'absence de négation. Nier est un acte. Et tout acte doit s'insérer dans le temps et s'exercer sur un contenu particulier. La négation de *tout* ne peut passer pour une activité destructrice: elle est la simple représentation de la notion négative en général. (p. 194)

Yet, while it is at this point that the manuscript breaks off, Sartre's argument here is in effect 'continued' in an earlier section. In Hegel's *Phenomenology of Spirit* sceptical consciousness is not yet fully aware of its own positivity nor of its self-contradictory nature as, on the one hand, certain of its freedom and, on the other, existing as a wholly contingent, single, separate, empirical consciousness. This full awareness is disclosed in the mode of 'unhappy consciousness', the next transition in Hegel's system towards the remote and implicit goal of Absolute Spirit – which Mallarmé once thought he had attained. Sartre, however, does not follow through Hegel's dialectical progression from scepticism to unhappy consciousness, although, in Hegel, that paradoxical oscillation between unchanging self-certainty and a determinate, changing, non-essential consciousness eventually becomes 'consciente pour soi de la réconciliation de son existence singulière avec l'universel',[54] thereby anticipating, albeit at a more abstract level, Sartre's 'universel singulier'. Sartre simply asserts that Mallarmé *is* 'la Conscience malheureuse' (p. 192), the battleground of metaphysical contradiction: 'en lui vont s'affronter, pour le compte de tous, le Singulier et l'Universel, la Cause et la Fin, l'Idée et la Matière, le Déterminisme et l'Autonomie, le Temps et l'Eternel, l'Etre et le Devoir-Etre' (p. 192). However, it is Mallarmé in his mundane vicissitudes who may move towards Hegel's 'conscience pour soi de la réconciliation' and become the exemplary 'témoin': 'le professeur chahuté', 'le fonctionnaire humilié', 'l'homme de ressentiment', 'l'impuissant', 'prêtera ses yeux et sa pensée à la Poésie et à l'Humanité pour qu'elles puissent s'atteindre et se voir' (p. 192).

But the process of reconciliation can never be complete, for the 'universel singulier' must live in and through the paradox of language, which man creates, but which he experiences as a mode of alienation. It is through Mallarmé's struggle to free language from its contingencies that Sartre learns to recognise its resistance as an element of the 'pratico-inerte' – a recognition not developed until *Critique de la raison dialectique*[55] but anticipated in *L'Engagement de Mallarmé*: 'Sur quoi travaillerait-on sinon sur des combinaisons de hasard, dont la dispersion même et l'extériorité réciproque contestent le tour synthétique qu'on leur veut donner? Et *avec quoi* sinon avec des mots hasardeux et fatidiques, agglutinés dans nos mémoires selon d'antiques affinités que nous subissons sans les connaître?' (p. 192). The transparency and directness of prose is no longer possible. But Mallarmé's poetry suggests the solution – the allusiveness which enables the poets of 'Orphée noir' to subvert the language of oppression, and which the writer of *Plaidoyer* must exploit in his mission to 'rendre compte du *tout* sur le mode du non-savoir, du vécu' (*S* VIII, pp. 452–3); 'l'écrivain [. . .] donne à saisir sous forme d'un objet (l'œuvre) la condition humaine prise à son niveau radical (l'être-dans-le-monde). Mais cet être-dans-le-monde n'est pas présenté comme je fais en ce moment par des approximations verbales qui visent encore l'universel [. . .]. L'écrivain ne peut que témoigner du sien en produisant un objet ambigu qui le propose allusivement' (p. 444). Mallarmé's philological reverie on rich pluralities of meaning suggests to the Sartre of *Plaidoyer* the positive value of ambiguity: 'l'écrivain [. . .] se sert de l'histoire des vocables et de la syntaxe pour créer des sursignifications aberrantes' (p. 448) – a value earlier dismissed in *Qu'est-ce que la littérature?*, in which he recommends a 'nettoyage analytique qui débarrasse [les mots] de leurs sens adventices' (*S* II, p. 305). It is Mallarmé, again in *Les Mots anglais*, who defines language as the medium of the *vécu* – that transparent 'présence à soi' and opaque 'absence de soi': '"le langage, distinguant l'homme du reste des choses, imitera encore celui-ci en tant que factice dans l'essence non moins que naturel, réfléchi que fatal, volontaire qu'aveugle"' (*EM*, p. 193; *O.c.*, p. 901). And in his practice of writing, Mallarmé revolutionises for Sartre its very 'conditions of possibility': 'Depuis qu'il a décidé d'écrire pour lancer le Verbe dans une aventure dont on ne revient pas, il n'est pas un écrivain si modeste soit-il, qui se risque dans un livre sans risquer la Parole avec lui. La Parole ou l'Homme: c'est tout un' (*EM*, p. 193). The poet has become the exemplary writer.

In his intense confrontation of private despair and of the 'organisation sociale inachevée' (*O.c.*, p. 866) of his time, Mallarmé changes poetry, language and, thereby, history. He also, *toute proportion gardée*, changes Sartre.

POSTSCRIPT

For Sartre, then, Mallarmé's exemplary writing, and all writing since, risks the highest stakes: 'la Parole ou l'Homme'. Yet Sartre's younger contemporaries, structuralist and post-structuralist alike, claim that these two key concepts are precisely those which he himself failed to put in question. His more superficial critics would see him as the obstinate exponent of a facile humanism, and as the victim of a naive view of language. For Sartre, it is suggested, the human subject is the centre of enquiry and the source of meaning, fully present to itself; transparent language gives direct access to thought and world, and to the meaning which is present in the mind of the speaker at the moment of speech. Sartre is castigated for failing or refusing to see that the subject is simply the point of intersection of a number of forces which work through it, or that language is a mobile, differential system whose elements refer not to 'truth' or 'reality' but to other elements within that system. In short, Sartre is thought to represent in a pure and dogmatic form the 'logocentric' tradition of the Western 'metaphysics of presence'. The characteristics of that tradition are most powerfully defined, as a prelude to its critique, by Jacques Derrida. It is a tradition which takes

[le] sens de l'être en général comme *présence*, avec toutes les sous-déterminations qui dépendent de cette forme générale et qui organisent en elle leur système et leur enchaînement historial (présence de la chose au regard comme *eidos*, présence comme substance/essence/existence (*ousia*), présence temporelle comme pointe (*stigmè*) du maintenant ou de l'instant (*nun*), présence à soi du cogito, conscience, subjectivité, coprésence de l'autre et de soi, intersubjectivité comme phénomène intentionnel de l'ego).[1]

Logocentric thinking, it is argued, is organised in terms of oppositions of which one term is given priority: examples in Sartre's work, interpreted from this point of view, would be perception/imagination, presence/absence, activity/passivity,

198

reason/emotion, prose/poetry. It is a tradition which takes the laws of identity and contradiction as the unquestioned framework of its logic. Within this tradition, Sartre is seen by his critics to exemplify a misguided assumption of mastery over the object of knowledge, with the authority of the subject as the source of that mastery: an assumption of which Sartre's emphasis on 'totalisation' is taken to be a symptom.[2] Such a centring of cognitive control within the subject ignores, it is suggested, the power of discourse itself. It also rejects the open ambiguity, the recognition of undecidability and the displacement of logical categories which characterise a 'deconstructive' method – a method calculated to undo the rigid dualities of traditional thought in order to suggest their permeability, and to reveal the differences within, rather than between, each term.

The foregoing chapters will have indicated that such views fail to do justice to Sartre's originality and complexity. The Sartre whose writing is alleged to postulate a unitary subject (as distinct from the 'split' subject, the 'decentred' subject or the 'disappearing' subject of his apparently more radical contemporaries) is a straw man. As we have seen, the Sartrean subject as Ego is a paradoxical construct created by consciousness in an attempt to escape from its own temporal dispersal and from its pre-personal insubstantiality. It is a construct which may at any moment dissolve – a dissolution enacted syntactically in, for instance, Roquentin's elision of the 'I' (see above, pp. 36 and 43). Consciousness is a 'glissement hors de soi' (*S* I, p. 33). The precarious act of reflection is itself far from unitary. Self-knowledge – a potential source of stability – is secondary, and its findings only probable: consciousness's 'certain' grasp of its own activity is a form of (self-)questioning. The 'soi' of the *pour-soi* is never, *pace* Derrida, fully present to itself: 'le pour-soi est toujours en suspens parce que son être est en perpétuel sursis' (*EN*, p. 713). For Sartre, the body as subject is not a basis for the stability of the self, but an uneasy vacillation between subjectivity and objectivity, fluctuating between instrumentality, resistance and complicity. In its lack of self-coincidence, consciousness invalidates the laws of identity.

The status of the subject as the source of historical knowledge and of social action is equally unstable. It is a 'subjectivité ignorante ignorée' dispersed in the 'prolifération décentrée' of events. Its attempts to explain, or even to represent or narrate, are paradoxically both frustrated and sustained by 'le non-savoir'. For Roquentin, the writing of history is as impossible a project as the writing of the self, while writing as creation or as would-be self-discovery is always haunted by traces of past writing. The authority of authorship as the source of truth, or, simply, of the text, is questioned: 'le poète est absent' (*S* II, p. 69). The 'truth' of Sartre's study of Flaubert is fictional (*S* x, p. 94). The author, whether of creative or discursive writing – if the distinction can still be said to hold – can never fully constitute or 'read' the meaning of his own writing.

Sartre's elusive subject cannot be said to be the central source of meaning, nor can language be said to be the transparent medium of that meaning. Such a view can be derived only from the first short section of *Qu'est-ce que la littérature?*. Elsewhere, both in his direct discussions of language and in the metalinguistic significance of his own writing, that view is radically questioned. The sense of the sense-giving word is never present in the object or quality which it designates: 'le vert *n'est jamais* vert' (*EN*, p. 243), nor is it fully present in consciousness at the moment when it speaks or writes. Would-be performative language – language as instrument, language as persuasion, language as seduction – depends upon but is inhibited by the codes which constrain its precarious transactions. And if meaning sometimes seems immanent in the *mot-chose* of poetry, it is felt as a haunting hesitation between presence and absence.

Sartre's handling of the presence/absence dichotomy belies perhaps most vividly the post-structuralist charge that he organises his thinking in terms of binary oppositions in which the first term is consistently privileged.[3] In other areas too it is clear that his dichotomies may be provisional and labile ones, and that he is intent upon exploring their margins: for instance, the permeable borderlines between imagination and intellection, or between desire, knowledge and creativity. The traditional pairing of concepts may be undermined: emotion, at one level, is seen as active and purposive, rather than passive. The tensions within concepts are brought to light and displace the difference between them. The distinction between emotion and reflection is less crucial than their overlapping interplay, and no more clear-cut than the divisions within each term. The eruption of the magical into the rational undermines the logic of contradiction. Knowledge itself is, as we saw, permeated and exceeded by 'le non-savoir'.

Sartre insists on the provisional nature of our constructs and of the hierarchies in which we seek to order them. He sees his need, and ours, as being to revise them constantly. Why, then, do younger critics charge him with claims of 'mastery' and of would-be total 'cognitive control' – those now apparently discredited goals of traditional philosophical enquiry? At the conceptual level, his emphasis on the 'totalising' function of consciousness may be responsible for such an interpretation. But the totalities created by our acts of consciousness are 'en perpétuelle désagrégation', and our interpretations of the movement of history are 'totalisations détotalisées'. Our attempts to grasp the objects of our consciousness as a totality are self-subverting: they can appear to succeed only in an imaginary world. But, in turn, the 'totalities' created in our imagination and, by extension, in our fictions, are open-ended, unstable or, quite simply, incomplete. Sartre's paradoxical 'mastery' of ellipsis is paralleled by his 'mastery' of the vast, unfinished fragment.

Sartre's assertive style may also suggest a claim to mastery. But it is most marked in polemical contexts where he tends temporarily to consolidate provisional positions which he will later qualify. And it is balanced by an attitude of authorial humility – one which he admires in Mallarmé's rejection of elective uniqueness and in his aspiration to anonymity, and one which he himself adopts when, in Les Mots, he finally refuses to see the writer as hero, or the act of writing as a form of salvation.

Or is such a posture simply a rhetorical ploy – a form of litotes designed to inspire greater confidence in the authority of writer and text? The pervasiveness of rhetoric both in Sartre's theoretical and in his literary texts might confirm such a view and, further, confirm the interdependence of literary and philosophical writing. For the overriding aim of all philosophical writing is to convince, and, short of couching its arguments in formally symbolic language, it will share the methods of persuasion also fundamental to literary writing. But in Sartre, rhetorical figures are not merely forms of persuasion or assertion; they are, additionally, forms of enquiry. Apparent tautologies, the negation of a term by itself, the identity of contradictory propositions, oxymoron, the 'category mistakes' of metaphor – these and other figures contest, in his theoretical work, the traditional limits of logic.[4] Further, his literary works do not so much incorporate as constitute extended figures in which these limits are both lived and transgressed in imagination. At the same time, his texts expose the rhetorical seductiveness of their own procedures. They thereby invite further enquiry into what we are doing when we read Sartre's writing: exploring the moving horizons of the rational and the irrational, of the active and the passive, of cognition and imagination, of complicity and resistance, of ideology and knowledge, of representation and meaning. The themes of Sartre's work are dramatised in the very process of our reading. We are not the recipients of a mastered body of knowledge. And as we are also invited to disclose the mobile relationships between and within his own texts, and between his own texts and those of others, the process of reflecting upon our reading of Sartre can never be complete.

NOTES

Unless otherwise stated, the place of publication for works mentioned below is Paris for books in French and London for those in English.

Introduction

1 See 'A Plea for Excuses', *Philosophical Papers*, Oxford, Clarendon Press, 1961, p. 130.

1 *La Nausée*

1 See Simone de Beauvoir, *La Force de l'âge*, Gallimard, 1960, p. 293.

2 The dates of publication (1938 for *La Nausée*, 1943 for *L'Etre et le Néant*) may not be an accurate guide to the relative dates of composition, but we know from Simone de Beauvoir that Sartre was already working on an early version of *La Nausée* in 1931 (*La Force de l'âge*, p. 111), while the actual preparation of *L'Etre et le Néant*, although based on philosophical research already under way in 1933, did not begin until 1940. A full account of the genesis and publication of *La Nausée* is given in the critical apparatus of Jean-Paul Sartre, *Œuvres romanesques*, éd. Michel Contat et Michel Rybalka, Bibliothèque de la Pléiade, Gallimard, 1981. (My references to *La Nausée* will indicate this edition.) One may safely assume that the writing of *La Nausée* coincided with the development of Sartre's philosophical thinking, but not that it illustrates a body of already fully constituted theory. Many of the ideas elaborated in *L'Etre et le Néant* refer to those of his earlier more exploratory philosophical works, and some of Roquentin's experiences in *La Nausée* can be related to *La Transcendance de l'Ego. Esquisse d'une description phénoménologique*, *Recherches philosophiques*, no. 6, 1936–7 (reprinted in an edition by Sylvie Le Bon, Vrin, 1965), to *Esquisse d'une théorie des émotions*, Hermann, 1939 (reprinted in 1965), and to *L'Imaginaire*, Gallimard, 1940. References will be given to the later editions of the first two works mentioned.

3 I shall concentrate upon the relationships within and between Sartre's own texts. For a more fully intertextual approach see Geneviève Idt,

La Nausée: analyse critique, Hatier, 'Profil d'une œuvre' 18, 1971, particularly ch. 6.

4 At some points, Sartre differentiates between consciousness and *l'être-pour-soi*: the *pour-soi* is the 'fondement ontologique de la conscience' (*EN*, p. 119) and consciousness is the 'noyau instantané' of the *pour-soi* (p. 111). But he frequently uses the terms interchangeably.

5 In *L'Etre et le Néant* Sartre describes contingency and facticity as follows: 'cet en-soi, englouti et néantisé dans l'événement absolu qu'est l'apparition du fondement ou surgissement du pour-soi demeure au sein du pour-soi comme sa contingence originelle. [...] Ainsi le pour-soi est soutenu par une perpétuelle contingence, qu'il reprend à son compte et s'assimile sans jamais pouvoir la supprimer. Cette contingence perpétuellement évanescente de l'en-soi qui hante le pour-soi et le rattache à l'être-en-soi sans jamais se laisser saisir, c'est ce que nous nommerons la *facticité* du pour-soi. C'est cette facticité qui permet de dire qu'il *est*, qu'il *existe*, bien que nous ne puissions jamais la *réaliser* et que nous la saisissions toujours à travers le pour-soi' (*EN*, pp. 124–5). Or, more briefly, facticity is 'le simple *fait* "d'être là"' (p. 126).

6 The typographical device of bracketing, as in 'conscience (du) corps' indicates that the consciousness involved is pre-reflective. Consciousness, by the very fact of being aware of its object, is pre-reflectively (self-)conscious: it is directly and explicitly aware of its object, but only indirectly and inexplicitly aware of its own activity.

7 Sartre distinguishes between several different forms of 'néantisation'. It can however be roughly defined as, first, the act whereby consciousness introduces a 'distance', a 'recul néantisant', between itself and the *en-soi*, thus creating the possibility of conferring meaning upon the *en-soi*, and, secondly, as the sustaining of a 'distance' within consciousness itself – a distance which distinguishes the *pour-soi* from the plenitude of the *en-soi*, and precludes total self-coincidence and identity.

8 I have adopted here the term used by Hazel Barnes in her translation of *L'Etre et le Néant* (*Being and Nothingness*, New York, Philosophical Library, 1956).

9 Sartre's distinctions between different levels of reflection and his theory concerning the constitution of the Ego are already established in *La Transcendance de l'Ego*, but the relationship between reflection, affectivity and the body are only fully elaborated in *L'Etre et le Néant*.

10 Sartre distinguishes sharply between consciousness and knowledge. At the levels both of pre-reflective (self-)consciousness and of pure reflection we do not 'know' ourselves, since we can only have knowledge of a transcendent object. The evidence of consciousness (whether 'conscience (de) soi', consciousness of being conscious of an object, or the intuitive 'présence à soi' of pure reflection) is, however,

certain, whereas empirical and reflective knowledge of an object is secondary, partial and probable. In 'impure' reflection we seek to have knowledge of ourselves by attempting to make ourselves transcendent objects for our own reflection, and the evidence derived from this form of reflection is, again, probable and corrigible. Sartre confuses the issue to some extent by maintaining at one stage in his discussion of pure reflection that it is, after all, 'une connaissance', but he qualifies this by arguing, with a play on words, that such a 'connaissance' is in fact a form of recognition: 'La réflexion est une connaissance, cela n'est pas douteux, elle est pourvue d'un caractère positionnel; elle affirme la conscience réfléchie. Mais [...] sa connaissance est totalitaire, c'est une intuition fulgurante et sans relief, sans point de départ ni point d'arrivée. Tout est donné à la fois dans une sorte de proximité absolue. Ce que nous nommons ordinairement *connaître* suppose des reliefs, des plans, un ordre, une hiérarchie. [...] Mais la réflexion qui nous livre le réfléchi non comme un donné, mais comme l'être que nous avons à être, dans une indistinction sans point de vue, est une connaissance débordée par elle-même et sans explication. En même temps, elle n'est jamais surprise par elle-même, elle ne nous *apprend* rien, elle *pose* seulement. [...] La réflexion est *reconnaissance* plutôt que connaissance. Elle implique une compréhension pré-réflexive de ce qu'elle veut récupérer comme motivation originelle de la récupération' (*EN*, p. 202). See also *EN*, pp. 18 and 19.

11 My italics. Unless otherwise stated, all italics in quotations are those of Sartre.

12 This characteristic of the *objets psychiques* of the Ego is summarised in *La Transcendance de l'Ego*: 'L'Ego [...] est synthèse d'intériorité et de transcendance' (p. 65).

13 The *noema* is the object-referent of an 'intentional' act of consciousness. The act itself is the *noesis*.

14 The term 'participation' is borrowed by Sartre from the anthropological work of Lucien Lévy-Bruhl, where it characterises certain attitudes more easily observed in primitive than in evolved societies, although they are in fact present in every human mind. They are primarily affective in character and involve an indifference to the law of contradiction. This is apparent, for instance, in the notion of a magical 'action à distance', which Sartre, as we shall see, also takes up. Lévy-Bruhl describes these attitudes thus: 'Les objets, les êtres, les phénomènes peuvent être d'une façon incompréhensible pour nous, à la fois eux-mêmes et autre chose qu'eux-mêmes. D'une façon non moins incompréhensible, ils émettent et ils reçoivent des forces, des vertus, des qualités, des actions mystiques, qui se font sentir hors d'eux, sans cesser d'être où elles sont. En d'autres termes, pour cette mentalité, l'opposition entre l'un et le plusieurs, le même et l'autre, n'impose pas la nécessité d'affirmer l'un des termes si l'on nie l'autre

ou réciproquement' (*Les Fonctions mentales dans les sociétés inférieures*, Alcan, 1910, p. 77).

15 In Roquentin's literal flight, we may find an image of the 'fuite' within consciousness which is so constant a theme in Sartre's work. In its purest form, it is simply the tendency of consciousness to 'tear itself away from itself' in its ambiguous duality, in an attempt to realise its projects and to transcend its contingency. In Roquentin's experience, this tendency is perhaps transformed into the literal, panic-stricken effort of a consciousness to escape the threat of facticity. (For the relationship between contingency and facticity, see note 5 above.)

16 This relationship is specifically described in Part ii, ch. 3 of *L'Etre et le Néant*, 'La Transcendance'. It is to this chapter that I shall have occasion to refer most frequently. There, Sartre's distinction between 'le monde' and *l'être-en-soi* is crucial. The world is already a 'humanised' structuring of the undifferentiated plenitude of being. For a masterly discussion of 'layers of thinghood' in Sartre, see Joseph P. Fell, *Heidegger and Sartre. An Essay on Being and Place*, New York, Columbia University Press, 1979, particularly Part i, ch. 3, and pp. 295–7.

17 Unlike the 'self-knowledge' of impure reflection described in note 10 above, 'connaissance' is to be taken here in the sense of an awareness of the object which is prior to a secondary or reflective knowledge and which is neither abstract nor conceptual. Indeed, as 'presence to' their object, 'conscience' and 'connaissance' in this context may seem to amount to the same thing, but in keeping with Sartre's basic rejection of 'l'illusion du primat de la connaissance' (*EN*, p. 18), 'conscience' is still seen, as in the introduction to *L'Etre et le Néant*, to be the ontological ground of knowledge: 'la loi d'être du sujet connaissant, c'est d'*être-conscient*' (p. 17).

18 The vocabulary of *La Nausée* is ambiguous here: 'le Monde tout nu' revealed to Roquentin towards the end of his vision corresponds more to the undifferentiated plenitude of *l'être-en-soi* than to a humanised 'world' (see note 16 above). The world seems to have collapsed, so to speak, into being-in-itself.

19 This ambiguity applies equally to other fundamental structures of consciousness: 'Ainsi l'ambiguïté de l'apparition et de la disparition vient de ce qu'elles se donnent, comme le monde, comme l'espace, comme la potentialité et l'ustensilité, comme le temps universel lui-même, sous l'aspect de totalités en perpétuelle désagrégation' (*EN*, p. 259). The structure of 'ustensilité' was, as we have seen, the first to disintegrate for Roquentin, and in Sartre's view it seems to follow that the sense of time should then disintegrate too; it can be recovered only when a sense of 'instrumentality' is restored: 'si l'on considère le Temps par lui-même, elle [la cohésion du temps] s'effondre aussitôt en une multiplicité absolue d'instants qui, considérés séparément, perdent toute nature temporelle et se réduisent purement et simplement à la

totale a-temporalité du *ceci*. Ainsi le Temps est pur néant en-soi qui ne peut sembler avoir un *être* que par l'acte même dans lequel le Pour-soi le franchit pour l'utiliser. [...] En effet notre première appréhension du temps objectif est *pratique*' (p. 267).

20 For the time being it can be noted that the role of imagination as a fundamental mode of consciousness, closely related to man's freedom and to his power of *dépassement*, is stressed by Sartre in *L'Imaginaire* (1940): 'Lorsque l'imaginaire n'est pas posé en fait, le dépassement et la néantisation de l'existant sont enlisés dans l'existant, le dépassement et la liberté *sont là* mais ils ne se découvrent pas, l'homme est écrasé dans le monde, transpercé par le réel, il est le plus près de la chose' (p. 237). The power to imagine is also seen to be closely linked to the sense-giving activity of consciousness: 'toute conscience du monde appelle et motive une conscience imageante comme saisie du *sens* particulier de la situation' (p. 238). In the light of Sartre's analysis in *L'Imaginaire*, Roquentin's experience of absurdity in the *Jardin public* is compatible, as we shall see, with a failure of his 'conscience imageante', which is partly reinstated in his intuition of the 'drôle de petit sens', and in the act of writing.

21 This earlier episode establishes a close relationship between an intuition of sense-giving form and of finality, a 'grand sentiment d'aventure' which purges the sensation of nausea, an awareness of identity, and the illusion of the coincidence of consciousness and world: 'j'ai traversé tout ce jour pour aboutir là, le front contre cette vitre, pour contempler ce fin visage qui s'épanouit sur un rideau grenat. Tout s'est arrêté; ma vie s'est arrêtée: cette grande vitre, cet air lourd, bleu comme de l'eau, cette plante grasse et blanche au fond de l'eau, et moi-même, nous formons un tout immobile et plein: je suis heureux' (*O.r.*, p. 68). Such an experience, its precariousness and its illusory timelessness, and the ontological implications of 'l'intuition esthétique', are described thus in *L'Etre et le Néant*: 'Cette fusion impossible et perpétuellement indiquée de l'essence et de l'existence [i.e. beauty] n'appartient ni au présent ni à l'avenir, elle indique plutôt la fusion du passé, du présent et de l'avenir, et se présente comme synthèse *à opérer* de la totalité temporelle. [...] La beauté représente donc un état idéal du monde, corrélatif d'une réalisation idéale du pour-soi, où l'essence et l'existence des choses se dévoileraient comme identité à un être qui, dans ce dévoilement même, se fonderait avec lui-même dans l'unité absolue de l'en-soi. [...] Mais le beau n'est pas plus une potentialité des choses que l'en-soi-pour-soi n'est une possibilité propre du pour-soi. Il hante le monde comme un irréalisable. Et dans la mesure où l'homme *réalise* le beau dans le monde, il le réalise sur le mode imaginaire. Cela veut dire que dans l'intuition esthétique, j'appréhende un objet imaginaire à travers une réalisation imaginaire de moi-même comme totalité en-soi et pour-soi' (*EN*, pp. 244–5). The description of Sunday at Bouville, which

includes the episode referred to above, and in which Roquentin moves towards a sense of pattern and fulfilment, momentarily seems to validate the possibility of writing as a mode of realising an 'intuition esthétique', but that possibility is immediately rejected at the beginning of the next diary entry: 'Se méfier de la littérature' (*O.r.*, p. 68).

22 On this point, Sartre's thought seems to have evolved between *La Transcendance de l'Ego* and *L'Etre et le Néant*. In the former the possibility of an 'impersonal' consciousness, devoid of an Ego, is categorically affirmed: 'la conscience transcendantale est une spontanéité impersonnelle' (*TE*, p. 79). In the latter, however, consciousness, even prior to the constitution of the Ego, is said to be personal: 'dès qu'elle surgit, la conscience, par le pur mouvement néantisant de la réflexion, se fait *personnelle*: car ce qui confère à un être l'existence personnelle, ce n'est pas la possession d'un Ego [...] mais c'est le fait d'exister pour soi comme présence à soi' (*EN*, p. 148). Sartre's more fully elaborated theory of reflection in *L'Etre et le Néant* may account for the transition, while the apparently more radical position of the earlier work is somewhat attenuated by his suggestion of 'prépersonnel' as a possible alternative for 'impersonnel'.

23 See *L'Etre et le Néant*, p. 147: 'l'Ego apparaît à la conscience comme un en-soi transcendant, comme un existant du monde humain, non comme *de la* conscience'.

24 See *La Transcendance de l'Ego*, p. 37: 'Le contenu certain du pseudo "Cogito" n'est pas "*j'ai* conscience de cette chaise", mais "*il y a* conscience de cette chaise".'

25 See 'Une Idée fondamentale de la phénoménologie de Husserl: l'intentionnalité', *Situations* i, Gallimard, 1947, pp. 31–5. (Written in 1933–4 and first published in 1939.)

26 Sartre's vocabulary in the passage under discussion also recalls that of *La Transcendance de l'Ego*. There, Sartre suggests that the role of the Ego may be 'de masquer à la conscience sa propre spontanéité' and that when this function is suspended, consciousness is revealed in its 'spontanéité monstrueuse', 'monstrueusement libre' (*TE*, pp. 80–1). Roquentin experiences a similar, negative sense of liberation: 'Elle [la conscience] se voit de part en part, paisible et vide entre les murs, libérée de l'homme qui l'habitait, monstrueuse parce qu'elle n'est personne' (*O.r.*, p. 202). It is interesting to note (particularly given the frequent critical view that Roquentin's experience is a symptom of neurosis) that for Sartre such an intuition is not the symptom, but the possible source, of 'psychasthenic' behaviour (*TE*, p. 80). The intuition itself, he maintains, is in no way aberrant; it is a suspension of the so-called 'natural attitude' which Sartre would later describe as being in *mauvaise foi* and which consists of 'un effort que la conscience fait pour s'échapper à elle-même en se projetant dans le Moi et en s'y absorbant' (p. 83). Such a suspension of 'l'attitude "naturelle"' is 'à

la fois un événement pur d'origine transcendantale et un accident
toujours possible de notre vie quotidienne' (p. 84). It occurs when 'la
conscience [se produit] soudain elle-même sur le plan réflexif pur'.
Roquentin's pre-reflective (self-)awareness may be moving, then, towards pure reflection, but his accompanying intuition of freedom
remains a negative one.

27 In, for instance, Roquentin's hypothetical autobiography, which a
false but inevitable teleology transforms insidiously into fiction: 'On a
l'air de débuter par le commencement: "C'était par un beau soir de
l'automne de 1922. J'étais clerc de notaire à Marommes." [...] Mais la
fin est là, qui transforme tout. Pour nous, le type est déjà le héros de
l'histoire. Sa morosité, ses ennuis d'argent sont bien plus précieux que
les nôtres, ils sont tout dorés par la lumière des passions futures. Et le
récit se poursuit à l'envers: les instants ont cessé de s'empiler au petit
bonheur les uns sur les autres, ils sont happés par la fin de l'histoire
qui les attire et chacun d'eux attire à son tour l'instant qui le précède:
"Il faisait nuit, la rue était déserte." La phrase est jetée négli-
gemment, elle a l'air superflue; mais nous ne nous y laissons pas
prendre et nous la mettons de côté: c'est un renseignement dont nous
comprendrons la valeur par la suite. Et nous avons le sentiment que le
héros a vécu tous les détails de cette nuit comme des annonciations,
comme des promesses, ou même qu'il vivait seulement ceux qui
étaient des promesses, aveugle et sourd pour tout ce qui n'annonçait
pas l'aventure. Nous oublions que l'avenir n'était pas encore là; le
type se promenait dans une nuit sans présages, qui lui offrait pêle-
mêle ses richesses monotones et il ne choisissait pas' (*O.r.*,
pp. 49–50). It is precisely to this narrative temptation and to the
temptation of reading the teleology of narrative into life itself that
Roquentin succumbs, to his subsequent disgust, in his next diary
entry: his description of Sunday in Bouville.

28 See the definition of the 'irrealising' function of the image in
L'Imaginaire: 'Poser une image, c'est constituer un objet en marge de
la totalité du réel' (*Im.*, p. 233). Furthermore, 'cet objet passif, main-
tenu en vie artificiellement [...] à tout moment est près de s'évanouir'
(p. 162). Rollebon as the subject of a biography is such an 'objet
passif': 'Et d'un seul coup, sans bruit, M. de Rollebon était retourné à
son néant' (*O.r.*, p. 115).

29 These threats to the *vraisemblance* of the novel *qua* diary are
frequent, but such is the reader's need to maintain a sense of
verisimilitude that critics have either failed to register them at all, or
have 'naturalised' them by taking them to be examples of the historic
present. But such readings miss the point that these strategies and
their disruptions of verisimilitude imply a 'third-order' questioning of
the possibility of representing 'first-order' experience in an unproblematic 'second-order' process of writing. The problem of
vraisemblance preoccupies Roquentin himself, who sees it as a matter

of fragile shared assumptions: 'Quand on vit seul, on ne sait même plus ce que c'est que raconter: le vraisemblable disparaît en même temps que les amis. Les événements aussi, on les laisse couler; on voit surgir brusquement des gens qui parlent et qui s'en vont, on plonge dans des histoires sans queue ni tête: on ferait un exécrable témoin. Mais tout l'invraisemblable, en compensation, tout ce qui ne pourrait pas être cru dans les cafés, on ne le manque pas' (*O.r.*, p. 12). The editors of Sartre's *Œuvres romanesques* (1981) emphasise his commitment to this theme: 'Sartre nous a dit qu'il voyait dans l'attaque contre la vraisemblance l'un des thèmes essentiels de *La Nausée*. Il tenait alors la vraisemblance, ou le vraisemblable, pour une catégorie de la pensée bourgeoise, qui ne se préoccupe pas du réel ou du vrai mais voit celui-ci à travers les voiles de ce qu'elle tient pour le possible. En d'autres termes, la vraisemblance est idéologique et s'oppose à la saisie brute du monde réel par la conscience immédiate, condition de l'accès au vrai et privilège de "l'homme seul". Dans la théorie qu'avait constituée Sartre au sortir de l'Ecole normale et dont *La Nausée* est encore, selon lui, largement tributaire, le vraisemblable et le certain étaient rejetés comme des catégories abstraites auxquelles s'opposait l'expérience concrète de "l'homme seul"' (p. 1730). One can conclude that both the formal and the thematic questioning of the *vraisemblable* in *La Nausée* are functional.

30 See *L'Etre et le Néant*, p. 597: 'L'unité verbale étant la phrase signifiante, celle-ci est un acte constructif qui ne se conçoit que par une transcendance qui dépasse et néantise le donné vers une fin. [...] Comprendre une phrase de mon interlocuteur, c'est, en effet, comprendre ce qu'il "veut dire", c'est-à-dire épouser son mouvement de transcendance, me jeter avec lui vers des possibles, vers des fins et revenir ensuite sur l'ensemble des moyens organisés pour les comprendre par leur fonction et leur but.' The instrumentality of language thus defined does not, however, preclude 'la part du diable' in language (*EN*, p. 600): 'une multiplicité de significations qui se hiérarchisent ou s'opposent pour une même phrase'.

31 See above, p. 16. For Sartre's reference to Alain, see *Esquisse d'une théorie des émotions*, p. 56, and 'Aller et retour', *S* I, 1947, p. 222 (an essay on the philosophy of Brice Parain first published in 1944).

32 Sartre is writing here of the implications of Parain's theory of language, but they are implications which, as we shall see, he anticipates and develops elsewhere on his own account.

33 Sartre's practice in *La Nausée* seems to anticipate, first, his theory of poetry, as set out in *Qu'est-ce que la littérature?* (1947); secondly, some of the objections which could be raised against the distinctions between prose and poetry established in the first part of his essay (and which are, as we shall see, covertly undermined within it); and finally, the redefinition of the writer's function which he formulates in the 1960s. (Recently published fragments of early works indicate that

Sartre was himself already questioning the position of *Qu'est-ce que la littérature?* shortly after its publication, thereby anticipating his arguments of the 1960s. See Chapter 6.)

34 Further implications of the distinction between *sens* and *signification* will be discussed later. For further analyses see Thomas R. Flynn, 'The Role of the Image in Sartre's Aesthetic', *Journal of Aesthetics and Art Criticism*, XXXIII, Summer 1975, pp. 431–42; Gérard Genette, 'Sens et signification: la théorie sartrienne du langage poétique', in *L'Analyse du discours/Discourse Analysis*, ed. Pierre R. Léon and Henri Mitterand, Montréal, Centre Educatif et Culturel Inc., 1976, pp. 193–201, and the last chapter, in particular, of Christina Howells, *Sartre's Theory of Literature*, MHRA, 1979.

35 Sartre's reservations concerning the attempt to convey 'le fleuve de la conscience' in a 'monologue intérieur', as exemplified by Schnitzler and Larbaud, are expressed in *Qu'est-ce que la littérature?*. They are based upon his distinction between *sens* and *signification*, and upon his emphasis (also attenuated elsewhere), on language as action: 'L'inconvénient de ce procédé c'est qu'il nous enferme dans une subjectivité individuelle et qu'il manque par là l'univers intermonadique, c'est en outre qu'il dilue l'événement et l'action dans la perception de l'un et de l'autre. Or la caractéristique commune du fait et de l'acte, c'est qu'ils échappent à la représentation subjective: elle en saisit les résultats mais non le mouvement vivant. Enfin ce n'est pas sans quelque truquage qu'on peut réduire le fleuve de la conscience à une succession de mots, même déformés. Si le mot est donné comme intermédiaire *signifiant* une réalité transcendante, par essence, au langage rien de mieux: il se fait oublier, il décharge la conscience sur l'objet. Mais s'il se donne comme *la réalité psychique*, si l'auteur, en écrivant, prétend nous donner une réalité ambiguë qui soit signe, en son essence objective, c'est-à-dire en tant qu'elle se rapporte au dehors, et chose en son essence formelle, c'est-à-dire comme donnée psychique immédiate, alors on peut lui reprocher de n'avoir pas pris parti et de méconnaître cette loi rhétorique qui pourrait se formuler ainsi: en littérature, où l'on use de signes, il ne faut user *que* de signes; et si la *réalité* que l'on veut signifier est *un mot*, il faut la livrer au lecteur par d'autres mots. On peut lui reprocher en outre d'avoir oublié que les plus grandes richesses de la vie psychique sont *silencieuses*' (*S* II, pp. 200–1). It could be argued that the recognition of intentionality implicit in Sartre's own use of 'stream of consciousness' technique rescues it from the charge of subjectivism. But it is also clear that Sartre does not 'user *que* de signes', and that Roquentin exemplifies what is later seen to be the poet's duty to 'faire du silence avec le langage' ('Orphée noir', *S* III, 1949, p. 247). Incidentally, Sartre exempts Joyce from the strictures quoted above. It is unfortunate that his lecture of the early 1930s on 'Le monologue intérieur: Joyce' has been lost. (See Michel Contat and Michel Rybalka, *Les Ecrits de Sartre*, Gallimard, 1970, p. 25.)

36 Much critical energy has been expended upon attempts to decide whether Roquentin actually writes the novel so tentatively envisaged at the end of *La Nausée*, and whether *La Nausée* itself is that novel. For a review of the conflicting hypotheses and an admirably close analysis of the text's hesitant conclusion, see Terry Keefe, 'The Ending of Sartre's *La Nausée*', *Forum for Modern Language Studies*, XII, no. 3, July 1976, pp. 217–35.

37 See Gérard Genette, 'Discours du récit', *Figures* III, Seuil, 1972, p. 72.

38 Ibid., p. 74.

39 Ibid., p. 229.

40 In *L'Imaginaire*, the force of the term 'représentation' is frequently a strong one: the object represented in imagination is 'made present', 're-presented' or embodied as a synthetic totality. This process is 'magical' in that it involves an irrational element, an 'action à distance'. Hence also its independence, as in the 'law of participation' discussed in note 14 above, of logical and perceptual categories.

41 Apart from its more radical distinction (following *Qu'est-ce que la littérature?*) between *signification* and *sens*, this passage summarises that part of the argument of *L'Imaginaire* which concerns the embodiment of *sens* in a particular 're-presenting' object. (The correlative role of a form of *savoir* will be discussed later.) One of the difficulties of Sartre's analyses in *L'Imaginaire* is that the word 'objet' is, according to the context, a form of shorthand for an existent object, for a 're-presented' object, or for an aesthetic object. This has in turn to be differentiated from the physical medium (sometimes an artefact – or object) which is its vehicle.

42 It could, of course, be argued that Roquentin is simply transcribing a memory, and that, for Sartre, the acts of consciousness involved in remembering and imagining are distinct. As he suggests in *L'Imaginaire*, a remembered event is *donné-présent au passé*, rather than *donné-absent* (*Im.*, p. 230). But in practice he often draws upon the activity of memory to provide examples of 'la nature de l'image', and 'certes le souvenir à bien des points de vue semble très proche de l'image' (p. 230). From this point of view his description of affective memory as a 'conscience imageante dont le corrélatif sera le sentiment d'hier irréellement présent' (p. 182) is particularly relevant. And as we saw earlier, apart from the 'analogical' rather than purely 'signifying' character of Roquentin's language, towards the end of his account he wonders if the experience evoked was not an imagined, dream-like event. (For Sartre's analysis of dream as an example of imagining consciousness see *L'Imaginaire*, pp. 205–25.)

43 Sartre envisages several different levels of the relationship between image and thought. Their hierarchy depends upon the extent to which the latter is unreflectively 'possessed' by the former: '*La pensée irréfléchie est une possession*. Penser une essence, un rapport, c'est sur

ce plan [i.e. of the 'idée comme image'] les produire "en chair et en os", les constituer dans leur réalité vivante (et naturellement sous la "catégorie d'absence" [...]) et c'est en même temps les voir, les posséder. Mais, en même temps, c'est les constituer *sous une certaine forme* et considérer cette forme comme exprimant exactement leur nature, comme *étant* leur nature. Ici la pensée s'enferme dans l'image et l'image se donne comme adéquate à la pensée. [...] En effet, l'objet considéré (essence, relation, complexus de rapports, etc.), ne se présente pas seulement comme une structure idéale: c'est aussi une structure matérielle. Ou plutôt structure idéale et structure matérielle ne font qu'un. [...] [La] subordination de structures matérielles aux structures idéales n'est possible que si l'on saisit les structures matérielles comme n'épuisant pas les structures idéales, que si l'on pose une indépendance relative des unes par rapport aux autres' (*Im.*, p. 151). In this context, Sartre gives priority to the 'structure idéale', but he is not entirely consistent in this. Hence the fluctuations in his positive or negative evaluation of the function of the image (pp. 146–55).

44　The attempt to think 'by analogy' is a dangerous one, according to the 'negative' emphasis in Sartre's analyses of imagination, unless the subject retains a 'savoir vide touchant la nature de l'idée pure en général' (*Im.*, p. 151). It could be argued that Roquentin's intellectual panic stems, in part, from the tension between the need to 'penser l'être' by analogy, and a sense of the inadequacy of the image, and of the threat it poses as a 'structure matérielle' to the relative (but also inadequate) purity of conceptual thinking. The resolution of this 'infra-aesthetic' tension on a positive level in the work of art is not fully developed thematically in the tentative ending of *La Nausée*. However, such a possibility, based upon an initial distinction between 'les choses' and 'la pensée' is theoretically envisaged by Sartre in (perhaps unexpectedly) *Qu'est-ce que la littérature?*: 'l'artiste a besoin d'une matière inassimilable parce que la beauté ne se résout pas en idées; même s'il est prosateur et s'il assemble des signes, il n'y aura ni grâce ni force dans son style s'il n'est sensible à la matérialité du mot et à ses résistances irrationnelles. Et s'il veut fonder l'univers dans son œuvre et le soutenir par une inépuisable liberté, c'est précisément parce qu'il distingue radicalement les choses de la pensée; sa liberté n'est homogène à la chose qu'en ceci que toutes deux sont insondables et, s'il veut réapproprier le désert ou la forêt vierge à l'Esprit, ce n'est pas en les transformant en idées de désert et de forêt, mais en faisant éclairer l'Etre en tant qu'Etre, avec son opacité, et son coefficient d'adversité, par la spontanéité indéfinie de l'Existence' (*S* II, pp. 158–9).

45　Sartre returns to this view in later works, and it is particularly relevant to *L'Idiot de la famille*. The rigid distinction between *sens* and *signification* set out as a general principle in the first part of *Qu'est-ce que la littérature?* and illustrated specifically in *Saint Genet* could, indeed, be said to be aberrant in relation to Sartre's work as a whole: 'si le sensible, dans son idiosyncrasie même, soutient des structures non-conceptualisables mais *objectives* au cœur même de la subjectivité (le goût "d'un plum-pudding" est à la fois une singularité vécue, non-conceptuelle et une sensation commune dont on peut réveiller le souvenir chez tous ceux qui l'ont éprouvée) ce non-communicable est, malgré tout, susceptible d'être transmis d'une certaine manière. Il faut, pourrait-on dire, renoncer à faire du langage un moyen d'information ou, en tout cas, subordonner la fonction informative à cette fonction nouvelle qu'on pourrait appeler *participation*. Autrement dit, il ne faut pas seulement nommer le goût du plum-pudding mais le donner à sentir; et la phrase lue remplirait parfaitement ce nouvel office si, tout en *signifiant* le lien conceptuel qui unit ce gâteau à sa consommation, elle *était* ce goût lui-même, entrant par les yeux dans l'esprit du lecteur' (*IF* II, pp. 1986-7).

2 *Les Mouches*: Emotion and Reflection

1 For an account of *Les Mouches* and *Huis clos* in the light of Sartre's ontology, see Peter Royle, *Sartre. L'Enfer et la liberté*, Québec, Presses de l'Université Laval, 1973. See also Francis Jeanson, *Sartre par lui-même*, Seuil, 1955, and Frederic Will, 'Sartre and the question of character in literature', *PMLA*, LXXVI, September 1961, pp. 455-60. For a discussion of *Les Mouches* in relation to other literary works of Sartre see Keith Gore, *Sartre: La Nausée and Les Mouches*, Edward Arnold (Studies in French Literature, no. 17), 1970.

2 These terms clearly involve problems of definition, for the difficulty of establishing distinctions between emotions, feelings and moods continues to preoccupy psychologists. In his *Esquisse* Sartre briefly acknowledges the problem by distinguishing between 'joie-sentiment' ('un équilibre, un état adapté') and 'joie-émotion' which is rather, in his view, an expression of the symbolic possession of a desired object (*ETE*, pp. 47-8). He also attempts, equally briefly, to distinguish between 'delicate' and 'weak' emotions (p. 55). For an analysis of Sartre's classification of emotions see Joseph P. Fell, *Emotion in the Thought of Sartre*, New York, Columbia University Press, 1965, particularly chs 8 and 11. For a critical view of Sartre's approach see also Terry Keefe, 'Problems of identification and definition in some of Sartre's shorter philosophical works', *Australian Journal of French Studies*, XII, no. 2, 1975, pp. 220-40. In defence of Sartre it could be said that, like so many of his shorter essays, his *Esquisse* is essentially a polemical work. In questioning the validity of traditional theories and in offering a phenomenological interpretation of the significance and function of emotion, he tends to take clear-cut

examples of extreme or intense emotions (with the notable exception of 'la tristesse passive'). Such emotions can be sharply differentiated from the general 'affectivité intentionnelle' described in *L'Etre et le Néant* and referred to in my first chapter (see above, pp. 11–17), but they can be less clearly distinguished from the 'sentiments' described in *L'Imaginaire*.

3 References will be given in the text to the 1969 reprint of the first post-war edition of *Les Mouches* in Jean-Paul Sartre, *Théâtre*, Gallimard, 1947.

4 See the introduction to Sylvie Le Bon's edition of *La Transcendance de l'Ego*.

5 See Fell, *Emotion in the Thought of Sartre*, pp. 136–7.

6 See also Chapter 1, pp. 12–19.

7 For Sartre, this causality or 'creativity' is essentially magical, rather than rational: 'l'Ego est un objet appréhendé mais aussi *constitué* par la science réflexive. C'est un foyer virtuel d'unité, et la conscience le constitue en *sens inverse* de celui que suit la production réelle: ce qui est premier *réellement*, ce sont les consciences, à travers lesquelles se constituent les états, puis, à travers ceux-ci, l'Ego. Mais, comme l'ordre est renversé par une conscience qui s'emprisonne dans le Monde pour se fuir, les consciences sont données comme émanant des états et les états comme produits par l'Ego. Il s'ensuit que la conscience projette sa propre spontanéité dans l'objet Ego pour lui conférer le pouvoir créateur qui lui est absolument nécessaire. Seulement cette spontanéité, *représentée et hypostasiée* dans un objet, devient une spontanéité bâtarde et dégradée, qui conserve magiquement sa puissance créatrice tout en devenant passive' (*TE*, pp. 63–4). This view is developed in *L'Etre et le Néant*. The 'cohésion magique' of the Ego, which is distinct from the 'unité ontologique' of the *pour-soi* is maintained by the 'action à distance' which operates between its elements: 'cette influence se manifestera soit par pénétration, soit par motivation. Dans le premier cas, le réflexif appréhende comme un seul objet deux objets psychiques qui avaient d'abord été donnés séparément. Il en résulte soit un objet psychique neuf dont chaque caractéristique sera la synthèse des deux autres, soit un objet en lui-même inintelligible qui se donne à la fois comme tout l'un et tout l'autre, sans qu'il y ait altération ni de l'un ni de l'autre. Dans la motivation, au contraire, les deux objets demeurent chacun à sa place. Mais un objet psychique, étant forme organisée et multiplicité d'interpénétration, ne peut agir que tout entier à la fois sur un autre objet tout entier. Il s'ensuit une action totale et à distance par influence magique de l'un sur l'autre. Par exemple, c'est mon humiliation d'hier qui motive tout entière mon humeur de ce matin, etc. Que cette action à distance soit totalement magique et irrationnelle, c'est ce que prouvent, mieux que tout analyse, les efforts vains des psychologues intellectualistes pour la réduire, en restant sur le plan du

psychique, à une causalité intelligible par une analyse intellectuelle' (*EN*, pp. 215–16).

8 This aspect of emotional behaviour is closely related to Sartre's theory of imagination: 'L'acte d'imagination [...] est un acte magique. C'est une incantation destinée à faire apparaître l'objet auquel on pense, la chose qu'on désire, de façon qu'on puisse en prendre possession. Il y a, dans cet acte, toujours quelque chose d'impérieux et d'enfantin, un refus de tenir compte de la distance, des difficultés. Ainsi le tout jeune enfant, de son lit, agit sur le monde par ordres et prières. A ces ordres de la conscience les objets obéissent: ils apparaissent. Mais ils ont un mode d'existence très particulier. [...] D'abord mon incantation [tend] à les obtenir tout entiers, à reproduire leur existence intégrale' (*Im.*, p. 161). See also Chapter 5, p. 144.

9 See G. Girard, R. Ouellet, C. Rigault, *L'Univers du théâtre*, PUF, 1978, p. 12, for a definition of the relationship between festival, ritual and theatre: 'Activité festive [...] en ce sens qu'elle [la comédie] renferme la mixité de la *fête* simultanément religieuse, cérémonielle, donc *rituelle* (ce qui permet son identification) et récréative, libre, inventive, c'est-à-dire *ludique* (ce qui la rend manifeste). La fête se définit comme rite producteur de liberté, de spontanéité collective. Par là éminemment symbolique [...], la fête privilégie tous moyens d'expression (chants, danses, paroles, etc.) capables d'exprimer l'objet célébré. Elle se rapproche ici du "jeu dramatique" et du jeu tout court. [...] Comme le théâtre, le jeu est, pour reprendre certaines idées de J. Huizinga et R. Caillois, une activité libre, aquotidienne, matériellement improductive, le plus souvent collective et ressentie comme *fictive*, à l'issue incertaine ou imprévue.' Compared with the 'negative' ritual of the 'Fête des morts' instituted by Egisthe, Electre's may superficially exemplify and invoke freedom and spontaneity; more basically, however, it too involves an element of captive fascination. Unlike 'le jeu et la fête à participation collective' (*L'Univers du théâtre*, p. 17), it is essentially 'spectacular'.

10 Again an irrational (or 'magical') response, which occurs when 'le producteur est passif par rapport à la chose créée' (*TE*, p. 63).

11 I.e., as we saw in Chapter 1, although the source of the action is literally 'at a distance', its effect is felt as though that distance did not exist.

12 'Forgers of Myths: the young playwrights of France', *Theatre Arts*, xxx, no. 6, June 1946. Reprinted in French as 'Forger des mythes' in *Un Théâtre de situations*, éd. Michel Contat et Michel Rybalka, Gallimard, 1973, pp. 55–67. In this and subsequent chapters, references will be given to this version.

13 In *L'Imaginaire* Sartre distinguishes between determinism and fatalism with some relevance to the case of Electre, although the immediate context is that of the fascinated 'captivity' of consciousness by hypnagogic imagery: 'Le caractère essentiel de la conscience

enchaînée nous paraît être la fatalité. Le déterminisme – qui ne saurait en aucune façon s'appliquer aux faits de conscience – pose que, tel phénomène étant donné, tel autre doit suivre nécessairement. Le fatalisme pose que tel événement doit arriver et que c'est cet événement futur qui détermine la série qui mènera jusqu'à lui. Ce n'est pas le déterminisme, c'est le fatalisme qui est l'envers de la liberté. On peut même dire que la fatalité, incompréhensible dans le monde physique, est, au contraire, parfaitement à sa place dans le monde de la conscience. [...] Dans la conscience captive, en effet, ce qui manque c'est la représentation du possible, c'est-à-dire la faculté de suspendre son jugement. Mais toute pensée captive la conscience et l'enchaîne – et la conscience la joue, la réalise en même temps la pense' (*Im.*, p. 68).

14 Our fundamental project is – and should be – always subject to the possibility of a radical 'conversion' (*EN*, p. 555).

15 But such an intuition, particularly if it has the character of a 'conversion', may *appear* as an instant: 'qu'on se rappelle l'*instant* où le Philoctète de Gide abandonne jusqu'à sa haine, son projet fondamental, sa raison d'être et son être; qu'on se rappelle l'*instant* où Raskolnikoff décide de se dénoncer. Ces instants extraordinaires et merveilleux, où le projet antérieur s'effondre dans le passé à la lumière d'un projet nouveau qui surgit sur ses ruines et qui ne fait encore que s'esquisser, où l'humiliation, l'angoisse, la joie, l'espoir se marient étroitement, où nous lâchons pour saisir et où nous saisissons pour lâcher, ont souvent paru fournir l'image la plus claire et la plus émouvante de notre liberté' (*EN*, p. 555). And yet, 'l'instant n'est lui-même qu'un néant car, où que nous portions notre vue, nous ne saisirons qu'une temporalisation continue, qui sera selon la direction de notre regard, ou bien la série achevée et close qui vient de passer, en entraînant son terme final avec elle – ou bien la temporalisation vivante qui commence et dont le terme initial est happé et entraîné par la possibilité future' (*EN*, p. 545).

16 See also *La Transcendance de l'Ego*, p. 76: 'si Pierre et Paul parlent tout deux de l'amour de Pierre, par exemple, il n'est plus vrai que l'un parle en aveugle et par analogie de ce que l'autre saisit en plein. Ils parlent de la même chose; ils la saisissent sans doute par des procédés différents, mais ceux-ci peuvent être également intuitifs. Et le sentiment de Pierre n'est pas plus *certain* pour Pierre que pour Paul. Il appartient pour l'un et pour l'autre à la catégorie des objets qu'on peut révoquer en doute. Mais toute cette conception profonde et nouvelle reste compromise si le Moi de Pierre, ce Moi qui hait ou qui aime, demeure une structure essentielle de la conscience'.

17 This emphasis can be explained by Sartre's desire to substitute a 'philosophie de la transcendance' for 'la philosophie douillette de l'immanence' according to which emotions would be 'in the mind' (*S* 1, p. 33).

3 *Huis clos*: Distance and ambiguity

1　For instance: Robert Campbell, *Jean-Paul Sartre ou une littérature philosophique*, Edition revue et augmentée, Pierre Ardent, 1946, pp. 128–40; Marie-Denise Boros, *Un Séquestré: l'homme sartrien*, Nizet, 1968, p. 62; Hazel E. Barnes, *Sartre*, Quartet Books, 1973, p. 73.

2　*Huis clos*, sc. v, p. 182, in Jean-Paul Sartre, *Théâtre*, Gallimard, 1947. All references, henceforth given in the text, are to the 1969 reprint of this edition.

3　See Marilyn Gaddis Rose, 'Sartre and the ambiguous thesis play', *Modern Drama*, VIII, no. 1, Summer 1965, pp. 12–19. Dr Rose bases her argument on an abridged translation of Sartre's lecture published in 1961 as 'Beyond bourgeois theatre', trans. Rima Drell Reck, *Tulane Drama Review*, v, no. 3, March 1961. The complete lecture was eventually published in *Un Théâtre de situations*, pp. 104–51. Reference will be given to this version.

4　Rose, 'Ambiguous thesis play', pp. 15–16.

5　See, for instance, Brecht, 'Notes to *Die Mutter*', in *Brecht on Theatre* (1964), ed. and trans. J. Willett, Eyre Methuen, 1978, pp. 59–60: 'In every case she [Helene Weigel] picked, out of all conceivable characteristics, those whose awareness promoted the most comprehensive political treatment of the Vlassovas (i.e. special, individual and unique ones) [...]. Among the differences that distinguish individuals from each other, there are quite specific ones that interest the political being who mixes with them, struggles with them and has to deal with them [...]. There is no point for him in stripping a given man of all his peculiarities until he stands there as Man (with a capital M), i.e. as a being who cannot be altered further.' (First published in *Versuche*, 7, Berlin, 1933.) Or, from later Brecht, see 'A short organum for the theatre', Section 39, *Brecht on Theatre*, p. 191: 'If a character responds in a manner historically in keeping with his period, and would respond otherwise in other periods, does that mean that he is not simply "Everyman"? It is true that a man will respond differently according to his circumstances and his class; if he were living at another time, or in his youth, or on the darker side of life, he would infallibly give a different response, though one still determined by the same factors and like anyone else's response in that situation at that time. So should we not ask if there are any further differences of response? Where is the man himself, the living, unmistakeable man, who is not quite identical with those identified with him? It is clear that his stage image must bring him to light, and this will come about if this particular contradiction is recreated in the image.' (First published in 'Kleines Organon für das Theater', *Sinn und Form*, Sonderheft Bertolt Brecht, Potsdam, 1949.) Indeed, Brecht associates an emphasis on 'Everyman' with bourgeois rather than epic theatre; see

'Alienation effects in Chinese acting', *Brecht on Theatre*, pp. 96–7: 'The bourgeois theatre emphasized the timelessness of its objects. Its representation of people is bound by the alleged "eternally human". Its story is arranged in such a way as to create "universal" situations that allow man with a capital M to express himself: man of every period and every colour. [...] This notion may allow that such a thing as history exists, but it is none the less unhistorical. A few circumstances vary, the environments are altered, but Man remains unchanged.' (First published in *Life and Letters*, London, 1936.)

6 Sartre here goes on to assert that the passions depicted in the action of the bourgeois play 'marquent ainsi l'éternité du caractère humain' – an apparent echo of Brecht's views as quoted in the previous note.

7 *TS*, pp. 130–3. It is only in non-bourgeois theatre (the examples given are Chinese opera and a Barrault mime) that 'les objets [sont] créés par l'action qui s'en sert' (p. 130), to the extent, indeed, that the object can remain imaginary without destroying the illusion: the gesture of killing creates the dagger, the action of rowing creates the boat.

8 In about 1936, Brecht wrote thus on the need to subvert the spectator's assumptions about what is natural, predetermined and unalterable: 'The spectator was no longer in any way allowed to submit to an experience uncritically [...] by means of simple empathy with the characters in a play. The production took the subject-matter and the incidents shown and put them through a process of alienation: the alienation that is necessary to all understanding. When something seems "the most obvious thing in the world" it means that any attempt to understand the world has been given up. What is "natural" must have the force of what is startling. This is the only way to expose the laws of cause and effect. People's activity must simultaneously be so and be capable of being different.' ('Theatre for pleasure or theatre for instruction', *Brecht on Theatre*, p. 71, first published in *Schriften zum Theater*, Frankfurt, Suhrkamp, 1957.)

9 'Jean-Paul Sartre nous parle de théâtre', *Théâtre populaire*, no. 15, septembre-octobre 1955. Reprinted as 'Théâtre populaire et théâtre bourgeois' in *Un Théâtre de situations*, pp. 68–79.

10 Sartre might have written these words of Brecht's: dramatists should break 'with the orthodox theatre's habit of basing the actions on the characters and having the former exempted from criticism by presenting them as an unavoidable consequence deriving by natural law from the characters who perform them' ('The street scene. A basic model for an epic theatre', *Brecht on Theatre*, p. 124, first published in *Versuch*, 10, 1950, written in 1938).

11 'L'Auteur, l'œuvre et le public', *TS*, pp. 97–8.

12 'Brecht et les classiques', *TS*, p. 84.

13 'Théâtre populaire et théâtre bourgeois', *TS*, p. 73.

14 Its very familiarity may, however, prevent its significance from being

recognised. One of the few critics to do so is R. Lorris in *Sartre dramaturge*, Nizet, 1975, p. 55.

15 'Pour un Théâtre de situations', *TS*, p. 20. First published in *La Rue*, no. 12, novembre 1947.

16 For the *dénouement* of a 'situation fausse' in rectitude and *attendrissement* see, among other plays, Sardou's *Fernande* and *Odette*; for the reconciliation of comedy, satire and 'la dignité humaine', Augier's *Ceinture dorée*; for the attempt to combine melodrama and the *bienséances*, his *Le Mariage d'Olympe*; for the resolution of the 'eternal' triangle in the sardonic mode Dumas *fils*'s *Une Visite de noces* and, in the melodramatic mode, his *La Femme de Claude*.

17 For example B. Lecherbonnier, *Huis clos: analyse critique*, Hatier, 'Profil d'une œuvre', 31, 1972, p. 42.

18 *EN*, pp. 596 and 501. See also p. 614: 'le bourgeois se fait bourgeois en niant qu'il y ait des classes'.

19 Sartre's tendency to consider such *employés* as belonging to the *petite bourgeoisie* rather than to the working class is borne out by his criticism of the *TNP*, in which he equated 'populaire' with 'ouvrier' and accused the *TNP* of failing to reach a genuinely 'popular' audience ('Théâtre populaire et théâtre bourgeois', *TS*, p. 69). Jean Vilar took exception to Sartre's distinction: 'En France, aujourd'hui, un public populaire n'est pas uniquement un public ouvrier. [...] Un employé des postes, ma dactylo, un petit commerçant qui travaillent eux aussi huit heures par jour, tous font partie du peuple. Pourquoi Sartre les rejette-t-il?' (*L'Express*, 24 novembre 1955. Quoted in *TS*, p. 79). However, to regard *employés* as separate from the working class is in accordance with Marxist theory; and, more relevantly, the distinction was widely recognised in French intellectual circles at the time of the composition of *Huis clos* (1943). It was elaborated, for instance, by the non-Marxist Maurice Halbwachs (to whom Sartre refers on page 596 of *L'Etre et le Néant*) in 'Les Caractéristiques des classes moyennes', *Inventaires*, III, Alcan, 1939. See, particularly, his section 'Les fonctionnaires' (pp. 38 *et seq.*) in which he refers explicitly to 'les agents des P.T.T.', and analyses the characteristics which distinguish 'petits fonctionnaires' from the working class and place them in a marginal relationship to the bourgeoisie. (Halbwachs was appointed to the chair of Social Psychology at the Collège de France shortly before his arrest by the Gestapo in July 1944. He died in Buchenwald in February 1945.)

20 In *Abhandlungen und Aufsätze*, 2 vols, Leipzig, Engelmann, 1915. A later edition, to which bibliographical references are often given, was incorporated in *Vom Umsturz der Werte*, the third volume of Scheler's *Gesammelte Werke*, Berne, Francke Verlag, 1955. A French translation, *L'Homme du ressentiment*, was published by Gallimard in 1933. References in the present chapter are given to *Ressentiment*, ed. Lewis A. Coser, trans. W. W. Holdheim, New York, Schocken

Books, 1961. (The French word *ressentiment* is a technical term in German thought. It was used in Nietzsche's arguments, and the implications of the word itself were then developed and modified by Scheler.)

21 *Ressentiment*, p. 50.
22 Ibid., p. 66.
23 Ibid., p. 48.
24 Ibid.
25 Ibid., pp. 52–3.
26 Ibid., p. 54.
27 Although she is a member of the *haute bourgeoisie*, Estelle is, like Garcin and Inès, marginal to her class. As Lecherbonnier points out (*Sartre: Huis clos*, p. 42) she had been 'adoptée par la bourgeoisie'.
28 'Brecht et les classiques', *TS*, p. 84.
29 *TS*, p. 305. (First published as '"*Les Séquestrés d'Altona* nous concernent tous", entretien avec Bernard Dort', *Théâtre populaire*, no. 36, 4ᵉ trimestre, 1959.)

4 *Les Mains sales*: Words and deeds

1 'Le Style dramatique' is the text of a lecture given by Sartre at the invitation of Jean Vilar in 1944, a few days after the *générale* of *Huis clos*. It was first published in *Un Théâtre de situations* in 1973, and references will be given to this edition. References to *Les Mains sales* will indicate the Gallimard edition of 1948.
2 See J. L. Austin, *How to Do Things with Words*, Oxford, Clarendon Press, 1962, and John R. Searle, *Speech Acts. An Essay in the Philosophy of Language*, Cambridge University Press, 1969. For a further discussion of illocutionary acts, see p. 105 above. My later argument does not imply that Sartre anticipated Austin's analyses, but rather that speech-act theory provides an appropriate framework for a discussion of Sartre's practice. Austin himself took the view that the performative utterances of literature are 'void', or 'parasitic' upon our normal use of language, and, as such, not serious (p. 22). He therefore excluded such utterances from his consideration. Nevertheless, speech-act theory is increasingly taken as a relevant basis for literary analysis. For a polemical discussion based on a critique of the Formalist distinction between literary and non-literary language see Mary Louise Pratt, *Toward a Speech Act Theory of Literary Discourse*, Bloomington, Indiana University Press, 1977. The relevance of speech-act theory to the analysis of drama is discussed in Keir Elam, *The Semiotics of Theatre and Drama*, Methuen, 'New Accents', 1980.
3 This could be taken to mean that a prior choice pre-exists and 'causes' present action. Sartre argues, however, that in acting I constantly renew, reaffirm or call into question earlier choices and projects: 'je me choisis perpétuellement' (*EN*, p. 560).

4   Reprinted as 'Forger des mythes' in *Un Théâtre de situations*, pp. 55–67. References will be given to this version.

5   Sartre, in theory, rejects the view that the will is autonomous, that it exemplifies our freedom more fully than does our emotional behaviour, and that it is morally superior to such behaviour in that it can 'décider soudain de briser l'enchaînement des passions' (*EN*, p. 520): 'la liberté, étant assimilable à mon existence, est fondement des fins que je tenterai d'atteindre, soit par la volonté, soit par des efforts passionnels. Elle ne saurait donc se limiter aux actes volontaires. Mais les volitions sont, au contraire, comme les passions, certaines attitudes subjectives par lesquelles nous tentons d'atteindre aux fins posées par la liberté originelle. [...] Il n'y a, par rapport à la liberté, aucun phénomène psychique privilégié' (*EN*, pp. 520–1).

6   Sartre's emphasis in the mid-1940s on the importance of conflicts of will and the affirmation of rights in the theatre seems to derive in part from his reading of Hegel. Greek tragedy is analysed by Hegel in terms of such conflicts both in his *Aesthetics* and in his *Phenomenology of Spirit*, which Sartre certainly read in Hyppolite's translation in the early 1940s. Sartre refers specifically to Hegel's commentary on Sophocles' *Antigone* (*TS*, pp. 59, 96 and 136–8). See also the introduction to *Un Théâtre de situations* by Michel Contat and Michel Rybalka.

7   This 'cohésion magique' differs from the 'unité d'être' of the *pour-soi*, of which it is simply an objectification. See also Chapter 2, note 7.

8   The complexities of the political background may, indeed, be eclipsed by the foreground of the action: for both reader and spectator, *Les Mains sales* is one of Sartre's most allusive plays. The political situation and events (in the order of their occurrence rather than in the order of their representation) are as follows. In 1943 Illyria is ruled by the fascist government of the Regent and the Prince, which collaborates with the Axis. The clandestine opposition consists of the nationalist bourgeois party, led by Karsky, and of the Parti Prolétarien, which has united in an uneasy coalition the P.A.C. (the communist party to which Olga, Hoederer, Louis and Hugo belong) and the social democrats. In March 1943 Hoederer proposes the policy that in anticipation of an eventual German defeat, and of a Russian advance into Illyria, the Parti Prolétarien should persuade the other two parties to form an alliance with it, in order to obtain for itself a minority share in the post-war government. The rationale behind this policy is that if the Left were to seize power for itself by exploiting Russian military strength, the unpopularity of the measures it would need to take, and the people's resentment of the occupying Russian army, would lead to its rapid defeat, whereas a form of power-sharing would enable it to consolidate its position. A further motive is a more humanitarian one. As Hoederer explains to Hugo: 'si nous traitons avec le Régent, il arrête la guerre; les troupes illyriennes attendent gentiment que les Russes viennent les désarmer;

si nous rompons les pourparlers, il sait qu'il est perdu et il se battra comme un chien enragé; des centaines de milliers d'hommes y laisseront leur peau' (v, iii, p. 211). Hoederer's proposal is carried by a social-democrat majority of votes against the wishes of the P.A.C. hard-liners, represented by Louis, who wish to press for sole communist power. They decide to 'liquidate' Hoederer, in the absence of any directive from Russia. Hugo, the young bourgeois 'idealist' who sees Hoederer's policy as a form of compromise, undertakes to do so. He witnesses and tries to interrupt Hoederer's meeting with the Prince and Karsky, but his own intervention is frustrated by a bomb attack. Hugo, who out of growing regard for Hoederer fails to fulfil in cold blood his mission of assassin, does so when he finds his wife Jessica in Hoederer's arms. Hugo is sentenced to five years' imprisonment, but is released after two years, having survived an attempt on his life three months previously. At the time of his release, he learns that Hoederer's policy had been approved by Russia and adopted by the P.A.C., that the power-sharing pact had been established, thereby saving many Illyrian lives, but that Germany had invaded the country. The play opens with the news of the German retreat before the Russian army. Hugo, who is now asked in the interests of the Party to 'forget' his assassination of the rehabilitated Hoederer, decides to claim it as a consciously political act, thereby ensuring his own death.

In the order of representation, the first and last *tableaux* are set in March 1945, at the time of Hugo's release from prison. The events of March 1943 are represented in flashback in *tableaux* II to VI.

9 See Ch. Perelman and L. Olbrechts-Tyteca, *The New Rhetoric. A Treatise on Argumentation*, University of Notre Dame Press, 1969, p. 444. (First published in 1958.)

10 For an analysis of the distinction between fictive utterances and natural utterances, and for a definition of literature (and, particularly, of poetry) as the representation of verbal acts, see Barbara Herrnstein Smith, *On the Margins of Discourse: The Relation of Literature to Language*, University of Chicago Press, 1978. Within a given literary text, quotations from other texts, or the utterances involved in language games, could be regarded as fictive to the second degree. From this point of view, the 'quoting' of commonplaces, which will also be discussed later, has an interesting marginal status.

11 See Karl R. Popper, 'Prediction and prophecy in the social sciences', in *Conjectures and Refutations*, Routledge & Kegan Paul, 1963, and, particularly, p. 338.

12 It is one of the play's ironies that Hoederer's code-name derives, whether by accident or design, from that of Count Kuehn-Hedérváry who, as the Hungarian Ban of Croatia, was one of those responsible for suppressing the highly vocal Illyrist national movement in the late nineteenth century. Hoederer, too, from a rather different political position, is impatient of Illyrian nationalist pretensions as

exemplified by Karsky, the leader of the bourgeois party: 'L'Illyrie, l'Illyrie seule: je connais la chanson. Vous l'avez chantée pendant deux ans à la bourgeoisie nationaliste' (IV, iv, p. 155). The vicissitudes of Illyrian aspirations to nationhood are more likely to be familiar to a French audience than to a British one, distracted by irrelevant Shakespearean associations. Napoleon occupied and annexed the Illyrian provinces, as they were then called, in 1809; in 1814 one group reverted to Austria, while another became an 'allied kingdom' or a subject province (depending on one's point of view) of the Hungarian crown.

13 See I, iii, p. 29.

14 *Lire le théâtre*, Editions sociales, 1978, pp. 207–8. Further page references will be given in the text.

15 See vol. I: 'Première partie: La Constitution, vi: Père et fils, A: Retour à l'analyse régressive', passim.

16 See Sartre's preface to Georges Michel, *La Promenade du dimanche*, Gallimard, 1967, pp. 7–10. The passages quoted are from pages 7–8. Sartre's text first appeared in the programme of the original production in 1966. Already, in his preface to Nathalie Sarraute, *Portrait d'un inconnu* (1948), shortly after the publication of *Les Mains sales*, Sartre summarises the effects of the *lieu commun* upon character and, by implication, upon characterisation. The *lieu commun* is 'rassurant pour autrui, rassurant pour moi-même puisque je me suis réfugié dans cette zone neutre et commune qui n'est tout à fait l'objectif, puisqu'enfin je m'y tiens par décret, ni tout à fait subjective puisque tout le monde m'y peut atteindre et s'y retrouver, mais qu'on pourrait nommer à la fois la subjectivité de l'objectif et l'objectivité du subjectif. Comme je prétends n'être que cela et comme je proteste que je n'ai pas de tiroirs secrets, il m'est permis, sur ce plan, de bavarder, de m'émouvoir, de m'indigner, de montrer "un caractère" et même d'être un "original", c'est-à-dire d'assembler les lieux communs d'une manière inédite: il y a même, en effet, des "paradoxes communs". On me laisse, en somme, le loisir d'être subjectif dans les limites de l'objectivité. Et plus je serai subjectif entre ces frontières étroites, plus on m'en saura gré: car je démontrerai par là que le subjectif n'est rien et qu'il n'en faut pas avoir peur' (*S* IV, pp. 11–12).

17 Hugo's formulation seems to approximate here to what Searle describes as an utterance made in a 'detached anthropological sense', which implies a distinction between the speech of a 'committed participant' and a 'neutral observer': 'Why can't I speak in a detached anthropological sense? It seems obvious to me that one can say "He made a promise", meaning something like "He made what they, the people of this Anglo-Saxon tribe, call a promise". And that is a purely descriptive sense of promise which involves no commitment to evaluative statements at all' (*Speech Acts*, p. 196). What Hugo does seem to be betraying is his increasing detachment from the 'hard line' of his

party colleagues. The conclusion of Searle's argument is that the adoption of the 'detached anthropological standpoint' has, as its price, 'that words no longer mean what they mean. [...] The retreat from the committed use of words ultimately must involve a retreat from language itself' (ibid., p. 198). Hugo's final speech-act is an attempt, in a world where words no longer seem to 'mean what they mean' to restore meaning and commitment to language, at the price of a retreat from life.

18 Since, for Sartre (or, at least, for a 'sloganised' Sartre) man is the sum of his acts, and since man's acts reveal his intentions, one might expect it to follow that his acts could be judged 'objectively'. Sartre frequently takes issue, however, with the closely related communist definition of objectivity. See, for instance, 'Matérialisme et révolution' (1946): 'Les trotzkystes, lui dit-on, se trompent; mais ils ne sont pas, comme vous le prétendez, des indicateurs de police: vous *savez bien* qu'ils ne le sont pas. – Au contraire, vous répondra-t-il, je sais parfaitement qu'ils en sont: ce qu'ils pensent au fond m'indiffère; la subjectivité n'existe pas. Mais *objectivement* ils jouent le jeu de la bourgeoisie, ils se *comportent* comme des provocateurs et des indicateurs, car il revient au même de faire inconsciemment le jeu de la police ou de lui prêter délibérément son concours. On lui répond que, précisément, cela ne revient pas au même et que, en toute *objectivité*, les conduites du trotzkyste et du policier ne se ressemblent pas. Il rétorque qu'elles sont aussi nuisibles l'une que l'autre et qu'elles ont toutes deux pour effet de freiner l'avance de la classe ouvrière. Et si l'on insiste, si on lui montre qu'il y a plusieurs manières de freiner cette avance et qu'elles ne sont pas équivalentes, même en leurs effets, il répond superbement que ces distinctions, fussent-elles vraies, ne l'intéressent pas: nous sommes en période de lutte, la situation est simple et les positions bien tranchées: pourquoi raffiner? Le militant communiste ne doit pas s'embarrasser de tant de nuances. Nous voilà revenus à l'utile: ainsi cette proposition "le trotzkyste est un indicateur" oscille perpétuellement de l'état d'opinion utile à celle de vérité objective' (*S* III, pp. 170–1). In a different register, the notion is also the target of Sartre's satire in *Nekrassov* (1955).

19 J. Huizinga, *Homo Ludens*, Routledge & Kegan Paul, 1949, p. 13. (First published in 1938.)

20 See Gregory Bateson, 'A theory of play and fantasy', in *Steps to an Ecology of Mind*, St Albans, Granada, Paladin, 1973. (The essay was first published in 1955.)

21 The play was warmly welcomed by the Parisian bourgeois audience, and condemned by the communist press, for what both took to be, contrary to Sartre's intentions, its anti-communist theme. For an account of the reception of the play see *Les Ecrits de Sartre*, pp. 177–82. For Sartre's own comment, see *Un Théâtre de situations*, pp. 246–65. In the light of his negative view of the notion of

'objectivity' (see note 18 above), it is perhaps ironic that in 1964 Sartre concedes the following point: 'On ne peut nier, objectivement, qu'à un certain moment, étant donné les circonstances dans lesquelles elle sort, une pièce assume un sens objectif qui lui est attribué par un public. Il n'y a rien à faire: si toute la bourgeoisie française fait un succès triomphal aux *Mains sales*, et si les communistes l'attaquent, cela veut dire [...] que la pièce est devenue *par elle-même* anticommuniste, objectivement, et que les intentions de l'auteur ne comptent plus' (*TS*, p. 251).

5 *Les Séquestrés d'Altona*: Imagination and illusion

1 References will be given in the text to the edition of *Les Séquestrés d'Altona* published by Gallimard in 1960. For a useful critical edition of the play, see *Les Séquestrés d'Altona*, ed. Philip Thody, University of London Press, 1965.

2 See Thody's comment in the introduction to his edition of *Les Séquestrés* (p. 27): 'The impression given by *La Critique de la raison dialectique* is that as long as man continues to work under the pressure of scarcity and need – and Sartre insists at length that these form an inherent part of the human condition – he will inevitably fall victim to his own creations. What this leads to is the fundamentally anti-Marxist view that man will always be alienated from himself by the unpredictable effect of his own actions, and that no authentic moral acts are therefore possible.' See, in contrast, the interpretation of the *Critique* and of *Les Séquestrés* offered by Michel Contat, *Explication des Séquestrés d'Altona de Jean-Paul Sartre*, Minard, Archives des Lettres Modernes, 1968 (5), no. 89, pp. 18–19: 'L'homme crée lui-même la nécessité et l'Histoire fait l'homme dans l'exacte mesure où il la fait. Autrement dit, la liberté est à la fois le fondement de la dialectique historique et la condition d'une histoire humaine. C'est pourquoi les conflits qui opposent entre eux les "Séquestrés" et les déchirent en eux-mêmes nous apparaissent comme une aliénation sociale liée à notre histoire et, par là-même, transitoire, c'est-à-dire *surmontable*. En ce sens [...] on pourrait dire que, par le fait même que cette tragédie est historique, *Les Séquestrés d'Altona* est, en définitive, une pièce plus optimiste que *Huis clos*.'

3 Questions of the 'Was Hamlet mad?' variety are often provoked by Frantz's behaviour, and with equally inconclusive results. His attitudes do in many ways conform, however, to Sartre's descriptions of what he calls 'pathological imagination' in *L'Imaginaire*. The fact that Frantz's imaginary world is consciously, indeed voluntarily, created and maintained is in a sense irrelevant. In a Sartrean perspective, the actions and attitudes of the schizophrenic are as consciously chosen as those of any other individual: 'Le schizophrène sait fort bien que les objets dont il s'entoure sont irréels: c'est même pour cela qu'il les fait apparaître' (*Im.*, p. 190). He chooses to flee not only the content of

reality (disappointment or failure), but its form: 'son caractère *de présence*, le genre de réaction qu'il demande de nous, la subordination de nos conduites à l'objet, l'inépuisabilité des perceptions, leur indépendance, la façon même que nos sentiments ont de se développer. Cette vie factice, figée, ralentie, scolastique qui, pour la plupart des gens n'est qu'un pis-aller, c'est elle précisément qu'un schizophrène désire. Le rêveur morbide qui s'imagine être roi ne s'accommoderait pas d'une royauté effective; même pas d'une tyrannie où tous ses désirs seraient exaucés. C'est que, en effet, jamais un désir n'est à la lettre exaucé, du fait précisément de l'abîme qui sépare le réel de l'imaginaire. L'objet que je désirais, on peut bien me le donner mais c'est sur un autre plan d'existence auquel je devrai m'adapter. Le voici maintenant en face de moi: si je n'étais pressé par l'action, je devrais longtemps hésiter, surpris, ne reconnaissant pas cette réalité pleine et riche en conséquences: je devrais me demander: "Est-ce bien *cela* que j'ai voulu?" Le rêveur morbide lui, n'hésitera pas: ce n'est pas *cela* qu'il voulait' (*Im.*, p. 189). The reader recalls Leni's words to Frantz, which suggest more than a simple acknowledgement of responsibility: 'Tu seras invulnérable, si tu oses déclarer: "J'ai fait ce que j'ai voulu et je veux ce que j'ai fait"' (ii, i, p. 92). Frantz's answering question suggests his inability to recognise, let alone adapt to, either the reality of his past actions or of their present consequences: 'Qu'est-ce que j'ai fait, Leni?' (p. 92). In the words of *L'Imaginaire* 'Le présent exige une adaptation qu'il [le rêveur morbide] n'est plus capable de fournir; il y faut même une sorte d'indétermination de nos sentiments, une réelle plasticité: c'est que le réel est toujours nouveau, toujours *imprévisible*' (p. 189). Hence Frantz's fear of new emotional experiences or new emotional demands, summed up in one of the many notices posted in his room: '"Il est défendu d'avoir peur"' (ii, i, p. 81). Hence, too, his obsessive desire to sustain existing responses: 'les sentiments du rêveur morbide sont solennels et figés; ils reviennent toujours avec la même forme et la même étiquette; le malade a eu tout le temps de les construire; rien n'est laissé en eux, au hasard, ils ne s'accommoderaient pas de la plus légère dérogation. Corrélativement les traits des objets irréels qui leur correspondent sont arrêtés pour toujours. Ainsi le rêveur peut choisir au magasin des accessoires les sentiments qu'il veut revêtir et les objets qui leur correspondent, comme l'acteur choisit ses costumes. [...] C'est un monde pauvre et méticuleux, où les mêmes scènes se répètent inlassablement, jusqu'au moindre détail, accompagnées du même cérémonial où tout est réglé à l'avance, prévu; où, surtout, rien ne peut échapper, résister ni surprendre' (*Im.*, pp. 189–90). It would appear that for Sartre the distinction between 'normal' and pathological imagination and role-playing is one of degree rather than of kind.

4 Despite, or because of, his theoretical concern to establish a sharp

distinction between imagination and perception, Sartre is fascinated by imagination's *imitation* of perception, or by those hybrid acts of consciousness in which imagination seems to have the density of perception. Hence, too, his sometimes uneasy interest in types of theatre which transgress the conventional relationship of perception and imagination exploited by 'participation' theatre – for instance, his concern with the 'dramatised' religious ritual of the Cuban National Theatre, psychodrama, 'documentary' theatre, or the 'happening'. (See 'Théâtre épique et théâtre dramatique' and 'Mythe et réalité du théâtre' in *Un Théâtre de situations*.) This fascination may also explain his predilection (a 'cratylist' predilection, according to Gérard Genette) for poetic words which seem to embody in their visual aspect or sound the quality of the object or the atmosphere which they evoke, thereby achieving, unlike the conventional sign, a synthesis of absence and presence. (See Gérard Genette, 'Sens et signification: la théorie sartrienne du langage poétique'.)

5 ‘"*Les Séquestrés d'Altona* nous concernent tous", entretien avec Bernard Dort', *Théâtre populaire*, no. 36, 4ᵉ trimestre 1959, pp. 1–13. Reprinted in *Un Théâtre de situations*, pp. 299–314. In connection with the 'évanouissement du mirage théâtral', Sartre invokes Corneille's *L'Illusion comique* rather than Brecht. In its interplay of 'trompe l'œil' and distance, illusion and the puncturing of illusion, of representations within representations which sometimes offer their own suspect versions of 'truth' and of imaginary worlds within imaginary worlds, the effect of *Les Séquestrés d'Altona* is quite strictly baroque.

6 Commitment and writing

1 'Les Ecrivains en personne', interview with Madeleine Chapsal, 1960, reprinted in *S* IX, Gallimard, 1972, p. 14.

2 'Question de méthode', published in 1960 as the introductory section of *Critique de la raison dialectique* (Gallimard), first appeared separately, but without its concluding pages, in *Les Temps modernes*, no. 139, septembre 1957, and no. 140, octobre 1957. For analyses of *L'Idiot de la famille* see Christina Howells, *Sartre's Theory of Literature*, MHRA, 1979, and Hazel E. Barnes, *Sartre and Flaubert*, University of Chicago Press, 1981.

3 *S* VIII, Gallimard, 1972. (The transcript of three lectures given in Japan in 1965.) Henceforth either *Plaidoyer* or *S* VIII.

4 *Obliques*, no. 18–19, éd. Michel Sicard, pp. 249–62. (See also a more recent and extensive transcript of Sartre's notes, which appeared too late to be taken into account in the present study: *Cahiers pour une morale*, Gallimard, 1983. The *Obliques* version corresponds to pp. 26–56 of the Gallimard edition.)

5 In *Les Ecrivains célèbres*, t. III, éd. Raymond Queneau, Mazenod, 1953, pp. 148–51. The essay is more often read as the preface to the

1966 Gallimard edition of Mallarmé's *Poésies*, and is reprinted in *S* ix, pp. 191–201.

6 *Obliques*, no. 18–19, pp. 169–94.

7 'Sur *L'Idiot de la famille*', *S* x, Gallimard, 1976, p. 113.

8 'Orphée noir' first appeared as an introduction to Léopold Sedar Senghor, *Anthologie de la nouvelle poésie nègre et malgache de langue française*, Presses Universitaires de France, 1948. Reprinted in *S* iii, Gallimard, 1949, pp. 229–86.

9 For an illuminating consideration of these terms in relation to 'committed' intellectuals writing before Sartre, see David L. Schalk, *The Spectrum of Political Engagement*, Princeton University Press, 1979. The chronological limits of Schalk's study (1920 to 1945) mean that his analysis concentrates upon the attitudes of Mounier, Benda, Nizan and Brasillach. There are frequent references to Sartre, but substantive discussion of his position is reserved for a two-page epilogue.

10 See Michel-Antoine Burnier, *Les Existentialistes et la politique*, Gallimard, 1966, and Mark Poster, *Existential Marxism in Post-war France*, Princeton University Press, 1975.

11 'Présentation des *Temps Modernes*', *S* ii, p. 12.

12 See 'la parole est un certain moment particulier de l'action et ne se comprend pas en dehors d'elle' (*S* ii, p. 71), or 'parler c'est agir: toute chose qu'on nomme n'est déjà plus tout à fait la même, elle a perdu son innocence' (*S* ii, p. 72).

13 The contradiction between the 'antinomie entre la parole et l'action' referred to here and the views quoted in the previous note remains unexplained.

14 See the section 'Oppositions de l'action éthique' in G. W. F. Hegel, *La Phénoménologie de l'esprit*, traduction de Jean Hyppolite, Aubier, t. ii, 1941, pp. 34–8. In this section, Hegel reaches the point in his dialectic of action at which 'la conscience de soi éthique fait maintenant l'expérience de la nature développée de l'action *effective*' (p. 36), and at which '*l'accomplissement* énonce de lui-même que ce qui est *éthique* doit étre *effectif*; car l'*effectivité* du but est le but de l'action' (p. 37). ('Effectivité' is Hyppolite's translation of *Wirklichkeit*, which in English versions of Hegel is usually rendered as 'actuality'.)

15 These antinomies still confront the intellectual in *Plaidoyer* over fifteen years later, and mean that his study of society can never be a fully objective one. In *Plaidoyer*, however, the possibility of a dialectical solution is envisaged, but Sartre avoids a rigorous definition of the method by maintaining that, unlike the procedures available to the 'technicien du savoir pratique', explicit knowledge of it is not available to the intellectual. See *S* viii, pp. 402–3.

16 The need for such a theoretical framework is recognised in 'Matérialisme et révolution' (*Les Temps modernes*, no. 9, juin 1946, reprinted in *S* iii, Gallimard, 1949, pp. 135–225): 'Il faut [...] une théorie philosophique qui montre que la réalité de l'homme est action et que

l'action sur l'univers ne fait qu'un avec la compréhension de cet univers tel qu'il est, autrement dit, que l'action est dévoilement de la réalité *en même temps* que modification de cette réalité' (*S* III, p. 184). But the essay concentrates largely on a negative critique of the doctrine of materialist determinism in contemporary Marxist theory; it invokes, but does not develop, a 'philosophie rigoureuse' which would eventually elucidate the notions of 'situation' and 'être-dans-le-monde' in terms of 'l'entière et métaphysique liberté humaine' (p. 223).

17　See *L'Etre et le Néant*, p. 717: 'Tout se passe donc comme si l'en-soi et le pour-soi se présentaient en état de *désintégration* par rapport à une synthèse idéale. Non que l'intégration ait jamais *eu lieu*, mais précisément au contraire parce qu'elle est toujours indiquée et toujours impossible'.

18　Later, Sartre sees his discussion of *praxis* in *Critique de la raison dialectique* as a provisional contribution to the solution of this problem. See *CRD*, pp. 129–35.

19　Like so much of Sartre's vocabulary in the mid and late 1940s, the term 'le non-savoir' echoes Hyppolite's translation of Hegel's *Phénoménologie de l'esprit*. There it occurs both in Hegel's analysis of 'Les oppositions de l'action éthique' (t. II, pp. 34–8) and in his discussion of tragic action (t. II, pp. 246–54): 'L'esprit *agissant*, comme conscience, se pose en face de l'objet sur lequel il est actif et qui ainsi est déterminé comme le *négatif* de l'élément qui sait; celui qui agit se trouve donc dans la situation de l'opposition du savoir et du non-savoir. [...] En effet ce savoir est dans son concept immédiatement le non-savoir, parce que la *conscience* est en soi-même dans le fait d'agir cette opposition. [...] La différence du savoir et du non-savoir tombe dans *chacune des consciences de soi effectives* – et c'est seulement dans l'abstraction, dans l'élément de l'universalité qu'elle se répartit en deux figures individuelles' (pp. 249–51). Or, as Hyppolite's annotation puts it: 'l'opposition du *Savoir* et du *Non-savoir* [...] se trouve à l'intérieur de chaque personnage' (p. 251). In short, 'le non-savoir' is an essential moment in Hegel's dialectic of action and aesthetic representation, and seems to have encouraged Sartre's increasing recognition of an element of opacity in human reflection and action.

20　Sartre's use of the term 'compréhension', which he distinguishes sharply from both 'connaissance' and 'intellection' is technical rather than idiosyncratic. In its application to both individual and social life, and in its inclusion of both rational and intuitive elements, it is indebted, as I have already suggested, to the German tradition referred to in Chapter 3, p. 88, and, particularly, to Karl Jaspers' *verstehende Psychologie*. For an analysis of that tradition which includes a discussion of Sartre see William Outhwaite, *Understanding Social Life. The Method called 'Verstehen'*, Allen & Unwin, 1975. Sartre already uses the term in relation to psychoanalysis in *L'Etre et le Néant*, where 'connaissance' of human behaviour is shown to be based on a more fundamental 'compréhension', whether or not 'le psychanalyste et le sujet de la psychanalyse ne font qu'un' (p. 659). For a discussion of the *Verstehen* tradition in psychology and psycho-analysis see Gerald N. Izenberg, *The Existentialist Critique of Freud. The Crisis of Autonomy*, Princeton University Press, 1976.

21 These terms recall those in which, in *L'Etre et le Néant*, Sartre refers to the subject's 'projet fondamental': 'Mais si le projet fondamental est pleinement *vécu* par le sujet, et, comme tel, totalement conscient, cela ne signifie nullement qu'il doive être du même coup *connu* par lui' (p. 658). But as we shall see, the notion of 'conscience' will undergo certain modifications.

22 '[Les mots] n'étaient plus à lui, ils n'étaient plus lui; mais dans ces miroirs étrangers se reflétaient le ciel, la terre et sa propre vie' (*S* II, p. 67).

23 Despite this acknowledgement of Surrealism, Sartre attempts to inte-grate the movement of literary history into the 'dialectic' of socio-cultural development: the debt of the black poets to white Surrealism is itself subverted and *dépassé*. For Sartre, the dialectical pretensions of Surrealism itself are hollow: it is more concerned with a 'calme unité des contraires', than with the 'perpétuel dépassement' of, for instance, Césaire (*S* III, p. 257). See also Sartre's critique of Surrealism in *Qu'est-ce que la littérature?* (*S* II, pp. 317–26).

24 This priority is still maintained in *Plaidoyer pour les intellectuels* (1965): 'L'intellectuel [...] reste, lui, *sans pouvoir* même s'il est lié à la direction du Parti. Car cette liaison lui rend, à un autre niveau, son caractère de fonctionnaire subalterne des superstructures et, tout en l'acceptant par discipline, il doit le contester sans cesse et ne jamais s'arrêter de dévoiler le rapport des moyens choisis aux fins organi-ques. En tant que tel, sa fonction va du témoignage au martyre: le pouvoir, quel qu'il soit, veut utiliser les intellectuels pour sa propa-gande mais s'en méfie et commence toujours ses purges par eux' (*S* VIII, p. 428–9).

25 For an analysis of the relationship between the experience of *échec*, the imagery of the sacred and the theme of aesthetic creation in Sartre, see Thomas M. King, *Sartre and the Sacred*, University of Chicago Press, 1974, and particularly the section 'The image as nega-tive theology'. King discusses the relationship with particular refer-ence to *L'Idiot de la famille*.

26 The reference to 'la loi du cœur' alludes to the section of Hegel's *Phénoménologie de l'esprit* in which the opposition between 'la loi du cœur' and 'la loi de la réalité effective' is described. The former is the internalising of the universal law, creating a 'singularité universelle' which then confronts a 'réalité effective'; this 'réalité' is then itself seen to be dual in character: 'une telle réalité effective est, d'une part une loi par laquelle l'individualité singulière est opprimée, un ordre

du monde, ordre de contrainte et de violence, qui contredit la loi du cœur, et est d'autre part une humanité pâtissant de cet ordre, une humanité qui ne suit pas la loi du cœur, mais est soumise à une nécessité étrangère' (t. I, p. 303). Here Hegel also, perhaps, inspires Sartre's view of 'négritude' as a form of *témoignage* ultimately more generally human than specifically racial in its aims: 'cette individualité tend donc à supprimer cette nécessité contredisant la loi du cœur, et à supprimer la souffrance provoquée par elle. L'individualité [...] est la gravité d'un dessein sublime qui cherche son plaisir dans la présentation de l'excellence de sa propre essence et dans la production du *bien-être de l'humanité*' (p. 304). This synthesis of metaphysical and humanitarian concerns seems to anticipate Sartre's own descriptions of the committed 'universel singulier'. (Sartre's interest in Hegel, already prominent in *L'Etre et le Néant*, was undoubtedly fostered in the late 1940s by two influential commentaries: Jean Hyppolite, *Genèse et structure de la Phénoménologie de l'esprit de Hegel*, Aubier, 1946, and Alexandre Kojève, *Introduction à la lecture de Hegel*, Gallimard, 1947. The available evidence indicates that Sartre – unlike, for instance, Jacques Lacan and Maurice Merleau-Ponty – did not attend the lectures on Hegel which were given by Kojève at the Ecole des Hautes Etudes from 1933 to 1939, and which formed the basis of his *Introduction*.)

27 Stéphane Mallarmé, *Œuvres complètes*, Bibliothèque de la Pléiade, Gallimard, 1951, p. 883. References given in the text and notes will be abbreviated as *O.c.* My own quotations from Sartre or Mallarmé will be given in single quotation marks; quotations from Mallarmé within quotations from Sartre will be given in double quotation marks.

28 See *Les Ecrits de Sartre*, pp. 32 and 33.

29 'Orphée noir', *S* III, p. 248; *O.c.*, p. 400. See also *Saint Genet, comédien et martyr*, Gallimard, 1952, pp. 331–2.

30 *Saint Genet*, p. 444; *O.c.*, p. 300. That Sartre was at this stage also preoccupied with Mallarmé's work is suggested by the frequency of his references to it in *Saint Genet*.

31 It is Mallarmé's own interest in Hegel which stimulates Sartre's recourse to Hegelian terminology in this particular analysis. He asserts that Mallarmé's knowledge of Hegel was derived from Villiers de l'Isle-Adam (*EM*, p. 193) and makes no reference to Eugène Lefébure in this connection. For the seminal account of Hegelian elements in Mallarmé's thought and of their derivation, see L. J. Austin, 'Mallarmé et le rêve du "Livre"', *Mercure de France*, CCCXVII, no. 1073, janvier 1953, pp. 81–108.

32 For Sartre, the limitations of orthodox Marxist 'reflection' theory lie in the fact that it postulates an initial separation and an ultimate parallelism between the elements of economic 'infrastructure' and institutional and ideological 'superstructure'. For an analysis of Sartre's

divergence from classical Marxist theory in this connection, see Fredric Jameson, *Marxism and Form*, Princeton University Press, 1971, particularly Chapter 4. For Sartre, 'the economic base is therefore inert matter which is transformed by human action, and which, in the act of transformation, leaves its traces within the new act as a kind of inert structure or skeleton; in other terms, it may be seen as the past [...] transcended [...] by the act of the historical agent. The Sartrean model is therefore closer to the original Hegelian one of a datum which is both negated and sublated (*aufgehoben*) or preserved: and this rearticulation of the reflection model into two consecutive moments, into situation and freely invented response, gives a more realistic content to the idea of alienation itself, as something which circumstances force us to *do to ourselves*, and that without clearly knowing it' (pp. 290–1). The point of view discussed here is most fully set out in the *Critique de la raison dialectique*, but is clearly anticipated in *L'Engagement de Mallarmé*.

33 An approximate rendering. See Stéphane Mallarmé, *Correspondance*, I, Gallimard, 1959, p. 241 (henceforth referred to as *C*, I).

34 *EN*, pp. 659–62.

35 Sartre fails to do justice to the 'intentional' elements of human behaviour analysed by Freud. For a general account of the relationship between existential and Freudian psychoanalysis, see Izenberg, *The Existentialist Critique of Freud*. For Sartre's later views on Freud see Christina Howells, 'Sartre and Freud', *French Studies*, XXXIII, no. 2, April 1979, pp. 157–76.

36 Charles Mauron, *Introduction à la psychanalyse de Mallarmé*, Neuchâtel, A la Baconnière, 1950, p. 149.

37 See, in contrast, the analyses of J.-P. Richard in *L'Univers imaginaire de Mallarmé*, Seuil, 1961.

38 *EN*, pp. 88–93 and 658–69.

39 Sartre's familiar distinction between consciousness and explicit knowledge is fundamental to many of his arguments but is not consistently sustained. It is particularly relevant to his concept of 'compréhension'.

40 'Sartre par Sartre' (1970), in *S* IX, Gallimard, 1972, p. 112.

41 *Plaidoyer*, *S* VIII, p. 453.

42 'Sartre par Sartre', *S* IX, p. 111.

43 *EN*, pp. 301–7 and 484–6.

44 To those who wish to attempt a Freudian psychoanalysis on Sartre, such terminology may suggest the 'cannibalistic' or 'oral' stage in Freudian theory and its association with the libidinal incorporation and appropriation of the object. But again Sartre differs from Freud: the image of appropriation refers not to a stage in psychosexual development but to the desire to know (*EN*, pp. 669), which refers, in turn, to the primary 'désir d'être': 'Connaître, c'est manger des yeux. [...] Pour l'enfant, connaître, c'est manger effectivement' (p. 667).

Knowledge does, however, have both sexual and alimentary implications for Sartre. (See pp. 666–9).

45 These changes may owe something to Merleau-Ponty's analyses of consciousness in *Phénoménologie de la perception* (1945), in which he criticises some of the more extreme positions of *L'Etre et le Néant* and takes greater account of the world of infancy and childhood. Apart from one explicit reference to Merleau-Ponty (see note 48 below) Sartre borrows his vocabulary – for instance 'l'insertion dans le monde' (this specific debt is not acknowledged until *Plaidoyer, S* VIII, p. 440) – and some of the spatial imagery associated with it. Merleau-Ponty does not ascribe a primarily negating function to consciousness, and in a passage clearly directed against Sartre's assertion of the radical freedom of consciousness and choice, he maintains that our embodied *être-au-monde* is prior to our sense-giving choices: 'Il y a un sens autochtone du monde qui se constitue dans le commerce avec lui de notre existence incarnée et qui forme le sol de toute Sinngebung décisoire' (*Phénoménologie de la perception*, p. 503). The world is not simply the 'facticity' of one's choice, as it was earlier for Sartre. Furthermore, Merleau-Ponty recognises the priority of *Mitsein* (p. 518). In short, Sartre's unusually lyrical evocation of infancy seems to be a transposition of our inherence in the world as described by Merleau-Ponty.

46 'Sur *L'Idiot de la famille*', *S* x, p. 97.

47 See Mauron, *La Psychanalyse de Mallarmé*, p. 13.

48 *Phénoménologie de la perception*, p. 188.

49 For Sartre, the anticipated crime of *Pauvre enfant pâle* and its punishment in death is a 'meurtre et martyre, assassinat qui, au fond, est un suicide' (*EM*, p. 187). He alludes throughout his essay to the tension in Mallarmé between the temptation of suicide and the imperative to create. The projected suicide of Igitur, last of his race, even becomes genocide (p. 193). But Mallarmé's survival expresses the desire to 'assumer en pleine Conscience la folie de ses ancêtres' (p. 193). The extremism of this 'dialectic' of self-sacrifice and creation in Mallarmé as interpreted by Sartre seems to constitute in his view a form of valiant *témoignage*. In another connection it may be noted that the 'môme trop vacillant pour figurer parmi la race' of *Réminiscence* is invoked in *Saint Genet* to characterise the alienation of the orphan Genet (pp. 21–2).

50 'Où Kant […] avait vu la Loi Morale, Mallarmé percevait sans doute l'Impératif d'une poésie: une Poétique.' *Variété* II, Gallimard, 1930, p. 198.

51 For a similarly Hegelian but more measured analysis of the same passage see L. J. Austin, 'Mallarmé', p. 97.

52 Sartre chooses to emphasise the positive aspects of Mallarmé's complex attitude towards 'la foule'. In the Mallarmé manuscript he does not refer in any detail to the problem of communication, which is

none the less central to a theory of committed literature. In 1960, however, defending Mallarmé against the charge of 'un engagement dans le refus', and alluding, it would seem, to *L'Action restreinte, Catholicisme*, and *Autobiographie*, he replies: 'Il refusait son époque, mais il la conservait comme une transition, comme un tunnel. Il souhaitait qu'on jouât un jour devant ce qu'il appelait alors "la foule" – et qu'il concevait comme un public de masse (plutôt dans une cathédrale athée que dans un théâtre) – la Tragédie. La seule, l'unique, qui serait à la fois le drame de l'homme, le mouvement du monde, le retour tragique des saisons et dont l'auteur, anonyme comme Homère, serait mort, ou bien, perdu parmi l'assistance, assisterait au déroulement d'un chef-d'œuvre qui ne lui appartiendrait pas, que *tous* lui donnerait comme à tous. Mallarmé liait ses conceptions orphiques et tragiques de la poésie à la communion d'un peuple plutôt qu'à l'hermétisme individuel. Celui-ci n'était qu'un refus de la sottise bourgeoise' ('Les Écrivains en personne', *S* IX, pp. 14–15).

53 G. W. F. Hegel, *La Phénoménologie de l'esprit*, traduction de Jean Hyppolite, t. I, p. 171.

54 Ibid., p. 179.

55 The term 'pratico-inerte' in Sartre designates matter in which past *praxis* (see above, p. 161) has become absorbed. Human acts and meanings thereby become alienated, and are seen as inert, materialised facts. Sartre's analysis of the event in *La Grande Morale* may be said to anticipate this view. For a description of language as an example of the 'pratico-inerte' see *Critique de la raison dialectique*, pp. 180–1. See also *Plaidoyer*, *S* VIII, p. 436.

Postscript

1 *De la Grammatologie*, Minuit, 1967, p. 23. For a critique of Sartre's humanism which exempts *La Nausée* see Derrida, 'Les Fins de l'homme', *Marges de la Philosophie*, Minuit, 1972, pp. 129–64. For a series of succinct essays on post-Sartrean thought in France, see John Sturrock (ed.), *Structuralism and Since*, Oxford University Press, 1979.

2 See, for instance, the evaluation of Sartre from a post-structuralist viewpoint in Dominick LaCapra, *A Preface to Sartre*, Methuen, 1979, p. 222: 'In Sartre, knowledge tends to be identified with power and cognitive control of the object. The denial or de-emphasis of ambiguity, repetition, play, and supplementarity fosters equivocation, empty repetition, and unthematized inconsistency'. Sartre's 'blind quest for "totalization"' is contrasted with a 'dialectical project of totalization [which] must remain open and give rise to continually displaced "centers", or final terms and referents'. Other critics imply, without adducing evidence, that Sartre's project of totalisation can be associated with right-wing totalitarianism. See J.-P. Faye, 'Sartre entend-il Sartre?', *Tel Quel*, no. 27, 1966, pp. 286–302.

3 For a defence of Sartre against the contention that, for him, being – whether *en-soi* or *pour-soi* – is fully 'present', see Christina Howells, 'Qui perd gagne: Sartre and Derrida', *Journal of the British Society for Phenomenology*, XIII, no. 1, January 1982, pp. 26–34. For a critique of Sartre's alleged dependence upon binary oppositions see LaCapra, *Preface to Sartre*, p. 127: Sartre's 'logic of mastery and domination [...] affirms alienated oppositions or fatal splits. Each of a pair of opposites [for instance, the for-itself and the in-itself] is internally a totality that expels all alterity onto the "other". It is forbidden to recognize sameness in the other or otherness in the same.' It can be argued against LaCapra that, for Sartre, consciousness is precisely not 'the same', because it carries alterity with itself. (This 'otherness', incidentally, has nothing to do with the way in which consciousness may seek its own objectification in the eyes of an empirical 'other'.) 'Que peut être, en effet, l'altérité, sinon le chassé-croisé de reflété et de reflétant que nous avons décrit au sein du pour-soi, car la seule façon dont l'autre puisse exister comme autre, c'est d'être conscience (d')être autre. L'altérité est, en effet, négation interne et seule une conscience peut se constituer comme négation interne. Tout autre conception de l'altérité reviendrait à la poser comme un en-soi' (*EN*, p. 712).

4 For the role of rhetoric in philosophical argument see Ch. Perelman and L. Olbrechts-Tyteca, *The New Rhetoric. A Treatise on Argumentation* (1958), University of Notre Dame Press, 1969.

WORKS CITED

For a full bibliography of Sartre's writings up to 1969 see Michel Contat and Michel Rybalka, *Les Ecrits de Sartre*, Gallimard, 1970. Supplements to this work, by the same compilers, are included in the English translation, *The Writings of Jean-Paul Sartre*, Evanston, Northwestern University Press, 1973, and in 'Les Ecrits de Sartre (1973–8)', *Obliques*, no. 18–19, mai 1979, éd. Michel Sicard, pp. 335–44.

Unless otherwise stated, the place of publication for works mentioned below is Paris for books in French and London for those in English. The date of first publication, where relevant, is given in parentheses.

Works by Sartre

Cahiers pour une morale, Gallimard, 1983.
Critique de la raison dialectique (précédé de Question de méthode), vol. I, *Théorie des ensembles pratiques*, Gallimard, 1960.
L'Engagement de Mallarmé, *Obliques*, no. 18–19, mai 1979, éd. Michel Sicard, pp. 168–94.
Esquisse d'une théorie des émotions (1939), Hermann, 1965.
L'Etre et le Néant. Essai d'ontologie phénoménologique, Gallimard, 1943.
'*La Grande Morale*, extraits d'un *Cahier de notes* (1947)', *Obliques*, no. 18–19, mai 1979, éd. Michel Sicard, pp. 249–62.
Huis clos (1944), in *Théâtre*, Gallimard, 1947 (1969 reprint).
L'Idiot de la famille, Gallimard, vols I and II, 1971; vol. III, 1972.
L'Imaginaire. Psychologie phénoménologique de l'imagination, Gallimard, 1940.
Les Mains sales, Gallimard, 1948.
Les Mouches (1943), in *Théâtre*, Gallimard, 1947 (1969 reprint).
La Nausée (1938), in *Œuvres romanesques*, éd. Michel Contat et Michel Rybalka, Bibliothèque de la Pléiade, Gallimard, 1981.
Nekrassov, Gallimard, 1955.
'Préface' to Georges Michel, *La Promenade du dimanche*, Gallimard, 1967, pp. 7–10.
Saint Genet, comédien et martyr, Gallimard, 1952.
Les Séquestrés d'Altona, Gallimard, 1960.
    ed. Philip Thody, University of London Press, 1965.

237

Works cited

Situations:
'Aller et retour' (1944), *Situations* I, Gallimard, 1947, pp. 189–244.
'Les Ecrivains en personne' (1960), *Situations* IX, Gallimard, 1972, pp. 9–39.
'Une Idée fondamentale de la phénoménologie de Husserl: l'intentionnalité' (1939), *Situations* I, Gallimard, 1947, pp. 31–5.
'Matérialisme et Révolution' (1946), *Situations* III, Gallimard, 1949, pp. 135–225.
'Orphée noir' (1948), *Situations* III, Gallimard, 1949, pp. 229–86.
Plaidoyer pour les intellectuels, *Situations* VIII, Gallimard, 1972, pp. 375–455.
'Portrait d'un inconnu' (1948), *Situations* IV, Gallimard, 1964, pp. 9–16.
'Présentation des *Temps Modernes*' (1945), *Situations* II, Gallimard, 1948, pp. 9–30.
Qu'est-ce que la littérature?, *Situations* II, Gallimard, 1947, pp. 55–330.
'Sartre par Sartre' (1970), *Situations* IX, Gallimard, 1972, pp. 99–134.
'Sur *L'Idiot de la famille*' (1971), *Situations* X, Gallimard, 1976, pp. 91–115.
Un Théâtre de situations, éd. Michel Contat et Michel Rybalka, Gallimard, 1973.
La Transcendance de l'Ego. Esquisse d'une description phénoménologique (1936–7), éd. Sylvie Le Bon, Vrin, 1965.

Books and articles which refer to Sartre

Barnes, Hazel E., *Sartre*, Quartet Books, 1973.
Sartre and Flaubert, University of Chicago Press, 1981.
Beauvoir, Simone de, *La Force de l'âge*, Gallimard, 1960.
Boros, Marie-Denise, *Un Séquestré: l'homme sartrien,* Nizet, 1968.
Burnier, Michel-Antoine, *Les Existentialistes et la politique*, Gallimard, 1966.
Campbell, Robert, *Jean-Paul Sartre ou une littérature philosophique.* Edition revue et augmentée, Pierre Ardent, 1946.
Contat, Michel, *Explication des Séquestrés d'Altona de Jean-Paul Sartre*, Minard, Archives des Lettres Modernes, 1968 (5), no. 89.
Derrida, Jacques, *Marges de la Philosophie*, Minuit, 1972.
Faye, J.-P., 'Sartre entend-il Sartre?', *Tel Quel*, no. 27, 1966, pp. 286–302.
Fell, Joseph P., *Emotion in the Thought of Sartre*, New York, Columbia University Press, 1965.
Heidegger and Sartre. An Essay on Being and Place, New York, Columbia University Press, 1979.
Flynn, Thomas R., 'The role of the image in Sartre's aesthetic', *Journal of Aesthetics and Art Criticism*, XXXIII, Summer 1975, pp. 431–42.
Genette, Gérard, 'Sens et signification: la théorie sartrienne du langage

Works cited

poétique', in *L'Analyse du discours/Discourse Analysis*, ed. Pierre R. Léon and Henri Mitterand, Montréal, Centre Educatif et Culturel Inc., 1976, pp. 193–201.

Gore, Keith, *Sartre: La Nausée and Les Mouches*, Edward Arnold (Studies in French Literature, 17), 1970.

Howells, Christina, 'Qui perd gagne: Sartre and Derrida', *Journal of the British Society for Phenomenology*, XIII, no. 1, January 1982, pp. 26–34.

'Sartre and Freud', *French Studies*, XXXIII, no. 2, April 1979, pp. 157–76.

Sartre's Theory of Literature, MHRA, 1979.

Idt, Geneviève, *La Nausée: analyse critique*, Hatier, 'Profil d'une œuvre', 18, 1971.

Izenberg, Gerald N., *The Existentialist Critique of Freud. The Crisis of Autonomy*, Princeton University Press, 1976.

Jameson, Fredric, *Marxism and Form*, Princeton University Press, 1971.

Jeanson, Francis, *Sartre par lui-même*, Seuil, 1955.

Keefe, Terry, 'The Ending of Sartre's *La Nausée*', *Forum for Modern Language Studies*, XII, no. 3, July 1976.

'Problems of identification and definition in some of Sartre's shorter philosophical works', *Australian Journal of French Studies*, XII, no. 2, 1975, pp. 220–40.

King, Thomas M., *Sartre and the Sacred*, University of Chicago Press, 1974.

LaCapra, Dominick, *A Preface to Sartre*, Methuen, 1979.

Lecherbonnier, Bernard, *Huis clos: analyse critique*, Hatier, 'Profil d'une œuvre', 31, 1972.

Lorris, Robert, *Sartre dramaturge*, Nizet, 1975.

Outhwaite, William, *Understanding Social Life. The Method called 'Verstehen'*, George Allen & Unwin, 1975.

Poster, Mark, *Existential Marxism in Post-war France*, Princeton University Press, 1975.

Rose, Marilyn Gaddis, 'Sartre and the ambiguous thesis play', *Modern Drama*, VIII, no. 1, Summer 1965, pp. 12–19.

Royle, Peter, *Sartre. L'Enfer et la liberté. Etude de Huis clos et des Mouches*, Québec, Presses de l'Université Laval, 1973.

Schalk, David L., *The Spectrum of Political Engagement*, Princeton University Press, 1979.

Will, Frederic, 'Sartre and the question of character in literature', *PMLA*, LXXVI, September 1961, pp. 455–60.

Other literary, critical and philosophical works

Austin, J. L., *How to Do Things with Words*, Oxford, Clarendon Press, 1962.

Philosophical Papers, Oxford, Clarendon Press, 1961.

Austin, L. J., 'Mallarmé et le rêve du "Livre"', *Mercure de France*, CCCXVII, no. 1073, janvier 1953, pp. 81–108.

Bateson, Gregory, *Steps to an Ecology of Mind*, St Albans, Granada, Paladin, 1973.

Works cited

Derrida, Jacques, *De la Grammatologie*, Minuit, 1967.

Elam, Keir, *The Semiotics of Theatre and Drama*, Methuen, 'New Accents', 1980.

Genette, Gérard, *Figures* III, Seuil, 1972.

Girard, G., Ouellet, R. and Rigault, C., *L'Univers du théâtre*, Presses Universitaires de France, 1978.

Halbwachs, Maurice, 'Les Caractéristiques des classes moyennes', *Inventaires*, III, Alcan, 1939.

Hegel, G. W. F., *La Phénoménologie de l'esprit*, traduction de Jean Hyppolite, Aubier, t. I, 1939, t. II, 1941.

Huizinga J., *Homo Ludens* (1938), Routledge & Kegan Paul, 1949.

Hyppolite, Jean, *Genèse et structure de la Phénoménologie de l'esprit de Hegel*, Aubier, 1946.

Kojève, Alexandre, *Introduction à la lecture de Hegel*, Gallimard, 1947.

Lévy-Bruhl, Lucien, *Les Fonctions mentales dans les sociétés inférieures*, Alcan, 1910.

Mallarmé, Stéphane, *Correspondance*, Vol. I, 1862–71, éd. Henri Mondor et Jean-Pierre Richard, Gallimard, 1959.

Mallarmé, Stéphane, *Œuvres complètes*, éd. Henri Mondor et G. Jean Aubry, Bibliothèque de la Pléiade, Gallimard, 1951.

Mauron, Charles, *Introduction à la psychanalyse de Mallarmé*, Neuchâtel, A la Baconnière, 1950.

Merleau-Ponty, Maurice, *Phénoménologie de la perception*, Gallimard, 1945.

Perelman, Ch. and Olbrechts-Tyteca, L., *The New Rhetoric. A Treatise on Argumentation* (1958), University of Notre Dame Press, 1969.

Popper, Karl R., *Conjectures and Refutations*, Routledge & Kegan Paul, 1963.

Pratt, Mary Louise, *Toward a Speech Act Theory of Literary Discourse*, Bloomington, Indiana University Press, 1977.

Richard, Jean-Pierre, *L'Univers imaginaire de Mallarmé*, Seuil, 1961.

Scheler, Max, *Ressentiment* (1915), ed. Lewis A. Coser, trans. W. W. Holdheim, New York, Schocken Books, 1961.

Searle, John R., *Speech Acts. An Essay in the Philosophy of Language*, Cambridge University Press, 1969.

Smith, Barbara Herrnstein, *On the Margins of Discourse: The Relation of Literature to Language*, University of Chicago Press, 1978.

Sturrock, John (ed.), *Structuralism and Since*, Oxford University Press, 1979.

Ubersfeld, Anne, *Lire le Théâtre*, Editions sociales, 1978.

Valéry, Paul, *Variété* II, Gallimard, 1930.

Willett, John (ed. and trans.), *Brecht on Theatre*, Eyre Methuen, 1978.

INDEX

241

Index

Index

Index

mediation, 25, 49, 59, 159, 162, 176, 186–7, 191, 193–4
Merleau-Ponty, Maurice, 192, 231 n. 26, 234 nn. 45, 48
metaphor, 2, 47–9, 51, 53, 190, 201
Michel, Georges, 224 n. 16
Mondor, Henri, 186
motivation, 98–9, 102, 105, 110–11, 113, 136; and *mobile*, 99–102, 104, 111, 114; and *motif*, 99–102, 114
Les Mots, 201
Les Mouches, 1, 2, 62–83, 85, 86–7, 99, 101, 103, 106–7, 110, 158

narrative, 39–40, 44, 46, 113, 115, 117, 120, 199, 209 n. 27; and *histoire, narration, récit*, 46–53, 56–8
nature, 55, 102, 171, 177, 181–2; human, 85–7, 89, 91, 126
nausea, 12, 14–19, 82, 158, 207 n. 21
La Nausée, 1, 2, 4–61, 76, 83, 199, 206 nn. 15, 18, 19, 207 nn. 20, 21, 208 n. 26, 209 nn. 27, 28, 29, 210 n. 33, 211 n. 35, 212 nn. 36, 42, 213 n. 44, 235 n. 1
le néant, 9, 13–14, 18–19, 28–31, 57–8, 76, 125, 138–9, 145, 151, 174, 192, 217 n. 15
néantisation (nihilation), 10, 14–15, 18–19, 25, 57, 82, 109, 139–40, 191, 204 nn. 5, 7, 208 n. 22, 210 n. 30
negation, 25, 27–8, 44–5, 49, 56, 58, 61, 152, 161, 165–6, 182, 190–2, 195, 201, 234 n. 45, 236 n. 3; and image, 138–9, 146–7, 152, 154
Nietzsche, Friedrich, 220 n. 20
noema, 205 n. 13
noesis, 205 n. 13
Nekrassov, 225 n. 18
le non-savoir, 61, 175–7, 182, 189, 197, 199–200, 230 n. 19

Olbrechts-Tyteca, L., 223 n. 9, 236 n. 4
'Orphée noir', 2, 164, 175, 176–84, 197, 211 n. 35, 229 n. 8, 232 n. 29
Ouellet, Réal, 216 n. 9
Outhwaite, William, 230 n. 20

Parain, Brice, 210 nn. 31, 32
participation, 16, 54, 120, 131–2, 155–6, 205 n. 14, 212 n. 40, 213 n. 45
participation theatre, 84, 88, 107, 123, 142, 227 n. 4
Pascal, Blaise, 168
passion, 73, 85–6, 91–2, 101–2, 222 n. 5; *see also* emotion

passivity, 10, 15–23, 48, 63, 65–6, 72–4, 81, 107–8, 127, 140, 145, 171, 176–8, 183, 186–7, 190, 193, 198, 202, 209 n. 28, 215 n. 7, 216 n. 10
perception, 5, 24–6, 30–7, 45, 48–9, 54, 59, 63, 80, 138, 140–5, 148, 152–3, 155–8, 169, 179, 198, 212 n. 40, 226 n. 3, 227 n. 4
Perelman, Ch., 223 n. 9, 236 n. 4
perlocution, 105, 114–17, 119, 121, 129, 131
Phidias, 194
Plaidoyer pour les intellectuels, 61, 161–3, 172, 175–6, 190, 197, 228 n. 3, 229 n. 15, 231 n. 24, 233 n. 41, 235 n. 55
poetry, 2, 41–2, 48, 54, 60, 63, 75, 78, 80–1, 162, 164–5, 176–97 passim, 199, 200, 210 n. 33
Popper, Karl R., 223 n. 11
Poster, Mark, 229 n. 10
post-structuralism, 198, 235 n. 2
pour-soi, 5, 9–37 passim, 48, 67, 79, 109, 113–14, 189–90, 199, 204 nn. 4, 5, 7, 206 n. 19, 207 n. 21, 215 n. 7, 222 n. 7, 230 n. 17, 236 n. 3
pratico-inerte, 196, 234 n. 55
Pratt, Mary Louise, 221 n. 2
praxis, 161, 169–70, 173, 230 n. 18, 235 n. 55
'Préface' to Georges Michel: *La Promenade du dimanche*, 127, 224 n. 16
presence, 13, 25, 27, 33, 41, 43, 54, 58, 138, 152, 155–6, 177, 190, 197, 198, 200, 208 n. 22, 226 n. 3, 227 n. 4; and absence, 54, 138, 155–6, 190, 227 n. 4, 236 n. 3
prise de conscience, 85, 87, 92, 96, 103, 132, 158, 161, 168, 175
progressive–regressive method, 159–61, 164
project, 5, 7–14, 18, 20, 23–4, 39, 45, 99, 101, 103–4, 106, 109, 111–12, 114, 160–1, 164, 166, 183, 189–90, 206 n. 15, 217 nn. 14, 15, 221 n. 3, 231 n. 21
prose, 161–2, 165, 178–83, 197, 199, 210 n. 33
psychoanalysis, 159, 176, 184, 186–8, 190–1, 195, 230 n. 20, 233 nn. 35, 44

quality, 25, 26, 33, 49, 54, 57–8
Qu'est-ce que la littérature?, 2, 41–3, 59–60, 80–2, 108–9, 159, 161, 163, 164–75, 178–83, 189, 197, 200, 210 n. 33, 211 n. 35, 212 n. 41, 213 nn. 44, 45, 229 nn. 12, 13, 231 nn. 22, 23

244

Index

245

Index